THE DAWN OF THE PACIFIC CENTURY

Other Books by the Author

1989   *Voyages to Utopia*

1986   *Paths to Progress* (with Arline McCord)

1982   *The Psychopath and Milieu Therapy*

1977   *Power and Equity* (with Arline McCord)

1977   *Urban Social Conflict* (with Arline McCord)

1977   *American Social Problems* (with Arline McCord)

1968   *Life Styles in the Black Ghetto* (with John Howard, Edwin Harwood, and Bernard Friedberg)

1965   *Mississippi: The Long Hot Summer*

1965   *The Springtime of Freedom*

1964   *The Psychopath*

1960   *Origins of Alcoholism* (with Joan McCord and Jon Gudeman)

1959   *Origins of Crime* (with Joan McCord and Irving Kenneth Zola)

1955   *Psychopathy and Delinquency* (with Joan McCord)

THE DAWN OF THE PACIFIC CENTURY

Implications for Three Worlds of Development

William McCord

Transaction Publishers
New Brunswick (U.S.A.) and London (U.K.)

Second Printing, 1993

Copyright © 1991 by Transaction Publishers, New Brunswick, New Jersey 08903.

Library of Congress Catalog Number: 90-11111
ISBN: 0-88738-367-X
Printed in the United States of America

Library of Congress Cataloging-in-Publication Data

McCord, William Maxwell, 1930-
    The dawn of the Pacific century: implications for the Third World/William McCord.
    p.   cm.
    Includes bibliographical references (p. 207).
    ISBN: 0-88738-367-X (cloth)
    1. East Asia—Economic conditions. 2. East Asia—Politics and government. 3. Asia, Southeastern—Economic conditions. 4. Asia, Southeastern—Political and government—1945-   5. Pacific Area—Economic conditions. 6. Pacific Area—Politics and government.
    I. Title.
HC460.5.M37   1990
330.9—dc20   90-11111
                                                            CIP

For my friends, students, and colleagues in Asia
who continue to fight for freedom

Contents

Acknowledgments

A grant from the Ford Foundation initially introduced me to the complexities of Southeast Asia. The generosity of the National University of Singapore gave me an acquaintance with that fascinating city-state and allowed voyages to Malaysia, China, Hong Kong, and Japan. The Chung Hua Institution of Tapei offered a fine opportunity to explore the rapidly changing nature of Taiwan, while the Daewoo Foundation provided the means to analyze Korea. The City University of New York graciously allowed the time for these travels. I wish to express my gratitude to these institutions for their essential backing.

Arline McCord, Peter Chow, and William Helmreich took time from their own research to criticize the book. Myron Kolatch of *The New Leader,* Owen Harries of *The National Interest,* and Gerald Segal of *The Pacific Review* meticulously crafted the parts of the book that originally appeared in their journals. Irving Louis Horowitz and Mary E. Curtis both encouraged and edited the book, while Marilyn Santomauro had the difficult job of making sense out of my scribblings.

I would particularly like to thank my Chinese friends for their able assistance but—for the moment—it is wiser that they remain anonymous.

1

The Rise of the Pacific

> *The Pacific Ocean will play the same role as at present the Atlantic . . . and the Atlantic Ocean will sink to the level of a great lake such as the Mediterranean is today.*
> —Karl Marx, 1865

In 1903, Theodore Roosevelt issued a prophecy similar to that of Karl Marx. "The Atlantic era," he said, "is now at the height of its development and must soon exhaust the resources at its command. The Pacific era, destined to be the greatest of all, is just at its dawn."[1]

Such oracles may have been a bit premature. It is clear, however, that the relative power of Europe and America has been eroded, although not eclipsed. The surging Pacific Basin can legitimately be regarded as the most economically dynamic region of the globe. A confluence of trade, technology, telecommunications, and training has brought together Asia, Australia and the American continents in a swell of economic, political, and cultural interplay that no one power can control. By 1984, Prime Minister Nakasone of Japan could confidently assert, "The Pacific era is now an historic inevitability."[2]

The basic thesis of this book is that East Asia, allied with Southeast Asia, has a tryst with destiny. Barring nuclear catastrophe, the region will assume a dominant strategic position in the world during the twenty-first century. It will serve as the beacon and perhaps the financier for those nations still caught in the quagmire of poverty. Europe, America, and the Soviet Union cannot remain aloof to these developments. My goal is to explore the opportunities, and the hazards—some grave—implied in the rise of this great Pacific arc and to examine the possible scenarios of its development.

I do not intend to play the role of Nostrodamus and make uncompromis-

1

ing predictions about the future. I will deal only with reasonable projections based upon the premise that post-1992 Europe (perhaps infusing the Soviet bloc with new economic vigor) will not, as many Japanese believe, turn into a cultural antique or that North America will collapse as a "paper tiger." East Asia will continue its economic growth—slower in the more mature regions, faster in those that are just entering the ranks of industrial societies. The fact remains that an Asian third force has already emerged on the world scene and that it can be ignored only at great peril.

The transformation of the Pacific began, of course, in Japan. In 1953, after recovering from the devastation of war, Japan embarked on a period of economic growth which averaged 9.7 percent annually, far higher than the rate of any other industrial nation in the world. Without natural resources, Japan increased her car production one hundred times between the end of the 1950s and the 1980s. By 1987, Japan had a higher per capita industrial GNP than America. The Japanese ousted America as the leading producer of radios, television sets and electronics; overtook Switzerland in the making of watches; displaced Germany in the production of cameras; and developed a larger steel capacity than the entire EEC.[3]

The turnabout in Japanese fortunes proceeded at an unprecedented pace, even when compared with its original "take off" in 1868. In 1960, Japanese firms had to beg loans from the Bank of California; by 1988, Japanese banks bailed out the Bank of California from default. By 1986, Japan owned seven of the world's ten largest banks.[4] The general contours of the Japanese miracle are well known, and most Europeans and Americans, however reluctantly, have become accustomed to Ezra Vogel's depiction of "Japan as Number One."[5]

Yet, the full scope of the Pacific transformation has not yet been entirely comprehended by many Americans and Europeans. Since 1982, for example, IMF figures indicate that two-way trade across the Pacific has handily surpassed trans-Atlantic trade.[6] By 1983, intra-Pacific trade had dramatically increased and, by 1988, was worth twice the Pacific countries' trade with the United States, and three times their commerce with Europe.

A nation such as Australia sent 70 percent of her exports to other Pacific countries and received 60 percent of her imports from them in 1987. Asian migrants, particularly from Japan, Hong Kong and Vietnam, continued to flow into Australia—previously an "all-White," racist nation. Fifty percent of Asian children attended a university while 10 percent went on to a technical school. They graduated with three times more honors degrees than native-born Australians.[7] While the "Asian influx" precipitated a political reaction, there seemed little doubt that Australia, particularly bolstered by Hong Kong capital and people, would become a genuinely Euro-Asian nation in the next century.

Across the Pacific rim, Canada did more business in the Pacific in 1987 than with its usual European trading partners. Chile's newest direction of trade flowed to the Pacific.[8] Japan exchanged automobiles for fruit, timber, flowers, and even wine grapes. China imported Chile's copper and wood. In 1988, Australians purchased a gold mine in Chile's northern desert and bought 60 percent of Chile's largest unexploited copper deposits. Hong Kong secured 45 percent of the Chilean telephone system. Due to exports of minerals and forestry products, however, Chile maintained a favorable balance of trade with the Pacific region.

While still the leading economic power of the region, Japan faced stiff competition from other Pacific countries. In 1988, the combined trade of South Korea, Taiwan, Hong Kong, and the ASEAN countries exceeded that of Japan. Thus, a huge—and potentially self-sufficient—trading bloc emerged on the world scene. While America and Europe could still place obstacles in the growth of this new giant, it seemed unlikely that even a world boycott could cripple it for long. Asian economies are sufficiently complementary that, in a crisis, they could easily secure the technology, capital, labor, and resources from each other with an almost total disregard for the rest of the industrial world.

This transformation has already had great socio-economic consequences for the United States and Europe. In 1960, America's commerce with Asia was less than half of its trade with Europe; by 1987, Asia-bound trade surpassed commerce with all of Europe by 50 percent. While Europe used to account for most migrants to America, Pacific basin countries contributed nine out of ten legal migrants to the United States by 1987.[9] (Illegal migrants from Mexico, Central America, and Latin America immeasurably increased this influx.)

Moreover, the direction of Pacific attention decisively moved away from the industrialized West to the developing world. In 1989, Taiwan set aside $1 billion annually from her abundant reserves to subsidize developing countries. In 1990, according to the Japanese Ministry of Finance, 56 percent of that nation's imports (and 55 percent of its exports) flowed to and from the "Third World."[10] In 1988, Japan's direct foreign aid to developing countries from Madagascar to Bolivia first exceeded the absolute amount of America's assistance ($10 billion vs. $9.2 billion).[11] Japan gave twice as much to a nation such as the Philippines as did the United

States. This benevolence was not based purely on altruism. (Like America, Japan devoted only 0.31 percent of its GNP to foreign aid and tied it to imports from Japan while countries like Sweden, Denmark, and Holland proportionately expended three times as much. Similarly, Japan took in many fewer refugees from Southeast Asian countries than did Canada, Australia or the United States.) Nonetheless, with major reserves of foreign exchange invested abroad, Japan, in particular, could now afford mutually beneficial relationships with the "Third World"—particularly in Asia and especially when "tied" to the import of Japanese products.

Japan and Hong Kong also laid heavy bets on China's future. Although poor on a per capita basis, plagued by inflation, and vacillating in its political direction, China already exhibited its potential economic strength. In 1987, aided by a peasantry released from communes, China passed the Soviet Union in grain production. In spite of the introduction of austerity practices in 1988 and political tragedy in 1989, reasonable calculations indicate that China's GNP will move ahead of the GNP of any European country by 2010.[12]

Even excluding China from the calculations and using very modest standards (an overall growth rate of about 4.2 percent annually), World Bank projections indicated that the Asian-Pacific GNP would match Europe and America within two decades.[13] Again excluding China, one study, *Japan in the Year 2000,* estimated that the total production of the Asian-Pacific countries will have matched the GNP of the United States and Europe by the year 2000.[14]

Such a seismic shift in the world's distribution of income and power has strategic consequences for Europe, the United States, Latin America, and the Soviet Union. By the late 1980s, Japan had already become the world's largest creditor with a net foreign investment of $248 billion while the United States had sunk to the status of the world's largest debtor, with a net foreign obligation of almost $400 billion. Militarily, Japan (while spending only slightly more than one percent of its GNP on defense in 1988) ranked third in the world in defense expenditures ($38 billion annually), ahead of Great Britain and France.[15] Japan dispatched 53 destroyers to defend its home islands within a 1,000-mile radius, more than twice as many as the U.S. Seventh Fleet deployed in the Western Pacific and the Indian Ocean.[16]

This drastic alteration in the economic-political axis of the world raises seven basic questions:

Will the two giants of the Pacific—Japan and China—form an alliance, as Harvard professors Roy Hofheinz and Kent Calder once predicted, that "would transform Eastasia into the dominant region of the world in the twenty-first century"?[17] The political and economic (and possibly military) consequences of such a relationship would be enormous. Major obstacles—Chinese memories of Japanese occupation and Japan's constitutional ban on atomic weapons—make the relationship dubious. Nonetheless, the reciprocal benefits to both nations—Japan's capital and technology balancing China's markets and manpower—logically suggested a closer unity.

In what ways does the Asian "model" of development offer lessons for both the "Third World" (the poverty-stricken but diverse areas of Africa, South Asia, and Latin America) and for currently industrialized nations? The distinguished scholar Ronald Dore believes that the Asian experience presages emerging trends in other nations.[18] In contrast, Hofheinz and Calder argue that "the economic performane of East Asia rests heavily on political conditions so unique as to be unreproducible."[19]

How will the economic resurgence of East Asia affect what historian Paul Kennedy calls "the shifting power balances in world affairs"?[20] In the late 1980s, both Japan and China spent a small part of their GNP on armaments. Some observers considered this capping of military expenditures and the subsequent reduction in China's armed manpower an essential ingredient in the two countries' success. With Japan under pressure to "rearm," could conditions change this relative neglect of military power?

Will the Soviet Union expand its previously minor role as an Asian power? In 1987, by acknowledging China's claim for a revision in borders, eliminating missiles from Soviet Asia, and hinting at the return of several northern islands to Japan, Gorbachev had—in the opinion of academician Vladimir Lukin, an expert on the Far East—"signaled a decisive turn of the country to the Asian-Pacific region."[21]

Will a debt-ridden America and a newly unified Europe rock the world economy by creating ever higher protectionist barriers? Economic stagnation, isolationist impulses, as well as racial antagonisms run deep in Europe and in America. Even in the twenty-first century, by closing access to their markets more than they did in the past (exceeding Japan's tariffs), America and Europe could hurt the Pacific area. This "white peril" could trigger a major re-evaluation of Asian economic and political strategy.[22]

Can Japan sustain its prosperity and pursue the goal, outlined in the 1986 Maekawa Report, of assuming a truly international role and fulfilling the needs of its domestic market? Even by 1986, the phenomenal growth rate of Japan had dropped, housing shortages (inflated by the cost of scarce land) remained unmet, and the graying of the Japanese population propelled a steady rise in the cost of social services. As political scientist Robert Scalapino commented in 1987, "Japan is confronted with the need for nothing less than a sweeping cultural change."[23]

Although Chinese officials acknowledged in 1978 that China's future advance depended on sustained world interdependence, is it possible that China could turn inward again? Certain trends—the fact that Chinese agriculture had reached the technical limits of its growth in the late 1980s (without an expensive infusion of technology), the capping of migration to cities, restrictions imposed by a lack of transportation and energy supplies, and the student revolt of 1989—could result in economic dislocation, xenophobia, and more social discontent.[24]

These are grave, alarming issues, but thoughtful people in Asia and the rest of the world must face them now if Asia is to fulfill its possible destiny. To answer these questions may prove impossible; to ignore them, in matters as momentous as these, would be unforgivable.

Notes

1. Theodore Roosevelt, quoted in "The Pacific Rim," *U.S. News and World Report,* 20 August 1984.
2. Ibid.
3. Staffan Linder, *The Pacific Century* (Stanford: Stanford University Press, 1986).
4. See Joel Kotkin and Yoriko Kishimoto, *The Third Century* (New York: Crown Publishers, 1988).
5. Ezra Vogel, *Japan As Number One* (Cambridge: Harvard University Press, 1979).
6. Ibid.
7. "Australia Goes Asian," *New York Times Magazine,* 4 December 1988.
8. See Kotkin and Kishimoto, *The Third Century.*
9. Ibid.
10. Cited in *World Paper.*
11. Cited in *Newsweek,* 22 February 1988, p. 19.
12. Linder, *The Pacific Century.*
13. *Japan in the Year 2000,* quoted in Linder, ibid.
14. Ibid.
15. "From Superrich to Superpower," *Time,* 4 July 1988, p. 19.
16. Ibid.
17. Roy Hofheinz and Kent E. Calder, *The East Asia Edge* (New York: Basic Books, 1982), 252.
18. Ronald Dore, *Taking Japan Seriously* (Stanford: Stanford University Press, 1987), 117.

19. Hofheinz and Calder, *East Asia Edge,* 41.
20. Paul Kennedy, *The Rise and Fall of Great Powers* (New York: Random House, 1987), chap. 8, 310.
21. Vladimir Lukin, cited in *Time,* see note 15.
22. See Linder, *Pacific Century,* and Jagdish Bhagwatie, *Protectionism* (Cambridge: MIT Press, 1988).
23. Robert A. Scalapino, "Asia's Future," *Foreign Affairs* (Fall 1987): 85.
24. See Orville Schell, *Discos and Democracy* (New York: Pantheon Books, 1988).

Part I

THE GREAT ASCENT

Introduction

In the middle of the twentieth century, as the great colonial empires splintered into independent states and nationalism swept through the Third World, even the poorest of peasants experienced a revolution in expecttions. Usually mantled in the semi-religious rhetoric of socialism, magnetic leaders such as Nehru of India, Sukarno of Indonesia, Nkrumah of Ghana, Mao of China, and Nasser of Egypt promised their peoples a rapid and painless escape from the abyss of poverty. They offered their followers a "new" form of freedom, a revivification of authentic cultural traditions, and burgeoning prosperity based on enlightened planning.

Some Western leaders such as John Kennedy, Lester Pearson, and Willy Brandt envisaged an "alliance for progress" whereby Western capital and knowledge would soon equip indigenous leaders with the means to fashion reality from their dreams. Economist Barbara Ward argued in 1961 that "the need is to remove the work of world development from the subsidiary attention of the wealthy nations and to make it a central theme of their diplomacy, their international relations, their philosophy of world order."[1] Gunnar Myrdal foresaw that the Asian dilemma might be resolved by "a strong, induced impetus" from "large-scale state intervention."[2]

Yet, more somber observers warned of a sad outcome to experiments in development. Aware of population pressures, the need to accumulate capital at human expense, the paucity of administrative resources, and the inevitable lure of dictatorial rule, some prophets predicted disaster for the developing world. "Can we imagine a sequence of events that might lead eventually to industrialization of all peoples of the world?" Harrison Brown asked in 1959. "When we enumerate all the difficulties in which the human species can become embroiled, it would appear a priori that the probability of successful transition along any path would be extremely small."³ In his prescient works, *The Great Ascent* and *The Future As History*, Robert Heilbroner suggested in 1959 that the supposed efficiency of authoritarian regimes in promoting economic growth would mark "the commencement of a chapter of tragedy and sorrow," in developing regions.⁴ In 1974, remarking on the population explosion, the greenhouse effect, and the food crisis, Heilbroner became even more pessimistic. As he inquired into the human prospect, Heibroner noted:

> There is a question in the air, more sensed than seen, like the invisible approach of a distant storm, a question that I would hesitate to ask aloud did I not believe it existed unvoiced in the minds of many: Is there hope for man?
>
> The answer to whether we can conceive of the future other than as a continuation of darkness, cruelty, and disorder of the past seems to me to be no; and to the question of whether worse impends, yes.⁵

Garret Hardin, the biologist, extended this argument by asserting that it would be useless, even counterproductive, for the rich nations to help the poorer ones: "The sharing ethic of the spaceship is impossible. For the foreseeable future, our survival demands that we govern our actions by the ethics of the life-boat, harsh though they may be."⁶

By the 1980s, reinforced by dire predictions from the Club of Rome, an organization that used computers to predict the future, many reasonable people in both industrialized and developing countries agreed. They surveyed an underdeveloped world strewn with the debris of authoritarian regimes; elites arbitrarily directing ruined, state-owned economies; redeemers who promised but failed to deliver economic welfare; *Gleichshaltung* programs that treated humans as experiments in animal husbandry. Much of Africa had declined from its food-exporting status into near-starvation. Latin America's tremulous democracies rightly feared intrusions from their armies or guerrillas. The Middle East squandered its precious oil wealth on war and monuments. Many nations, socialist or capitalist, followed the siren call of independent self-sufficiency and suffocated under unpayable debts. Expressing a fin de siècle mood, Fouad Ajami wrote in 1982: "The sense of political and cultural despair over the Third World— the belief that it can't be taught public order—has its economic counterpart. Now the poverty of the Third World, too, is beyond hope."⁷

If the optimists of the 1950s and 1960s had fatally underestimated the obstacles to progress, the pessimists of the 1980s, from unregenerate Stalinists to "world systems theorists," studiously ignored events in

Asia—or dismissed them as aberrations, ephemeral enclaves of capitalist exploitation, or odd exceptions to the rule that the "periphery" could never become a central part of the world's "core."

To their credit, perceptive analysts of development such as Peter Berger, Chalmers Johnson, and Roderick MacFarquhar did not cavalierly dismiss the Asian experience. They recognized that by all the usual criteria of development—majestic increases in income, a growth in equity among social classes, a universalization of education, and major improvements in health—some of the Asian countries had approached or even exceeded the levels of advanced industrial nations.

From the ashes of Hiroshima and Nagasaki, Japan in 1988 boasted a higher GNP per capita ($19,566 annually) than did the United States ($18,400).[8] While these figures did not turn into a higher personal income for the Japanese, they lived longer than Americans and had reached a higher level of literacy. The Japanese example "turned conventional wisdom on its head. It has shown developing nations that industrial success can be accomplished without massive injections of foreign capital, without state control, and without social turmoil."[9]

Singapore, Hong Kong, Taiwan, and Korea formed a second tier of nations that increasingly matched the Japanese pace. From 1960 to 1985, Singapore emerged from bleak poverty into a city state with a per capita GNP of $7,000 a year. Modern medical techniques reduced infant mortality to a lower level than in the United States.[10] Korea surged from a per capita GNP in 1950 of $100 a year to $2,826 in 1988.[11] Taiwan experienced a similarly remarkable growth in real income. At the close of World War II, per capita GNP stagnated at $70 a year. By 1987, it surpassed $5,000 annually.[12]

All of these areas achieve economic growth in an environment charac-terized by export expansion, low inflation, full employment, and an equal-ization of income. Moreover, their rate of economic growth continued relatively unabated during the more protectionist atmosphere of the late 1980s. Japan grew at a real pace of 4.5 percent annually, Hong Kong at 7 percent, Singapore and Taiwan at 8 percent, and Korea at 10 percent.[13]

None of them possessed unique advantages. At the beginning of their great move forward, they lacked resources and capital. All had been ravaged by war and were forced to accept millions of penniless refugees. All depended upon sharp, uncontrollable changes in the world's political and economic environment. Yet, Japan and the NICs managed their great ascent in an unprecedentedly short period of time while dramatically improving the income, welfare, and health of their peoples.

A third tier of nations on the edge of the East Asian explosion has made great strides since the 1960s. Consciously, their governments often looked to the East Asian "model," and the results were extraordinary. In 1988, Indonesia expanded its actual GNP by 4 percent a year, Malaysia by 8 percent, and Thailand by 9 percent.[14] All of these countries were blessed with major, if largely unexploited resources; all had suffered from ethnic tensions and civil war; all had quite different cultures from their East Asian predecessors; and all had experienced direct or indirect colonization. Even the Philippines, wrecked by internal dissension, achieved a growth rate of 6.5 percent annually.[15]

On a fourth tier of development, the great and unpredictable nation of China seemed poised to join in the Asian renaissance. Since 1978 Deng Xiaoping and other reformers attempted to create a system of "commodity socialism" in the world's largest market place. The reformers hoped to transform China's Herculean economy and clean up its Augean political household. By dismantling 54,000 communes, the Dengists initiated a cycle in the countryside that increased agricultural production by 7 percent a year between 1978 and 1988. Heavy industry, stimulated by a decentralization of management and an incentive system for workers, grew at 10.2 percent a year in the 1980s.[16] The opening of free trade zones in China's coastal areas allowed them to jump far ahead of the interior. Although plagued by difficulties from inflation to strident demands for more democracy, the reformers created a mixed market economy, ended China's isolation from the rest of the world, and gingerly allowed a degree of scientific, economic, and intellectual freedom. The political repression of 1989 and (a perhaps needed) slowing of the pace of economic growth put the great experiment into question, but few Chinese scholars believed that pragmatic policies could be completely reversed.

Clearly, the Asians had made their astounding progress without following the orthodoxies of either Adam Smith or Karl Marx. They had abandoned the totalitarian mobilization advocated by Stalin and Mao, the strict hierarchialism of Confucius, and the passive acceptance of fate preached by Buddha. Except for a degenerating Burma or a decimated Indo-China, these nations had opened their doors to an invigorating flood of new ideas, new investments, and new technology. The truth is that pragmatic Asians—Japanese and Chinese, Malays and Thais—fashioned new trails, unmapped by doctrine, as an escape route from suffering and decadence.

The great Asian colossus had stirred and stretched its limbs with a vigor unknown for centuries. Comprehending the nature and scope of this transformation is a first, essential step toward understanding its portent for the future.

Notes

1. Barbara Ward, *New Perspectives on Economic Development* (Oxford: Oxford Conference on Tensions in Development, 1961), 8.
2. Gunnar Myrdal, *The Asian Drama* (New York: Pantheon, 1968) vol. 2, 718.
3. Harrison Brown, *The Challenge of Man's Future* (New York: The Viking Press, 1956), 228–9.
4. Robert Heilbroner, *The Future As History* (New York: Harper and Row, 1959), 80.
5. Robert Heilbroner, *An Inquiry Into the Human Prospect* (New York: W. W. Norton, 1974), 13, 22.
6. Garrett Hardin, "The Case Against Helping the Poor," *Psychology Today* 14 (September 1974): 126.
7. Fouad Ajami, "The Fate of Nonaligned Nations," *Foreign Affairs* 21 (Summer 1982): 1022.
8. "Newsletter," Japan Society, New York, 1988.
9. Peter Trasker, *The Japanese* (New York: E. P. Dutton, 1987), 30.
10. William McCord, "Singapore's Success Story," *The New Leader* (August 1985): 12–26.
11. Japan Society, New York, 1988.
12. Shirley W. Y. Kuo, *Development of the Taiwan Economy*, Chung-Hua Institution of Economics, Taipei, 14 November 1988.
13. *The Far East Economics Review,* 25 August 1988, 77.
14. Ibid.
15. Ibid.
16. Orville Schell, *Discos and Democracy* (New York: Pantheon Books, 1988).

2

The First Tier: Japan

*The history of postwar Japan has been one of the
most astonishing success stories of the century.*
—Jared Taylor, 1983

In 1945, Japan lay humbled by the ravages of war. B29's had leveled all
of her major cities except for the temple shrines of Nara, Kyoto and
Nikko. Hiroshima and Nagasaki had been levelled. Firebombing had
wrought terrible havoc in Japan's other cities. A single firebomb raid on
Yokohama on 29 May 1945 destroyed 80 percent of that city. The few
people on the rubble-strewn streets of Tokyo dressed their emaciated
bodies in rags. Many starved. Overseas, seven million defeated Japanese
troops awaited repatriation. Stripped of industries, divested of colonies,
terribly short of basic foods such as rice, Japan's very survival seemed at
issue.

Coal production had dropped to one-eighth of its prewar level, utilities
did not function, 80 percent of textile factories had been converted to a
wartime footing and now lay in cinders. Over two million Japanese had
died in the war and the rest starved; they needed the import of 3,500,000
tons of food merely to subsist through the first winter of defeat.[1] John
Gunther observed that "the bitter sting and humiliation of defeat" had
made the people "dazed, tottering, and numb with shock."[2]

No one at the time anticipated Japan's eventual emergence as a new
industrial giant, the world's greatest creditor, and the peaceful leader of a
genuine "co-prosperity" sphere. At the very most, as Lindesay Parett
wrote in late 1945, the Japanese economy was not ever "likely to expand
sharply. The prospect [is for] a return to Japan's status as a small, self-
contained nation."[3] As late as 1960, Karl Sax, a demographer, predicted
that "the people of Japan can expect only subsistence living standards."[4]

Such prophets ignored Japan's initial rise to world significance and the fact that its people already had some eighty years of experience transforming a rural society devoid of resources into a major economic and military power. (With hindsight, some have argued that Japan as well as Germany profited in the long run from the destruction of their industrial base. It allowed them to replace old, "rusting" industries with the most modern technology.)

The Meiji Regime

Japan's first economic revolution began in 1868 with the Meiji *restoration*. Until then, Japan had developed a small merchant class and circulated currency, but the nation had built only the vestiges of industry. The ruling Tokugawa clans had sealed off the country from contamination by foreign influences. In 1863 and 1864, however, European ships bombarded Satsuma and Choshu, decisively illustrating Western superiority in the martial arts. Humiliated by this encounter, a dissident group of samurai (the lesser, "outer clans" already alienated from their rulers) revolted against the Tokugawa and set Japan upon a determined course of modernization. They had a single goal: the achievement of military prowess. Using a child emperor as their excuse and their spokesman, they transformed Japan from a peasant society into a military power by 1900.[5]

In spite of a total lack of resources, Japan surpassed Europe's and Russia's growth in both scope and pace. From a largely feudal society in 1868, the Meiji reformers built railroads, a modern armaments industry, and enormous shipyards by 1896.[6] Between 1878 and 1887, the total national product increased by 42 percent. From 1900 through World War I, the amount of food doubled. Every ten years until the 1930s national production increased by 50 percent.[7] In their frontal assault on backwardness, the reformers used several techniques.

By redistributing what were formerly Tokugawa lands, the Meiji first ensured a surplus of food. They introduced new rice farming techniques and, indeed, Japan soon became a rice exporting nation.

The reformers consciously copied what they regarded as the most advanced techniques and policies from Western countries: ship-building from England, business practices from America, educational systems from France, and (unfortunately) a constitution from Germany. All of the modern industrial techniques from iron-smelting to silk-weaving came from abroad. Artfully, the Japanese adapted these foreign imports to their own needs either in the construction of armaments or the creation of major export industries, such as silk.

From the first, the Meiji emphasized the importance of education and, before the end of the century, Japan had become one of the most literate nations in the world. By the end of the twentieth century, the Japanese consumed more books and newspapers than any other people in the world.

While sending young people abroad to learn what the modern world had to offer, the reformers also tried to augment the ties that linked a person to his family, his community, his work, and the Meiji emperor. The new government made the individual legally responsible for the welfare of his family, the social security of his parents, and his role in the newly created factory system.[8] School teachers imparted modern skills but assumed that their prime role was to inculcate reverence for family and emperor. The Meiji also preserved or enhanced traditional symbols: the old Tokugawa nobles were allowed to retain their now useless swords; a new cult of reverence for the emperor was invented; and people had to register as members of their family and community, retaining that status forever.

Economically, the rulers accumulated investment capital for industry from the peasants. A land tax imposed in 1873 required farmers to pay the government 25 percent of the yield. By 1875, fortified by ever more abundant harvests, this revenue accounted for 85 percent of government income.[9] Initially, the government invested the capital in light, even cottage, industries, widely decentralized throughout the country. Thus, they made use of the talents of an overlarge supply of labor.

The Meiji vigorously took the lead in building an infrastructure of irrigation canals, railroads, and model factories. After starter industries demonstrated a profit in producing silk or cement, cotton or soap, the government sold the factory to private companies often headed by nobles from the same class. Controlling about 50 percent of investment in the nineteenth century, the government pursued a policy of *guided capitalism* as the stimulant for economic growth.

The reformers carefully attempted to merge economic modernization with the preservation of certain aspects of traditional life. Workers moved into new factories as groups, keeping their status from the original community. Because of a policy of light, decentralized industries, urbanization proceeded slowly and many economic activities were pursued within the family unit. As a possible consequence, rates of crime, alcoholism, and other symptoms of social malaise remained low. The incidence of crime and suicide actually decreased when the *koban* police system—a conglomerate of neighborhood police centers where the officers spent much of their time in social work—was introduced. Trade unions were not allowed to emerge until the 1920s and were often linked to specific enterprises.

Unblessed with the resources, land or capital of Europe, Russia, and America, Japan underwent an economic transformation. An agricultural revolution, income derived from peasants, an assiduous copying of Western techniques, an emphasis on education, guided capitalism, and a series of policies that reinforced traditional values allowed the Japanese rulers to build a mighty military machine. At the turn of the twentieth century, Japan's well-equipped and disciplined military forces easily defeated Tsarist Russia. By the 1930s, her nascent experiments with democracy in shambles, a nationalist Japan had overrun Manchuria, much of China, Korea, and Formosa. In 1941, threatened by an economic blockade and hungry for oil and minerals, Japanese militarists attacked Pearl Harbor, Malaysia, and Singapore. Temporarily, Japan defeated the combined American, British, Dutch, French, and Chinese forces. The Japanese survived for four dreadful years until Emperor Hirohito, convinced by the devastation wrought by atomic bombs, ordered his people to surrender and "to endure the unendurable." A new Japan had to be built from the rubble.

The MacArthur Era

Brilliant, vain, authoritarian, and Christian, General Douglas MacArthur, the supreme commander of Allied forces, hardly seemed the man to initiate a radical revolution among the Japanese people. Yet, between 1945 and 1952, he did just that. MacArthur not only put forward the policies that rebuilt Japan but laid a new economic base that, in some ways, was more revolutionary than the reforms of the Meiji. Among his more far-reaching and lasting changes, MacArthur demilitarized the country, instituted civil liberties, launched a major redistribution of land, created a stable democracy, granted the vote to women, and propelled Japan into an epoch of unparalleled economic growth.

One of MacArthur's most significant actions was the dismantling of Japan's feudal agricultural domain. In 1946, responding to drastic shortages of food and hyperinflation, the headquarters of the occupation forces ordered the government to pass a series of land reform laws in order "to break the economic bondage which has enslaved Japanese farmers."[10] The Diet dutifully complied with measures ensuring that the land of all absentee landlords above one hectare was purchased and resold to tenants. In spite of obstruction by over two million landlords who tried to subvert the program, the reform was completed within two years. The results were spectacular: the number of owner-cultivators rose to 75 percent of farmers, the proportion of absentee owners fell from 30 percent to 3 percent, and production soared.[11] As Ronald Dore, a distinguished expert on the Japanese transformation, remarked on the triumph of the program, it meant ''a subversion of traditional patterns of social relations which had held sway for decades or even centuries.''[12] (Later in the century, the original agricultural reforms presented some problems to the government. As a powerful voting bloc, the farmers demanded and received heavy subsidies and extended protection from foreign competition. As a result, rice in Japan cost six times the international rate.)

Following a slightly contradictory course, MacArthur enjoyed somewhat less success in breaking the power of monopolistic business concerns that had worked closely with previous military regimes. MacArthur dissolved the old family-owned holding companies that underpinned the *zaibatsu,* great combines of industrial power. Yet, he allowed Japanese businesses to reform into *keiretsu,* horizontal groupings of companies that usually contained a bank, an insurance company, a trading arm, and many industries in varied fields. These new corporations were not strict monopolies since they competed strongly against each other, but as a whole they formed an oligopoly.[13] The more prominent included old *zaibatsu* combines (Mitsubishi, Mitsui, Sumitomo) and corporations such as Fuji that were held together by a great bank.[14] The banks played a central role in each case since they advanced credit to their own subordinate companies without regard to immediate profits. Thus, the combines felt free to reinvest their earnings with the goal of achieving long-term growth. The central bank of Japan guaranteed, in effect, the investments of each *keiretsu* bank.[15] Unrestrained by the need to show an immediately favorable balance on their books, as did American businessmen, the leaders of the *keiretsu* worked for the long-term good fortune of their seemingly eternal institutions.

Technically, MacArthur also freed trade unions in 1945 to negotiate openly with the large business firms. Between 1945 and 1949, 34,000 unions had sprung up and exchanged increases in productivity for fast-rising wage rates, low unemployment, and a high degree of job security (including life tenure in major firms).[16] Nonetheless, MacArthur did not hesitate to ban general strikes that threatened violence and to purge

Communist leaders in 1949 and 1950. Many unions limited their activities to polite discussions within the "family" of their particular enterprises.[17]

Perhaps the most sweeping changes of the MacArthur era came with the introduction of a new constitution in 1947. Occupation laws had created a relatively free press, developed the power of police forces, introduced local government, and assured the independence of the judiciary.[18] Drafted in occupation headquarters, the new constitution's most striking feature was the "no-war" clause, article IX; "Aspiring sincerely to an international peace based on justice and order, the Japanese people forever renounce war as a sovereign right of the nation . . . land, sea and air forces as well as other war potential, will never be maintained." MacArthur himself had directed the inclusion of a prohibition against going to war in the present Japanese constitution.[19]

With the advent of the Korean War, however, MacArthur drained occupation troops from Japan and assented to the creation of a Japanese "Self-Defense Force."[20] Although the new troops trained with tanks and mortars, officials tried to disguise their activities as merely police-related. Most observers agreed that the creation of the Self-Defense Force violated the new constitution and represented the rearmament of Japan.[21] The dominant Liberal Democratic government, actually a conglomeration of conservatives, approved it.

Thus, with some degree of ambiguity, the MacArthur era achieved several goals: 4.7 million farmers gained freehold tenure, competitive business organizations grew, labor gained limited freedoms (as well as the fastest-rising wage rates in the industrialized world), and a stable liberal democracy took root. In sum, as Paul Johnson, the great commentator on modern times, commented, " 'The American era' . . . succeeded in destroying the mesmeric hold the state had hitherto exercised over the Japanese people. The American occupation of Japan was probably the greatest constructive achievement of American overseas policy in the whole postwar period."[22]

Export-Led Growth: the 1950s and 1960s

In the first move toward expanding its economy, Japan rebuilt its industrial base, concentrating on large, labor-intensive, export-oriented industries. Driven by the need for foreign exchange to finance the importation of her mineral and energy resources, the government cagily—but soon, energetically—promoted Japanese export trade.

At the beginning of her rapid growth, in spite of some privileges conferred by the MacArthur regime, Japan started with grave disadvantages. In 1952, it was still the most densely populated country on the globe, and food supplies had to be imported for her survival. Moreover, Japan had to import its oil, timber, iron ore, and most of its coal. Jobs had to be provided for millions of relatively young repatriates. The country could no longer exploit its labor at will, as it had once done during the Meiji time.

Japan's level of production amounted to little more than one-third that of France. Japanese electronic goods were far less competitive than America's or Germany's. In 1958, the nation produced less than 100,000 automobiles, many fewer than Great Britain.[23]

Between 1953 and 1970, however, Japan overcame these obstacles and emerged as the world's second largest exporter. Japanese textiles swamped the United States. Japanese exports of cameras, lenses, and optical equipment outperformed Germany. A flood of Toyotas, Nissans, and Hondas threatened (and eventually overwhelmed) American and German competitors. The British motorcycle industry, once distinguished, collapsed in the face of Japanese competition. Japan took the world lead in exporting everything from bicycles and pianos to pottery and even ski equipment.[24] Japan's gross domestic product expanded at a rate of 10.5 percent annually between 1950 and 1970, twice as fast as the rest of the world.[25] How did the reversal take place within the short span of two decades? The reasons for the success were straightforward. The Japanese elite, in both its political and business incarnations, had determined to make the nation *ichi ban* (number one) in industrial power, and the people agreed with this goal. The elite could count on "one priceless asset" produced by Japanese history and homogeneity—"a chilling degree of national consensus."[26]

In a race for economic supremacy, the Japanese "work ethic" reinforced a drive for economic efficiency. Indeed, as Ronald Dore later observed, the prime factor in Japan's renaissance was the obvious fact that "the Japanese worked hard."[27] Indeed, most workers at all levels worked six or even seven days a week; even school children attended their classes for many more days than Americans. As M. J. Wolf, a critic of Japan, commented, "Japan's national workforce has been mobilized, trained and deployed as an industrial army. . . . The Japanese worker serves because he has been trained for just that since his birth. A tradition of discipline from a feudal Japan . . . is still potent as a spiritual force."[28]

When such a devotion to work is allied with a national consensus to achieve the number one status in the world economy, miracles can occur. The mélange produced "a work culture where everyone in a company, from the top to the bottom, knows his or her correct place and . . . most important of all, they can all pull more smoothly in the same direction."[29]

On a more tangible level than celebrating the Japanese "work ethic," other concrete reasons lay behind the Japanese progress.

Japanese businesses invested at a high rate in productive enterprises and they borrowed liberally from foreign technology. A very high level of personal savings, often channeled through the post office system, backed the new ventures. Taxes, defense, and government spending remained at a low level. Windfall profits from the Korean and Vietnam wars helped the economy to expand but internal factors—including a strict educational policy geared to the needs of the economy—basically propelled the growth.[30]

In addition, as worker productivity rose and industrial wages increased (at a high but still slower pace), Japanese corporations and the government managed a remarkable degree of control over labor. Euphemistically called "wage restraint," the policy kept wages lower than the value added to the product. Partially, this was due to a corporate policy which nurtured a collective, even family atmosphere among tenured workers. Many Japanese firms sponsored uniforms, housing, meals, medical care, sports, "self-improvement committees" and sloganeering banners to exhort their workers to greater productivity.[31]

Temporary workers, a majority, were motivated more by fear of losing their jobs than by company propaganda and benefits.[32] As one journalist who worked as a seasonal employee at Toyota described the real situation, "Though I double my efforts, using twice as much energy, I just can't recover the lost seconds. It's like I imagine hell to be."[33]

During this period Japan protected her infant industries but, in fact, the total trade imbalance with America "lay not in Japan's protectionism but in America's inferior competitiveness and lack of interest in cultivating exports to Japan."[34]

Due to all of these factors, Japan emerged in the 1970s as the premier exporting nation in the world.

Surviving the World's "Shocks": the 1970s

In 1973 and again in 1978, Japan's pace temporarily slowed because of the "oil shock" imposed by petroleum exporting nations. Dependent for

99 percent of its oil on foreign lands, Japan had to readjust because of the precipitous rise in oil prices. Unlike Great Britain, Japan chose to ease out "old" industries like steel and ship-building, and to target the growth of newer, less energy-consuming industries like electronics. Japan increased its capital investments during the 1970s in assembling and processing industries while output rose again by 50 percent. Japan had begun her transition "from smokestack industries to shirt-sleeved brain industries."[35] Meanwhile, Japan stepped up its construction of nuclear-energy plants in order to reduce its reliance on foreign energy suppliers.

Other nations failed to react with such strategic foresight. At least partially, Japan continued to advance because of the efforts of MITI, the Ministry of International Trade and Industry. MITI was a planning body that set standards for modernization, the restructuring of industry, the launching of new enterprises, and the salvage of decaying industries. MITI did not possess pervasive powers or break up the new *keiretsu,* but MITI officials were so persistent in "their efforts to look after the welfare of Japanese industry that they [were] dubbed by their countrymen as *kyoiku mama,* over-anxious mothers who hover over their children and push them to study."[36]

In 1973, MITI determined to lead Japan into an epoch when business invested in service or information endeavors and developed construction projects in the Middle East—all with the goal of reducing Japan's dependence on foreign sources of energy as well as correcting its foreign exchange imbalance. MITI guided sectors of the economy, encouraged investment, helped promising companies to gain technology, arranged capital investment, "targeted" new areas of opportunity, and directed the flow of research funds.

Nonetheless, unlike "command economies," MITI could not order Japanese enterprises to follow its guidance. As Vogel wrote in 1979, MITI's success "derived not from statutory rules but . . . the voluntary cooperation of the business community."[37] (At times, businesses went against the recommendations of MITI. Earlier, MITI had suggested that it would be unwise for Japan to compete in the international automobile arena. Toyota, Nissan, and Honda soon demonstrated MITI's fallibility.)

Yet MITI was an intimate member of "Japan, Inc.," a combination of industrial, political, academic, and media power in Tokyo. Drawing an analogy to America, Chitoshi Yanago observed that it would be as if all major American organizations were located in Washington, and all "top executives would . . . claim the same alma mater [Tokyo University], belong to the same country clubs, maintain daily contact, and enjoy intimate relations with influential senators and congressmen."[38] Since MITI bureaucrats could influence banks, give guidance to industries and finance basic research, they inevitaly played a major role in Japan's export drive.

Switching to Domestic Needs: The End of the Century

By the 1980s, Japan faced increasingly severe export competition, particularly from the "NICs." Moreover, long-neglected domestic require-ments for more and cheaper consumer goods began to concern a public which had sacrificed its own immediate demands for the fulfillment of export goals. Housing emerged as a paramount need since the Japanese, however rich in external earnings, had paid little attention to their creature comforts. (My own relatives—a stock-broker and a teacher with good incomes—resided in one eight-by-sixteen-foot room near Tokyo. They folded their fudans each night into a closet, cooked on a microwave hidden in a corner, and ate off a miniscule table). Hugely inflated prices for land hindered housing development, but gradually a small boom in Japanese construction commenced.

A 1988 "White Paper on National life" underscored the need to pay close attention to domestic needs.[39] The government-sponsored report indicated that three-quarters of the people believed that disparities in land ownership and housing created unfair gaps among the people.[40] Only 50 percent of Japanese said that they were satisfied with their lives. Although blessed with a relatively equitable income distribution and a widespread perception that everyone belonged to "the middle class," some Japanese feared the possible onset of a degree of "social alienation like that of the United States."[41] The government responded by spending more money on parks, recreation facilities, and public amenities and by lowering the price of consumer goods.

Nonetheless, MITI engaged in detailed plans to develop nuclear fusion, biotechnology, microchips, and super computers. Known as "the next generation industries," the new enterprises targeted by Japan included the development of porcelains to replace heavy metals, biogenetics, solar power, aerospace, and gigantic fish farms. Led by MITI and financed by large research grants, primarily from business, Japan advanced rapidly in the making of the VA500, the world's most technologically advanced engine.[42] With equal vigor, Japan took over the world lead in building super computers, the fastest calculating devices on earth.[43] In a period of six years, Japan overcame American superiority in the field. American manufacturers suddenly found that their only choice was to buy critical components from Japan. Mutual cooperation in super computers and aerospace became necessary for survival. MITI's research groups had also made major progress in developing sophisticated "fifth generation" computers with artificial intelligence.[44]

Financed by $4 billion a year garnered mostly from privatizing old public monopolies, MITI pioneered in establishing "key technology centers," spurring Japan's effort to cross the frontiers of high technology.[45] Thus, by an intense devotion to advanced research, major advances in high technology, a postwar policy of creating a meritocracy through education, a fortunate collaboration between industry and government, and the creation of corporations that resembled families, Japan managed to navigate a treacherous path to the forward edge of advanced industrialization.

Japan's Stages of Growth

Japan's growth as a world power was stretched out over more than one hundred and fifty years. The country struggled to achieve military parity in the nineteenth century, sought to expand its empire in the 1920s and 1930s, suffered almost total destruction in the 1940s, and launched into a renaissance during the 1950s that has yet to end. Japan's chequered yet still majestic rise to eminence passed through five relatively distinct phases:

In the beginning, Japan underwent an agricultural revolution and managed to accumulate capital by squeezing it from a peasant surplus.[46] The land tax provided the necessary revenue to fund budding industries that later were bought by private entrepreneurs. Education and the copying of the West's technology took a high precedence as Japan's new elite pushed their country toward modernization.

Second, between 1868 and 1890, light industries such as silk took the lead in exports while the Meiji built an infrastructure of railroads, dams, and irrigation canals. By 1890, the Japanese had laid the foundations for heavy industries, particularly steel, shipbuilding, and armaments, that were still labor-intensive in nature. By reinforcing traditional culture, the Meiji created a highly disciplined force of civilians and soldiers. After defeating Russia, the Japanese militarists continued their search for power while drawing resources from newly conquered territories acquired between 1900 and the 1920s.

Third, after initial military advances in the 1930s and final defeat in 1945, Japan abandoned the quest for military supremacy and, under MacArthur's influence, set about restructuring its economy. Once again, agricultural reform, the creation of light industries, and the rebuilding of the infrastructure took precedence. By the 1950s and 1960s, Japan had developed a base of export-oriented, mass-production industries.

Fourth, in the 1970s and 1980s, MITI guided Japan in another major transition into the production of electronic goods, calculators, computers, and hi-fi equipment. Fueled by a high rate of savings, high investment, and low taxation, Japan conquered the world's export markets. Japan's achievements in this era cannot be attributed, as a former trade negotiator, Clyde Prestowitz, asserts, to a refusal to open its markets to foreign competition.[47] Rather, Japan's tariffs were lower than Europe's or America's and Japanese businesses did not benefit from official or semi-official barriers. An actual opening of the entire world market could well have resulted in a major increase in Japanese exports of cars, electronics, and machinery while Japanese agriculture and small-scale industries may have withered or collapsed.[48]

Fifth, by the end of the century, Japan had emerged as the most energetic economic influence on the Pacific Rim. In a new "age of information," Japan commanded the highest technology in electronics, microchips, computers, and telecommunications. Simultaneously, the country paid attention to its voracious consumers and made corporate alliances both in developing countries and in the industrial world to insure a continuing flow of resources, an expansion of markets, and access to advanced knowledge and technology.[49]

How has Japan been able to advance through its extraordinarily flexible history of industrialization into world preeminence? Advocates of two general schools of thought—the *culturalists* and the *structuralists*—proposed several generalizations. At some levels, these theories were incompatible; at others, they complemented each other.

The culturalists generally credited Japan's success to its extraordinary homogeneity, the people's belief in their uniqueness, a pervasive hierarchical structure that enforced discipline, an ambience of paternalism, and a resulting conformity.[50] Some theorists cited the "Confucian ethic" (melded with Shintoism), with its emphasis on order, thrift, and hierarchy, as the unifying force. Michio Morishima, for example, argued that Confucianism played a premier role in Japanese development.[51] More prudently, the distinguished sociologist Peter Berger contended that a "vulgar Confucianism" emphasizing respect for authority, education, and diligence provided a "dynamic trigger" for Japanese growth.[52] Chie Nakane has maintained that the paramount values of Japanese culture—"groupism" and hierarchy—have been transmitted from the *ie*, or household, to modern business organizations.[53] Peter Trasker emphasized that "the small civilities of life are still intact" in Japan despite rapid social change. He portrayed the Japanese emphasis on law and order, a derivative of Confucianism, as the key to peaceful transitions. Rhetorically, he asked:

> Picture a country where you never need to count your change; where the streets are free of litter, the walls free of graffiti; where no one feels compelled to vandalize public telephones; where people visit sports grounds not to engage in tribal warfare but to cheer good play; where there are no muggings, no skinheads, no hippie convoys; where the policemen are affable and courteous and the pistols they carry are only fired a couple of times a year for the entire force.[54]

That, according to Trasker, was Japan in 1987.

In contrast, the structuralists suggested that specific socio-economic policies accounted for Japanese success and stability. By implication, these policies could be adopted by people of an entirely different culture. The economist Gustav Papanek averred that "the principal element in economic success was the strategy adopted, which should be readily reproducible elsewhere."[55] Papanek stressed particularly the emphasis on labor intensive industry, government intervention designed to strengthen a market economy, high returns to investors, and an environment where personalistic decisions were minimized.

In his pioneering work on the Japanese model, Vogel concluded "that Japanese success has less to do with traditional character traits than with specific organizational structures, policy programs, and conscious planning."[56] Vogel noted Japan's attention to education, meritocracy, government-business cooperation, the copying of lessons from the West, and long-term corporate planning as among the key ingredients in Japan's progress.

Clearly, too, Japan has recognized education as a prime ingredient for both economic growth and national cohesion. Japanese investments in education at all levels have exceeded most countries since 1868. Beginning in the 1950s, I.Q. tests have reflected the large amounts of money and time that the Japanese invested in education. By 1987, Japanese children scored ten points ahead of Americans or Europeans; only 2 percent of Americans or Europeans had I.Q.s above 130, as opposed to 10 percent of Japanese.[57] (This disparity cannot be explained in racial terms. The Japanese of the 1980s scored seven points higher than the Japanese of the 1940s, a gain that defies a genetic rationale.)

The structuralists offered the hope that lagging industrial economies and underdeveloped countries might benefit from the adaptation of Japanese policies. Addressing an American audience, for example, Vogel suggested that America could replicate certain Japanese policies and that "America, like Japan, can master the new challenges, that we will respond with foresight rather than hindsight, with planning rather than crisis management, sooner rather than later."[58]

Whether you attribute Japan's past success to her specific policies or her original culture (because of the ramifications of this issue, we shall return to this debate in part 2), the nation clearly faced new obstacles as she entered the twenty-first century. Some of the problems emerged from the prospective international situation, others from changes in Japan's demography and culture.

A protectionist climate threatened Japan's robust exports. Europe and America severely restricted the products of key Japanese industries such as textiles, automobiles, and video cassettes. As a result, Japan turned inwards to her domestic market, developed new, high technology products for industrialized nations, and explored the possibilities for further collaboration with developing areas.

Since the proportion of older Japanese grew at a faster rate than any other industrialized country, new pension burdens swamped the social security system. By 2020, 22 percent of the population will be over the age of sixty-five (twice the level of 1987). Each older person will be supported by only three active workers.[59] Guaranteed life-time employment in large companies, a major source of Japan's tranquility in labor relations, could well be one casualty of this trend.[60] The advent of the robotic age, previously welcomed by Japan's labor unions, could further create tension in Japan's labor negotiations.[61]

The very success of Japan's economy created several new cultural trends and resulting tensions. Psychological studies between 1984 and 1988 indicated a new sense of individualism among teenagers, singles, and even people in their fifties and sixties.[62] Such individualism, which traditionalists might label as selfishness, could undermine group loyalties. At the same time, a new "leisure ethic" made its appearance. People took longer vacations, were more willing to change companies, and exhibited less loyalty to their bosses. As Robert Wilk, a marketing specialist, noted, "The work ethic . . . is changing significantly as people want and expect more from their jobs."[63]

Japan also came under pressure, both from the United States and some nationalist politicians, to increase her investment in armaments. Slowly, the proportion of the GNP spent on weapons increased while absolute spending went up dramatically. As historian Paul Kennedy warned, "Previous great powers lost their productive vitality . . . as a propensity to spend on the present (consumption and defense) rather than on the future" increased.[64]

In spite of warning signals such as these, "the huge and sustained expansion of the Japanese economy was decisive in creating a dynamic market environment for the entire Pacific area."[65] As Japan's phoenixlike record suggested, observers were wise to postpone prophecies of decadence in the twenty-first century.

Notes

1. See William Manchester, *American Caesar* (New York: Dell Publishing, 1978) for a graphic description of postwar Japan.
2. John Gunther, quoted in *American Caesar*, 544.
3. Lindsay Parett, quoted in Robert C. Christopher, *The Japanese Mind* (New York: Simon and Schuster, 1983), 19.
4. Karl Sax, *The World's Exploding Population* (Boston: Beacon Press, 1960), 133.
5. See George Sansom, *The Western World and Japan* (New York: Alfred Knopf, 1970).
6. See Henry Rossovsky, *Capital Formation in Japan* (New York: Free Press), 1961.
7. See Samson, *Western World*.
8. See James Abegglen, *The Japanese Factory* (New York: Free Press, 1958).
9. See Paul Baran, *The Political Economy of Growth* (New York: Monthly Review Press, 1956).
10. See Fukutake Tadashi, *Japanese Rural Society* (Tokyo: Oxford University Press, 1967).
11. See Ronald P. Dore, *Land Reform in Japan* (London: Oxford University Press, 1950).
12. Ibid.
13. See *Post-War Japan*, J. Livingston, J. Moore, and F. Oldfather, eds. (New York: Pantheon Books, 1973).
14. See Chitoshi Yanaga, *Big Business in Japanese Politics* (New Haven: Yale University Press), 1968.

15. James Abegglen, "The Economic Growth of Japan," *Scientific American* (March 1970).
16. Andra Boltho, *Japan* (New York: Oxford University Press, 1975).
17. See Okuchi Kazuo, *Labor in Modern Japan* (Tokyo: Science Council of Japan, 1958).
18. See Kazuo Kawai, *Japan's American Interlude* (Chicago: University of Chicago Press, 1960), and John Maki, *Court and Constitution in Japan* (Seattle: University of Washington Press, 1964).
19. See Robert E. Ward, *American Political Science Review,* 1956.
20. See John Dower, "The Eye of the Beholder," *Bulletin of Concerned Asian Scholars,* 2, no. 1 (October 1969).
21. Jon Halliday and G. McCormick, *Japanese Militarism Today* (Baltimore: Penguin Books, 1973).
22. Paul Johnson, *Modern Times* (New York: Harper and Row, 1983), 719.
23. Ezra Vogel, *Japan As Number One* (Cambridge: Harvard University Press, 1979).
24. Ibid.
25. Michael Smith, "Japan," in Michael Smith et al., *Asia's New Industrial World* (London: Methuen, 1985).
26. Ibid., 10.
27. Ronald Dore, *Taking Japan Seriously* (Stanford: Stanford University Press, 1987), 12.
28. M. J. Wolf, *The Japanese Conspiracy* (London: New English Library, 1984), 216.
29. Smith, "Japan," 6.
30. See Johnson, *Modern Times.*
31. See Abegglen, "Economic Growth of Japan."
32. See Satoshi Mamata, *Japan in the Passing Lane* (London: George Allen and Unwin, 1983).
33. Ibid., 25.
34. Vogel, *Number One,* 13.
35. Smith, "Japan," 10.
36. Vogel, *Number One,* 70.
37. Ibid., 73.
38. Chitoshi Yanaga, *Big Business in Japanese Politics* (New Haven: Yale University Press, 1968), 101.
39. Economic Planning Agency, *White Paper on National Life,* Tokyo, 1988.
40. See "Rich Man, Poor Man in Japan," *New York Times,* 26 Dec. 1988, 14.
41. Kumiko Inoguchi, quoted in ibid., A18.
42. Smith, "Japan."
43. See Robert Cohop, "A High Tech Lead in Danger," *New York Times,* 18 Dec. 1988.
44. See Bob Johnstone, "Easier Said Than Done," *Far Eastern Economic Review,* 22 Dec. 1988.
45. See Richard Cohop, "Japan Spurs Research and Development," *New York Times,* 15 Dec. 1988.
46. See Baran, *Economy of Growth.*
47. See Clyde Prestowitz, *Trading Places* (New York: Basic Books, 1985).
48. Peter Trasker, *The Japanese* (New York: E. P. Dutton, 1987).
49. Smith, "Japan."

50. See Jared Taylor, *Shadows of the Rising Sun* (New York: Quill, 1983), and Robert Christopher, *The Japanese Mind* (New York: Simon and Schuster, 1983).
51. See Michio Morishima, *Why Has Japan Succeeded?* (Cambridge: Harvard University Press, 1982).
52. Peter Berger, "An East Asian Development Model," in Peter Berger and Hsin-Huang Michael Hsiao, eds., *In Search of An East Asian Development Model* (New Brunswick and Oxford: Transaction Books, 1986), 76.
53. See Chie Nakane, *Japanese Society* (Berkeley: University of California Press, 1972).
54. Trasker, *The Japanese*, 71.
55. Gustav Papanek, "The New Asian Capitalism: an Economic Portrait," in *In Search of an East Asian Development Model*, see note 52, 77.
56. Vogel, *Number One*, ix.
57. Trasker, *The Japanese*.
58. Vogel, *Number One*, 256.
59. Japanese Economic Planning Agency and Ministry of Health and Welfare, Tokyo, 1988.
60. Peter Drucker, "Japan's New Economy," Japan Society, New York, 12 April 1988, 1.
61. Smith, "Japan."
62. Robert J. Wilk, "The New Japanese Consumer," Japan Society, New York, 28 June 1988, 1.
63. Ibid.
64. Paul Kennedy, "A Guide to Misinterpreters," *New York Times*, 15 June 1988.
65. Johnson, *Modern Times*, 722.

3

Tier Two: The Newly Industrialized Countries

*You have to learn how to succeed, to see who
performs better, and then copy them. . . . There
will be no distinctive life forms in the future, it will
be one interrelated and integrated world.*
—Lee Kuan Yew

Japan's awesome and sustained expansion acted as both "a direct
stimulus and an example" for the newly industrialized countries (NICs)—
Hong Kong, Korea, Taiwan, and Singapore.[1] At the start of their surge to
prosperity, all were impoverished regions, barren of resources. Unlike
Japan, they lacked a traned industrial force, accomplished administrators,
experienced entrepreneurs, or a history of industrial experimentation.
Subject to British and Japanese colonialism, they had gained an infrastructure of roads and port facilities, but they remained mere agricultural
suppliers or entrepôts for the Japanese Empire during World War II. Yet
the four NICs, as historian Paul Johnson noted, "brought into existence
an entirely new phenomenon: the Pacific free enterprise state, which by
the early 1980s was perhaps the most encouraging aspect of human
society."[2]

Brutalized by occupation and civil war, South Korea was transformed
into a middle-income industrial country between the 1950s and the end of
the century. Even in 1961, according to economist Bon-Ho-Koo, South
Korea was "poor, primitive, and agrarian" with a per capita income of
less than $100 a year.[3] By 1976, income had risen to $800 a year, by 1978
to $1,000, and by 1988 to almost $3,000.[4] In contrast, North Korea, a
dictatorial collectivized economy, had absorbed all of the "Hermit Kingdom's" meager industrial base in the border division between the Soviet
Union and America in 1945. Nonetheless, as South Korea advanced, North
Korea languished with a per capita income of $400 annually in the 1980s.

At the end of the Second World War, after thirty five years of Japanese occupation, 70 percent of South Koreans were peasants; by 1988, 65 percent were urban—"a vast, sudden uprooting."[5] In 1989, South Korea claimed the world's highest growth rate—12 percent—in annual gross national product. As one of the world's largest exporting nations, Korea had a $10 billion trade surplus with the United States. Amid student and labor demonstrations, Korea had gingerly entered an era of political democracy; indeed, opposition parties dominated parliament.

The transformation of Korea began in 1954 with a vast injection of foreign aid from America. Designed to rehabilitate Korea from the trauma of civil war, the aid amounted to 73 percent of national "savings." Even in 1961, foreign aid composed 51 percent of the government's revenue.[6] The aid went mainly to rebuilding Korea's infrastructure and countryside, but during the 1970s, major sums were expended by the government in building heavy and chemical industries.

With the end of foreign aid, Korea searched for a new policy. The real upsurge in the Korean economy occurred at the end of the 1970s when the government adopted a fundamentally new policy orientation.[7] Since then, "export-oriented industrialization has been intentionally and consistently pursued by the Korean policy authorities."[8] Great conglomerates or *chaebol* such as Daewoo, Hyundai, Samsung, and Lucky-Goldstar spearheaded the export drive and dominated the economy. Unlike other NICs, Korea borrowed heavily abroad to finance its expansion but promptly repaid her debts.[9] From its position as one of the world's beggars in the 1950s, Korea became a major Asian power in the 1980s.

A formerly malarial entrepôt and a British colony, Hong Kong necessarily followed a somewhat different path than Korea or Japan. A rocky, 400-square-mile enclave on the coast of China, Hong Kong was destined to be absorbed by China in 1997. It would be a valuable addition and, indeed, some predicted that Hong Kong's people would lead China into a new age. By 1989, Hong Kong had raised its per capita gross domestic product to $7,000 annually—far higher than China's—and provided 40 percent of the entire foreign exchange savings of the People's Republic.[10] Moreover, Hong Kong took in four million refugees from the mainland, more than four times the number of Palestinian exiles in the Arab world.[11] These refugees became "within a matter of months . . . converted into efficient workers in the capitalist system."[12] Although lacking China's natural resources, Hong Kong emerged as the world's third largest financial center and the tenth biggest global trading partner of the United States.[13]

More than the other NICs or Japan, Hong Kong followed a relatively pristine capitalist path to prosperity.[14] The colony's British governors maintained a stable rule of law and helped in planning Hong Kong's development, but they imposed no controls over imports, foreign exchange, foreign investment, wages, prices, or zoning. While severe disparities of wealth resulted from the unfettered free enterprise system, the people enjoyed a higher standard of living than in nations such as Argentina, Yugoslavia, and Portugal.[15] Life expectancy in Hong Kong reached an astonishing seventy-six years in 1985. Economists such as P. T. Bauer and Alvin Rabushka credited Hong Kong's expansion to fiscal responsibility, entrepreneurial talent, low taxes, free trade, and a dynamic market economy.[16] Hong Kong's prime resource was its workers and businessmen, some of whom had swum from the mainland seeking greater freedoms. At base, "the miracle of Hong Kong [was] . . . a miracle performed with Chinese labor and genius."[17]

Across the straits of Formosa, Taiwan more than matched Hong Kong's example. On this once poverty-stricken island, the dramatic economic rise of the Taiwanese went hand-in-hand with a lessening of economic gaps between the very rich and the indigent.

Taiwan: From Defeat to Prosperity

In 1989, the mountainous island of Formosa presented a series of anomalies. The Koumintang (KMT), Chiang Kai-shek's corrupt and humbled regime, had fled mainland China in 1949. Few expected that this defeated alliance of former landlords and warlords would produce an economic revolution. Yet even by 1986, Asian journalist David Aikman could truthfully declare, "Taiwan for several decades has simply been one of the best-governed, less-developed countries in the world."[18] The KMT had ruthlessly massacred native Formosans in the 1940s, but by 1989 a Formosan, Lee Teng-hui, was elected president. In the 1940s, the richest Taiwanese had an income 15 times that of the poorest; by 1982, the ratio had dropped to 4.29 to 1.[19] Meanwhile, real per capita income on the island had phenomenally increased from an annual sum of $70 in 1945 to more than $3,000 in 1985 and then leapt to $5,000 in 1989.[20] Taiwan's per capita income exceeded that of mainland China by a factor of 12.[21] The nation had become the fifth largest trading partner with the United States. The national primary schools enrolled 99.8 percent of all children, and 80 percent of families owned their own homes.[22]

In the midst of such affluence, as I found it in 1988, Chinese customs still provided the underpinnings of this economic dynamo. In Taipei's "snake alley," merchants gave their pitches on electronic amplifiers as they flayed snakes alive. Since the snake blood supposesdly increased male potency, the Western-dressed crowd eagerly drank up the resulting broth. The hills around Taipei were covered with ornate burial grounds where people worshipped their ancestors. Before a new skyscraper went up, workers in *dou-li* hats built bamboo scaffolding while *feng-shui* masters estimated the balance of wind and water on the site.

At the Taoist Hsing-tien temple, fortune-tellers plied their trade while incense-sellers at Lungshan temple supplied Buddhist worshippers. The government itself paid homage in Confucian temples to China's greatest sage. In a strange juxtaposition, economic planners targeted information technology, biogenetics, and precision machinery as Taiwan's next strategic industries.

Back in 1949, Chiang Kai-shek claimed that he was defending an ancient Confucian heritage while he spent vast sums maintaining his armed forces. The Republic of China on Taiwan considered the whole Chinese mainland as part of its domain, while China regarded Taiwan just as a rebellious province. With the American recognition of the Chinese People's Republic and the Sino-American agreement of 1972, these dreams began to fade. Only twenty-four countries, many of them tiny island states in the Pacific, maintained formal recognition of the Republic of China on Taiwan. Yet, subterfuge "embassies" such as the U.S. American Institute on Taiwan and Japan's Interchange Association allowed Taiwan to continue stable legal and financial ties to the world.

As the real threat of invasion lessened, Taiwanese leaders considered decreasing the army's size. The economy's growth had, in itself, created a shortage of skilled manpower and pushed the army to release men for civilian work. Only the Japanese conviction that Taiwan was an "unsinkable aircraft carrier" and the mainland Chinese's intention of reestablishing their rule on Taiwan kept the nation producing its own jet fighters with a tested performance greater than Mach 2. Nonetheless, real cuts in military expenditures both on Taiwan and in China reduced the chances of actual conflict.

Even as Taiwan became less militarized, the country's ability to manufacture sophisticated weapons testified to its technological abilities. Several attributes contributed to Taiwan's remarkable development.

Over time, the KMT grew into one of the most stable and yet flexible governments in the Pacific. When it ruled China, the KMT was character-ized by corruption, runaway inflation, government contempt for its own troops, and disciplinary measures that included such brutalities as burying dissidents alive in anthills.

On Taiwan, the ousted Nationalist regime, perhaps fearful of American reactions as well as an invasion from the mainland, magically corrected its excesses and transformed itself into a government run largely by techno-crats rather than idealogues or warlords. The resulting economic growth, the first upward march since the Qing dynasty surrendered the island to Japan in 1895, resulted in a reasonably high degree of loyalty to the KMT. "The ultimate point for most Taiwanese," Aikman wrote in 1986, "is that their fellow Chinese on the mainland all along not only endured far worse economic conditions than they did, but had to put up with tyranny along with poverty."[23]

A major element in the KMT's economic strategy to eliminate poverty was to use public corporations to counterbalance private companies. Although composing no more than 35 percent of industrial producers, public corporations in steel, aluminum, petroleum, fertilizer production, shipbuilding, and electric power had considerable influence on resource costs and the eventual prices for private industries. Thus, during particular crises, the public corporations could keep Taiwan competitive on the world market by holding down the prices charged to private industry. In addition, the Central Bank of China controlled monetary and foreign exchange policy, capping inflation at a low rate. Taiwan largely avoided the strong political intervention exercised by private conglomerates (as in Japan or Korea) and enjoyed "perhaps the smoothest, most 'apolitical' economic policy management of all Eastasian states."[24] After the economy had taken off, the government moved toward the privitization of public corporations and deregulation, which was similar to the style of Hong Kong.[25] Wisely, the government recognized the dangers of ossification in the public sector. Nonetheless, the Taiwanese approach to stimulating economic growth could not be considered as purely capitalistic; instead, the island repre-sented a successful blend of private and public endeavors.

Like Korea, between 1950 and 1965, Taiwan also benefited from enor-mous assistance from the United States—approximately $1.4 billion in aid for a population of some 16 million people.[26] Although this level of per capita foreign aid hardly matched that extended to Israel or the sums of foreign capital lent to Korea, it still contributed distinctly to the stability (as well as the transformation) of a fragile society.

A major portion of aid went into building Taiwan's infrastructure of dams, roads, and irrigation canals—critical necessities in a largely agricultural society. This, in turn, laid the base for Taiwan's early and highly significant land reform.

At the end of the Second World War, the majority of Taiwanese were farmers and 61 percent of these were impoverished tenants.[27] Landlords colleccted 50 to 70 percent of the crop yield and could evict tenants at will. Motivated by their disastrous experience on the mainland and unencumbered by direct ties to the agricultural oligarchy, the KMT rulers engineered a major rent reduction in 1949: Landlords could charge no more than 37.5 percent of the produce and had to guarantee a five-year tenure to the peasants. Between 1951 and 1953, the government forced landlords to sell all but three hectares of their land to the public sector. The owners received reimbursement in the form of bonds and stocks in public corporations. In turn, the government resold the land at extremely low prices to formerly landless tenants. Nearly 200,000 farm families gained from this "land-to-the-tiller" redistribution.[28] By 1982, the government provided funds for expanding and mechanizing agriculture as the peasants began to face stiff world competition.[29]

The results of rural rejuvenation were outstanding: "The land reform not only represented a substantial redistribution of income; it also gave the farmers a great incentive to work harder and make the land more productive."[30] As I observed tea farms, even the poorest peasant possessed not only his own land but also special machinery to harvest the tea leaves. In his cottage, he had a television set and refrigerator while a motorcycle sat in the courtyard.

Most peasants engaged in agricultural work only on a part-time basis since they had established their own small industries. With domestic demands for food fully met, agricultural entrepreneurs shifted their interests either to small industries or to such export crops as asparagus and mushrooms.

When agriculture blossomed and gained a technological base, surplus labor naturally moved into the burgeoning industrial sector of the Taiwanese economy. At first, the new factories were labor-intensive industries that allowed Taiwan to capitalize on its greatest comparative advantage: cheap and abundant labor. Taiwan's production of goods for export—tennis shoes, textiles, simple computers—increased impressively. Between 1953 and 1987, the total annual amount of trade with the outside world grew an incredible 275 times.[31] Industrial exports accounted for 94 percent of all trade in 1987, a total reversal of the 1953 pattern.[32]

Although workers in labor-intensive industries received lower wages than in highly industrialized countries, the fruits of economic progress soon spread to everyone. By 1983, virtually every household on Taiwan owned a color television, a refrigerator, a washing machine, and a motorcycle. There was one air-conditioner in every seven households, one automobile per thirteen families, even one piano for every eighteen homes.[33] Through an expansion in income of unskilled workers, labor intensive industry was a prime contributor to growth with equity.

Without great stress on education, it would have been impossible for Taiwan's labor force to make the transition from a poor rural economy to one oriented to industry and service activities. Between 1950 and 1988, the total number of schools at all levels increased 1.8 times and, in 1968, the government introduced a nine-year compulsory education program.[34] At the same time, the number of universities increased from three to sixty-eight. The government also opened the Hsinchu science-based industrial park in 1980, a "technology hothouse" where high-tech firms could be situated in close proximity to one another. The park played a major role in assimilating foreign technology. Overall, the advances in knowledge that resulted from these innovations accounted for 38 to 53 percent of Taiwan's economic growth.[35]

While advances in education were crucial for Taiwan's progress, the domestic economy alone could not have absorbed all of the better trained people. As an outward-looking economy developed, however, new opportunities opened for educated Taiwanese. Indeed, as economist Chi-ming Hou has argued, "the early adoption of an export expansion strategy was the most important factor contributing to Taiwan's success."[36] (While production for export was emphasized after 1955, the initial import substitution policy designed to aid selected industries was never totally abandoned in the later decades.)

The government deliberately launched an export expansion drive in 1955 by reducing taxes on industries geared for export, easing import controls on critical materials, and establishing tax-free zones designed to attract foreign capital. In addition, the government manipulated the exchange rate on the Taiwan dollar to favor exporters. The results were phenomenal. In 1952, exports amounted to only $116 million. In 1986, exports had soared to almost $40 billion yearly.[37] In fact, by 1987, Taiwan's 20 million people exported more goods than such resource-rich giants as Brazil, India, and Mexico.[38]

The pattern of export expansion in Taiwan had several important consequences. Small- and medium-size enterprises controlled 65 percent ot total exports. The export drive created a high degree of employment; jobs generated by exports constituted more than 50 percent of total employment in manufacturing during Taiwan's high growth decades. Export expansion also reduced income inequality, particularly because labor-intensive industries absorbed excess farm labor at higher wages.[39] Rather than taxing the rich, export expansion created an environment for the levelling upwards of basic wages.

The growth in export-oriented industries gained its strength from a policy of "labor restraint" that prevailed in Taiwan. Before 1984, wage workers had no official rights to bargain or to protest. Indeed, until 1987, martial law prevailed on Taiwan and the government kept a tight control on worker discontent. Although their real wages rose in a spectacular fashion, organized workers played little role in negotiating the increase in wages and benefits. Market forces, driven by a steadily increasing demand for previously unskilled workers, gave impetus to a striking growth in workers' income. After 1987, workers became more aggressive in asserting their demands and launched strikes at Shin Kong textiles, Nestlé of Switzerland, Ford Motor, and Philips of the Netherlands. One organizer of a new labor group, Su Chin-li, told me in 1989 that "Workers are very impatient. Taiwan is getting very rich and living standards are so high." Yet, she added, "It is not that way for the workers."

In reaction to "the revolution in expectations," farmers marched in Taipei demanding higher wages, students demonstrated for greater freedom, villagers stopped construction of a DuPont chemical plant, and a Hakka minority demanded its rights between 1988 and 1989.[40]

Pushed by these restive forces that were unleashed by great economic growth, Taiwanese authorities responded with flexibility and a degree of grace rather than the old repressive measures of the KMT. Chiang Ching-kuo, the son of Chiang Kai-shek and his successor, initiated basic political reforms. He ended martial law in 1987, released political prisoners, and allowed the formation of new political groupings. Upon his death in 1988, a battle ensued within the KMT. Authoritarians wanted the nonagenarian widow of Chiang, Madam Chiang Kai-shek, to assume dynastic power.[41] Nonetheless, with the support of a majority of the islanders and the army, a native Formosan, Lee Teng-hui, became president.

Lee allowed even greater freedom of speech, a loosening of controls over the press, and the emergence of the Democratic Progressive party (DPP), a Labor party, and a right-wing Democratic Freedom party. Although split into factions, the potentially significant DPP favored an independent Taiwan. That prospect provoked choleric responses from both the aging KMT leadership and mainland Chinese leaders, but they could not easily dismiss the prospect.

The move toward democratization allowed the sprouting of street demonstrations and the founding of fifty-eight independent newspapers. Environmentalists, feminists, consumers, and even army veterans took advantage of new opportunities to voice their concerns. One protest in May 1988 turned into a riot when farmers demanded higher prices for their produce. Over two hundred people were injured or arrested. Yet, the police did not resort to tear gas or live bullets. As even a government publication emphasized, "In a frightening but nonetheless clear way, the riot was proof of the growing political maturity of the people of Taiwan."[42] While hardly complete, the restructuring of a Taiwanese parliamentary system moved ahead. In 1989, although all of the new political parties were technically illegal, the legislative Yuan—including its "illegal" members—debated new laws governing civic organizations.

As Taiwan advanced towards a more liberal political order, informal economic ties with mainland China grew simultaneously until 1989. Taiwan funneled some $2 billion in trade annually (largely through Hong Kong) to the mainland, and Taiwanese authorities permitted 200,000 personal visits of Taiwanese to the mainland annually. The People's Republic of China offered resources, markets, and cheap labor to Taiwan. When Taiwan's average industrial wage exceeded $20 a day, China paid only $1.20,[43] an obvious lure for Taiwanese investment on the mainland. With a $71 billion foreign exchange reserve and a 40 percent annual rate of savings, Taiwan had plenty of money for investment in China. The truth was that Taiwan, as well as the other NICs, could provide a powerful impetus to China's development, and the opportunities were not lost to either side.

Taiwan's transformation from a colonized island of destitute peasants into a land of relatively free, increasingly prosperous, and internationalized people took only four decades to accomplish. The development was broad, rapid, equitable—and it affected even the most humble peasant. The reasons for the miraculous growth seem straightforward. Bolstered by American aid between 1950 and 1965, a sweeping land reform paved the way for growth and generated capital, labor, and consumer demands for industrial production. The government invested selectively in industries such as petrochemicals and power generation that were too risky for private investors. (Subsequently, in the 1980s, the government privatized the China Steel Corporation and the China Petrochemical Corporation by selling shares to the public.) Small industries employing less than fifty workers contributed 94 percent of the nation's total production and,[44] originally, labor-intensive industries offered the best opportunities for development.[45] A vast growth in the educational system provided the manpower for industrialization as well as widening opportunities for social mobility. Beginning in 1955, a surge in export-oriented industries "unleashed the power of the potential productive resources—especially labor—and made the accelerated modern economic growth in Taiwan possible."[46] In the late 1980s, accommodating new pressure groups, Taiwan's political structure opened up and the nation began a peaceful transition to democracy.

The KMT government, an unlikely purveyor of civic order, unexpectedly provided a solid and stable framework for growth. Early on, the government pursued a policy of export growth. It adopted a system that encouraged savings, particularly by requiring banks to pay high interest rates that exceeded inflation. The government allowed market forces to determine prices and wages as well as the value of national currency on the world market. By dismantling high tariffs and import restrictions, the government opened the way for an export economy. Meanwhile, the KMT took strict measures to curtail corruption within government ranks.

In the absence of these favorable policies, as Yun-Peng Chu of the Academica Sinica has pointed out, Taiwan's growth with equity could not have been achieved:

> Just imagine how a potential entrepreneur who was contemplating the construction of a labor-intensive export processing factory would fare if he found that (i) the foreign exchange he earned from exports must be sold to the government at a suppressed rate. (ii) the factory he planned to build would not have a reliable power supply (iii) he must pay a considerable amount of bribes to obtain the licenses necessary for constructing a factory, importing the raw materials and exporting the finished products (iv) it would not be easy for him to find a literate work force who could be trained to operate simple machinery, (vi) he could not hire labor at their true opportunity costs because of the government's effective minimum wage regulation, and (vii) it was uncertain that the international market would remain strong in the coming years, due to a possible upcoming world recession or protectionist policies.[47]

Whenever it could, Taiwan's government provided a favorable foreign exchange rate, a reliable infrastructure, honest officials, an educated work

force at relatively low wages, and an encouraging attitude toward participation in the world economy.

Clearly, in the next century, Taiwan faces a number of new challenges.
While attempting to move into high-technology industries, the country
must end a "brain drain" of its most highly educated people.[48] In a
protectionist world economy, Taiwan will need to shift from export-driven
growth to a balanced combination in which exports, service industries,
and social spending are emphasized.[49] Coping with the mainland and
building an ever more open political culture remains a grave challenge.[50]
The opportunities are there. The question is whether the Taiwanese—after
breath-taking economic growth—are ready to take advantage of them.

Could Taiwan's ascent be emulated without large doses of foreign aid?
Taiwan, as well as Korea, benefited during its initial stages of growth from
U.S. monies and military assistance. Even Hong Kong had the protections
bestowed by the British government and well-established trade links
throughout the world. Among the second-tier countries, only Singapore
had to stand alone in the world. Its experience demonstrates that development can occur without the bulwark of foreign gifts, advice, or military
aid.

Singapore: Confucian Capitalism

In the 1950s, Singapore—a small island of migrants from China, Malaysia, and India—seemed a most unlikely candidate to join the ranks of
developed countries. Unlike Taiwan, Singapore lacked even a semblance
of an agricultural base, cultural homogeneity, or American assistance. It
had no resources whatsoever and had to import oil, minerals, food, and
water. Moreover, it received no aid from foreign powers and faced potential Malay enemies, Indonesia and Malaysia, that directly bordered the
island territory.

The average Singaporean family earned $332 annually and had to eat
tapioca three times a day in the 1950s. The people of Chinatown lived in
windowless cubicles, bare of toilet facilities, and crowded with 1,800
inhabitants to a city block. More than half of the population of 1.6 million
lived in huts made of discarded planks without water, sewage, or electrical
facilities. Thirteen percent of people could find no work at all, and the
population grew at a disastrous rate of 3.6 percent a year.[51]

After British colonization and almost four years of brutal Japanese
occupation (1942–1945), the political situation hardly seemed promising.

In 1963, Singapore briefly merged with resource-rich Malaysia, but ethnic conflicts doomed the federation. In 1964, racial and religious riots decimated Singapore, students threw bottles at politicians, and the *Barsian socialis* (a radical party) fomented labor unrest, threatening a general strike. Thirty-five died in the ensuing battles. Adding to the economic confusion, the British announced the planned closing of their huge naval base, the country's prime source of employment, by 1970. Singapore's minister of finance estimated that 43,000 new jobs would have to be created each year before 1970 to fill in the gap. Capping the turmoil, Malaysia expelled Singapore from their ill-fated union in 1965.

With great reluctance, for he recognized the importance of Malaysian resources to Singapore, a teary-eyed Lee Kuan Yew, the prime minister, announced the creation of an independent Republic of Singapore. Lee, a brilliant, austere man who had taken a double-first at Cambridge, briefly flirted with socialism but soon turned to a "guided" capitalist system, heavily dependent on multinationals.

At the time, few observers held out much hope for an independent Singapore. Journalist David Bonavia, for example, declared that Singapore had no future outside of "a fresh accommodation with Malaysia to restore the natural economic relationship."[52] Scholar Iain Buchanan predicted an upsurge in social unrest that would topple the little nation.[53] Only Albert Winsemius, a Dutch economist who had headed a UN team in 1961, concluded "we don't see any reason why Singapore should not be able to industrialize, provided that it is determined to do so."[54] Events soon justified Winsemius's heretical optimism.

Within three decades, when I lived there, Singapore blossomed with majestic highrise buildings and terraced homes surrounded by red and purple hibiscus. Bustling factories in the Woodlands and the reclaimed swamps of Jurong produced tv sets, biochemicals, computers, telex machines, and even orchids for export. Singapore's harbor had gained a place as the second largest petrochemical center in the world, while the Changi international airport ranked as the undisputed first in Asia.

The people earned more than $7,000 annually in 1988, ahead of countries like Ireland and Israel. The majority of Singaporeans (74 percent) owned their own flats and houses, medical care was virtually free, and education was universal. Retiring at age 55, the average Singaporean could anticipate a reliable income from the Central Provident Fund. Most people (84 percent) lived in clean and comfortable public housing, bordered by flowering parks, swimming pools, and sports complexes. Crime, drug addiction, vandalism—even spitting—had almost disappeared from Singapore.

Singapore scored higher on measures of literacy and life expectancy than any of her Southeast Asian neighbors. On a scale of 100, Singapore rated 83. Even with much greater resources, the Philippines scored 71, Thailand 68, Malaysia 66, Vietnam 54, Burma 51, and Indonesia 48.[55] Including a striking decrease in infant mortality, Singapore had achieved major economic growth with a spread in equity.

A survey of ninety-three countries between 1974 and 1984, a critical decade of economic achievement, indicated that Singapore was the fastest growing economy in the world. Economists projected that Singaporeans would surpass the per capita wealth of the United States or Switzerland by the early part of the next century—if these countries continued to advance at their current rate.

Few people could reasonably expect Singapore to maintain its precipitous growth forever in a precarious world economy. In fact, between 1985 and 1986, Singapore suffered its first minor depression since the 1950s. By moving with typical speed and dexterity—offering more tax incentives to business, seeking "upmarket" industries such as financial services and biotechnology, and by cutting corporate contributions to the Central Provident Fund—Lee and the People's Action party (PAP) soon restored the Singaporean economy.[56] In 1989, Singapore was growing again at the astounding rate of 11 percent a year.[57]

Such a dizzying but relentless pace of economic advance, as the distinguished economist Ian M. D. Little noted, was "almost entirely due to good policies and the abilities of the people—scarcely at all to favorable circumstances or a good start."[58] The concrete socio-economic policies that propelled Singapore into an age of high technology resembled Taiwan's approach except that the Republic could not count on foreign aid or an agricultural base.

In the 1960s, the PAP government emphasized Singapore's most obvious comparative advantage, its preeminence as a port, to encourage the development of entrepôt and petrochemical industries. In the 1970s, Singapore used another comparative advantage—cheap, but diligent and relatively educated labor—to attract assembly and light industries from abroad. State-sponsored enterprises such as Keppel Shipyards, joint ventures, such as Singapore Petro-Chemical, and foreign companies including Phillips and IBM promoted industrial diversification. Simultaneously, trade unions were curbed and put under the control of a tripartite National

Wages Commission, a grouping of employers, unions, and government officials. Initially, this commission held wages low, but market forces gradually drove the wage level upwards until, in the mid-1980s, Singapore had almost priced itself out of the world labor market.

The republic's large investment in the basic infrastructure and the building of fully equipped industrial estates attracted the capital, technology, and markets of multinational corporations. Tax incentives, as well as a stable and incorrupt system of law, offered a welcoming environment to European, Japanese, and American corporations.

As the government rapidly moved the economy toward an export orientation after 1965, new industries such as computer services, biogenetics, aerospace, telecommunications, and "brain services" (that is, financial, legal, scientific, and technical advice) increasingly took precedence in the economy.

These activities, in turn, required substantial investments in all levels of education. The government sponsored free elementary schools, very inexpensive ($22 annually) secondary schools, many vocational schools, and a fine university. (Interestingly, women outnumbered men at the university and dominated in such unusual fields as science, law, business, and accounting.) Since 1984, English served as the language of instruction, quite a feat in a multilingual nation. In addition, the government cooperated with large multinationals—Tata of India, Phillips of the Netherlands, BBC Brown Boven of Germany—in creating specialized institutes for the training of machinists, tool and die workers, and experts in robotics. While equipping the students for specific vocations, this diversified system also provided a broad general education including instruction in Confucian ethics.[59] Without this innovative program—and government targeting of the required supply of people in each field—Singapore would not have advanced into the modern age.[60]

Singapore's Central Provident Fund provided both a ready stock of capital and a pension scheme. This compulsory savings program required workers to put 25 percent of their earnings into the CPF. Employers matched this sum with another 15 to 25 percent of salaries. The accumulated capital allowed the government to invest in such major programs as the building of schools, hospitals, and subways. Workers could withdraw from the fund to purchase a home or to invest in productive industries. If untouched, the fund accumulated with interest until retirees drew on it at age fifty-five.

A series of other social policies, all initiated by Lee, contributed to

Singapore's stability and growth. Extensive public housing not only provided decent and affordable shelter but, by a careful mixture of the country's diverse groups, reduced ethnic conflict. A combination of education, propaganda, and economic incentives brought the nation's population growth rate down to zero. (Singapore was the first developing nation to achieve this goal.) The PAP government created an extensive investigatory system and strict fines in order to eliminate corruption. A severe anti-drug program combining jail terms, counseling, after-care, and the death penalty for drug dealers virtually eradicated a once serious problem of opiate addiction on the island.

Lee and his advisors carefully promulgated, planned, and oversaw these policies. In a series of free elections, the PAP again and again won the people's approval and swept to overwhelming victories. Until the late 1980s, Lee allowed a relatively free press and an untrammeled judiciary to function as watchdogs over the government.

As his term neared an end, however, Lee took his victories and the growing prosperity of the nation as a mandate to impose his own Confucian ethic upon the people. He attacked the growth of individualism on the island, ridiculed dissenters, limited the circulation of foreign newspapers, and launched campaigns of social engineering designed to improve Singapore's "genetic pool."

When I worked in Singapore, I loved the city and its scattered islets but I also witnessed the chilling impact of Lee's policies on the brightest talent. A scientist at the university had to tape-record his own speeches, critical of Lee's genetic theories, for fear of misinterpretation. A PAP parliamentarian, a brilliant young woman, was scared to voice her feminist concerns publicly. An inept department chairman at the university, later caught as a molester of young girls, squashed all discussions of innovations in the school's curriculum. The most experienced of technocrats, both foreign and indigenous, schemed to leave the republic for new jobs—a very dangerous development for a nation totally dependent on its "human capital." Previously, Singapore had avoided such a "brain drain" and had attracted able foreigners to its hospitable shores. Nonetheless, as Lee's reign approached its announced end, the PAP regime tightened its controls over dissent and forced out all competitors.

In 1987, Lee directly attacked members of the foreign press who were the slightest bit critical of his policies. He also imprisoned twenty-two Singaporeans—church leaders, satirical playwrights, and even a former solicitor general—whom he ludicrously accused of hatching a Marxist plot.

Lee also forced the disbarment of one of the few parliamentary leaders of a competing political party. When the English Privy Council, the ultimate court of appeals for Singapore, cleared the man, Lee's government refused to restore him to Parliament. Wishing to impose a proper respect for social order on young people, Lee introduced a compulsory program in Confucian culture within the schools. Devan Nair, Singapore's ex-president, denounced the program as "humbugging" in a multicultural society.[61] Lee promptly sued him for "defamation."

Lee justified his authoritarianism as a useful part of Asian culture and as a necessary element in Singapore's growth: "I say without the slightest remorse that we wouldn't be here, would not have made the economic progress, if we had not intervened in various personal matters—who your neighbor is, how you live . . . what language you use. It was fundamental social and cultural changes that brought us here."[62]

Undeniably, Lee and his people had created a clean, prosperous, and healthy society. As his people became increasingly educated, however, Lee faced an insoluble spiritual problem: "How to separate Western science from Western ideas, English as a tool for practical use from English as a conduit for liberalism, Cambridge from Confucianism."[63] In a society whose only resource lay in its questing, creative people, attempts to force them into a conformist mold threatened to sap Singapore of its vitality.

The NICs Example

The newly industrialized countries—in spite of meager resources and external threats, energy shortages and originally illiterate populations—made the great ascent from poverty to prosperity in fewer years than any other region of the globe. Their policies were, in many ways, similar: state planning aimed at creating a capitalist economy, an export-oriented and (originally) labor-intensive program of industrialization, flexibility in adapting to their comparative advances, great emphasis on the development of human resources, and a receptive posture towards foreign aid, capital, technology, and ideas. In these areas, the stable governments simultaneously curbed wage demands and spread health care and education widely. Most remarkably, income gaps between the rich and the poor narrowed as development proceeded. In general, Chalmers Johnson, professor of political science at the University of California at San Diego, has dubbed Korea, Taiwan, Singapore (as well as Japan) as "capitalist development states"—political regimes that directly mobilize capital, subcontract to private entrepreneurs, and play the predominant role in organizing work-ers.[64]

Politically, the NICs followed somewhat differing paths. Johnson noted, "As the CDS progresses to advanced levvels of capital-intensive and knowledge-intensive industrialization, the resulting high levels of pluralism will create a crisis of stability than *can* lead to democracy."[65] The pattern was hardly inevitable: Hong Kong, within its colonial status, maintained liberal institutions such as a free press and a stable rule of law, but it was hardly a democracy; Taiwan and Korea moved from one-party military regimes into an era of incrreasing liberalization; Singapore, in contrast, appeared to have hardened its authoritarianism as the years passed. Thus, one of the great challenges for these areas is to welcome the pluralistic trends that prosperity and increased education engender without slipping back into dictatorship.

A second primary challenge for the NICs is their role in the world economy in the next century. The worst prospect for these outward-oriented economies is the possibility of worldwide recession, perhaps triggered by American protectionism, a further blockade by a united EEC, and an inward turn by Japan.

Wisely, the NICs increasingly began to focus on the Pacific Rim itself or the Third World for sustenance and markets. By 1985, Singapore had become the telecommunications and medical center for all of Southeast Asia.[66] In 1988, Taiwan resumed its role in the Asian Development Bank and allocated $1 billion annually for Third World aid.[67] In 1989, Korea increased its trade with mainland China to over $3 billion annually and explored ties with North Korea.[68] More than ever, Hong Kong played its central role in facilitating financial flows among Asian nations. Fortu-nately, the NICs were surrounded by great outlying areas, particularly China and the nations of Southeast Asia whose economic needs and resources complemented those of the NICs. As just one example: by 1988, Hong Kong had created two million manufacturing jobs in China, more than in the Colony itself.[69]

On the periphery, just at the start of major growth, nations such as Malaysia, Indonesia, and Thailand—replete with resources and potential markets—consciously "looked eastward" and poised to join in the great Pacific resurgence. If they succeeded, the Pacific Rim would turn into an arc of affluence.

Notes

1. Paul Johnson, *Modern Times* (New York: Harper and Row, 1983), 722.
2. Ibid., 718.

3. Bon-Ho-Koo, "An Overview of Korea's Economic Development," Taipei, Chung Hua Institution of Economics, November 1988.
4. Ibid.
5. Boyd Gibbons, "South Koreans," *National Geographic,* August 1988, 71.
6. Hung-Ki Kim, "Capital Formation: An Experience in Korea," Taipei, Chung Hua Institution of Economics, 15 Nov. 1988.
7. Ibid.
8. Ibid., 5.
9. Ibid.
10. David Aikman, *Pacific Rim* (Boston: Little Brown, 1986), 97.
11. See Johnson, *Modern Times,* 723.
12. Roy Hofheinz and Kent Calder, *The Eastasia Edge* (New York: Basic Books, 1982), 61.
13. See Jan Morris, *Hong Kong* (New York: Random House, 1988).
14. Alvin Rabushka, *Hong Kong: A Study in Economic Freedom* (Chicago: University of Chicago, 1979).
15. See Clark Kerr, *The Future of Industrial Societies* (Cambridge: Harvard University Press, 1983).
16. Rabushka, *Economic Freedom.*
17. Hofheinz and Calder, *Eastasia Edge,* 62.
18. Aikman, *Pacific Rim,* 111.
19. Ibid.
20. Shirley W. Y. Kuo, "Development of the Taiwan Economy," Chung-Hua Institution for Economic Research, Taipei, 14 Nov. 1988.
21. Aiken, *Pacific Rim.*
22. Ibid.
23. Ibid., 112.
24. Hofheinz and Calder, *Eastasia Edge,* 57.
25. Kuo, "Taiwan Economy."
26. Yu-kang Mao, "Land and Agricultural Policies in the Process of Economic Development of the Republic of China on Taiwan," Chung Hua Institution of Economics, 15 Nov. 1988, 29.
27. Ibid., 6.
28. Ibid., 8.
29. Ibid., 10.
30. Ibid., 11.
31. Ibid., 3.
32. Ibid.
33. Chi-ming Hou, "Relevance of the Taiwan Model of Development," Chung Hua Institution of Economics, Taipei, 16 Nov. 1988, 6.
34. See Chi Schive, "Education and the Assimilation of Foreign Technology," Chung Hua Institution of Economics, mimeographed paper, Taipei, 16 Nov. 1988.
35. Ibid.
36. Hou, "Relevance of Taiwan Model," 7.
37. Ibid.
38. Thomas Omestad, "Dateline Taiwan: A Dynasty Ends," *Foreign Policy* (Summer, 1988): 179.
39. Hou, "Relevance of Taiwan Model," 15.
40. *The Far Eastern Economic Review,* 19 Jan. 1989.

41. Omestad, "Dateline."
42. Republic of China, Government Information Office, Taipei, Sept. 1988, 1.
43. *Far Eastern Economic Review,* see n. 40.
44. Shim Jae Hoon, "Awash in a Sea of Money," *Far Eastern Economic Review,* 15 Sept. 1988.
45. See Yun-Peng Chu, "Towards a Theoretical Explanation of Taiwan's Development with Increasing Equality," mimeographed paper, Chung Hua Institution of Economics, Taipei, 16 Nov. 1988.
46. Hou, "Relevance of Taiwan Model," 7.
47. Chu, "Development with Equality," 19.
48. See Jonathan Moore, "The New Word on Campus: Flexibility," *Far Eastern Economic Review,* 15 Sept. 1988.
49. See Jonathan Moore, "Social Unease: the Price of Development," *Far Eastern Economic Review,* 15 Sept. 1988.
50. Omestad, "Dateline."
51. See John Drysdale, *Singapore's Struggle for Success* (Singapore: Times Books, 1984).
52. David Bonavia, *Far Eastern Economic Review,* 23 Feb. 1963.
53. Iain Buchanan, *Singapore in Southeast Asia,* quoted in Goh Chok Tong, "People's Action Party," Singapore, Petir 25th. Anniversary Issue, 1985, 65.
54. Albert Winsemius, "From A Distance," National Exhibition, Singapore, Ministry of National Development, 1984, 43.
55. Kerr, *Future of Societies.*
56. See John Andrews, "Singapore: Lee's Creation and Legacy," *Far Eastern Economic Review,* 22 Nov. 1988.
57. "Economic Indicators," *Far Eastern Economic Review,* 12 Jan. 1989, 65.
58. Ian M. D. Little, *Economic Development* (New York: Basic Books, 1982), 108.
59. See Viswanathan Selvaratnam, "Vocational Education and Training: The Singapore and Other Third World Initiatives," Chung Hua Institution, Taipei, 17 Nov. 1988.
60. For a general analysis, see Philip Coombs, *The World Crisis in Education* (New York: Oxford University Press, 1985). Typical Third World nations have suffered from an undersupply of skilled personnel, particularly in technical fields. A few, like India, have overproduced lawyers (and even engineers). Government targeting of vocational demand allowed Singapore to hit the right educational balance.
61. Nair quoted in Ian Buruma, "Singapore," *New York Times,* 12 June 1988, 10.
62. Lee Kuan Yew, quoted in Andrews, "Singapore," 9.
63. Buruma, "Singapore."
64. See Chalmers Johnson, "South Korean Democratization," *The Pacific Review,* 2, no. 1 (March 1989).
65. Ibid., 43.
66. *The Straits Times,* Singapore, 10 Feb. 1985.
67. Kuo, "Taiwan Economy."
68. Ken Yun, "Crossing the Yellow Sea," *The China Business Review,* Jan.–Feb., 1989.
69. Frank Ching, "The Emergence of Greater China," *Billion,* Hong Kong 1 (1988).

4

Tier Three: The Southeast Asian Rim

The center of world manufacturing and increas-
ingly that of finance, is shifting from the North
Atlantic to the Western Pacific.
—James Abegglen, 1989

The stunning success of the NICs encouraged some countries (notably Malaysia and Thailand) and some development agencies (particularly the World Bank) to advocate the adaption of export-oriented, labor-intensive, free-market policies in other areas of the world. Certain experts prematurely declared the World Bank policy a failure.[1] Economists Robin Broad and John Cavanaugh, for example, argued that "the result was two vicious battles—one to offer cheaper, more docile labor forces and more attractive financial incentives . . . and the other to win scarce export markets."[2] Broad and Cavanaugh contended that the NICs had already expropriated the world market, that new technologies and protectionism had eclipsed the potential comparative advantage of other countries, and that the debt crisis "left increasing numbers of people at the margins of market activity."[3]

The validity of such harsh assessments remained in doubt, particularly in those regions most directly affected by East Asian growth. The record of Southeast Asia—an area that was decisively inspired by Japan and the NICs—offered some startling evidence that the general pessimism of Western experts was not justified.

The history of the Southeast Asian rim demanded that "the debate on adjustment and development should be reopened."[4] In particular, three factors affected the destiny of this populous, tropical edge of Asia:

Rich with the foreign reserves, in need of commodities, and desirous of cheap consumer goods, Japan steadily invested in Southeast Asia. In the short period between 1983 and 1988, Japan increased her investments in Indonesia, Thailand, Malaysia, and the Philippines from $651 million to almost $15 billion.[5] Investment in Thailand grew fourteen times in five years while Japanese capital in Indonesia shot upwards twenty-seven times.[6] Although hampered by memories of the Japanese "co-prosperity sphere," Southeast Asians accepted the money with the hope that it would usher in a new era of intra-Pacific cooperation.

Other more developed Asian nations also opened a series of joint ventures with their Southeast Asian neighbors. Singapore, for example, agreed with Indonesia to exploit Batam Island in a cooperative fashion. The island, just south of Singapore, offered the possibility of easing congestion in Singapore's port facilities, becoming a new center for high technology, and aiding in the transshipment of liquefied natural gas. (Singapore had none while Indonesia was the world's largest producer.)[7] Korea and Taiwan shifted their production of plywood to Indonesia.[8] The ASEAN nations (Singapore, Indonesia, Brunei, the Philippines, and Malaysia) reached unprecedented agreements in 1985 to establish joint plants in the region, such as a fertilizer producer in northwest Sumatra.[9] Such regional endeavors presaged a new, if still fragile era of Pacific cooperation.

Meanwhile, the richer Asian nations, seeking to satisfy their own domestic needs at the lowest possible price, shed certain industries and built a new economic base in Southeast Asia and surrounding territories. Singapore abandoned its uneconomic production of pigs and imported the cheaper products of Australia and New Zealand. Japan started a rural success story in Thailand by sponsoring (and even insuring) the export of frozen food to the homeland.[10] With the assistance of Mitsubishi, Malaysia launched its Proton car upon an uncertain world market. Taiwan and Korea invested heavily in the Philippines, ensuring a growth rate there of 6.7 percent in 1988. Thus, as Japan and the NICs moved towards new forms of technology and changed their priorities, opportunities opened for Southeast Asia.

The pattern was not uniform for the southern rim. Ravaged by foreign invasions and civil war, Cambodia, Laos, and Vietnam remained stagnant economies. Indeed, as rice production dropped, the Indo-Chinese area registered its tenth consecutive year of a negative trade balance in 1987.[11] Vietnam exported raw materials and minerals, but 70 percent of its exports went to the Soviet Union in repayment for military aid.[12] Simultaneously, Vietnam continued to maintain a 1,260,000-man army, the second largest military force in Asia.

Although well-endowed with timber, oil, rice, minerals, and fisheries, Burma adapted a policy of socialism in 1974 and went into self-imposed exile. As a result, the economy remained agrarian, state-owned industries floundered, student riots and ethnic rebellions riddled the country, a black market flourished, and food production lagged behind population growth. In 1987, the silver jubilee of the socialist revolution passed without celebration since that year marked the point at which Ne Win, Burma's leader, asked the United Nations to designate his nation as among "the least developed countries" of the world.[13]

Like Burma, the great Philippine archipelago of 7,100 islands in the South China Sea possessed abundant resources. Under the corrupt, semi-feudal rule of Ferdinand Marcos between 1965 and 1986, however, this great potential went to waste. Between 1972 and 1985, per capita income declined to approximately $600 a year. While Marcos and his cronies lived in affluence, most Filipinos subsisted on $55 a month. Farm workers scraped by on less than $2 a day. Forty percent of the work force was totally unemployed.[14] Next to Bangladesh, the Philippines had the poorest economic record in all of Asia. Bernardo Villegas, an influential Philippine economist, declared in 1985 that "the Philippines is the economic basket case of Pacific Asia."[15]

Predictably, deteriorating economic conditions fueled a Communist insurgency in Luzon, a Muslim secessionist movement in Mindanao, and riots in Manila. Marcos declared martial law in 1972 and arrested opposition leaders, notably Benigno Aquino, and after imprisonment, sent them into exile. In August, 1983 assassins murdered Aquino as he was led down the steps of an airplane in Manila. This event marked the beginning of the end for the Marcos regime. Economic woes added to the political instability: inflation reached 20 percent annually in 1983, the peso halved in value, and foreign indebtedness rose to $27.5 billion. Merely paying the interest on these loans consumed one-third of Filipino foreign exchange earnings.[16] In 1986, Marcos fled to a luxurious asylum in Hawaii, and Corazon Aquino, the widow of the murdered politician, took over power.

President Aquino attempted to restore the economy, aid the poorer peasants, end rebellion, and strengthen the private sector. To a degree, she succeeded. In 1987, the GNP began to grow again, real per capita income increased, and the balance of payments turned favorable.[17] Aquino launched a land reform, but powerful landholders, assured of only 10 percent cash as recompense, opposed the move. Ideally, Aquino hoped to revitalize agriculture and to build rural-based industries, but lack of foreign capital, continuing insurrections, labor unrest, and the emergence of right-wing vigilante groups still held the Philippines back from fulfilling its potential.

Elsewhere in Southeast Asia—where neither a feudal regime nor a socialist ideology prevailed—other governments emulated the East Asian model more or less with success. Observers could reasonably anticipate that Malaysia, Thailand, and even troubled Indonesia might emerge as a new generation of economically progressive nations.

Malaysia: A Delicate Balance

Like the Philippines, Malaysia at its independence could lay claim to great reserves of natural resources—tin, rubber, oil, timber, and palm oil. Yet, with world commodity prices wildly fluctuating, few people expected this unusual land to lead in economic development. The peninsula and its territories in Borneo had endured centuries of Arab, Dutch, Portuguese, English, and Japanese exploitation.[18] The country had barely survived a Communist insurrection and it suffered from pronounced ethnic divisions (59 percent Malay, 31 percent Chinese, 10 percent Indians and others). Foreign-owned rubber plantations dominated the economy, aborigines were afraid to emerge from the great rain forests, and the mountainous inland still harbored cobras. Moreover, Islam was the predominant religion, and no other Islamic society had managed to distribute increasing wealth in an equitable fashion.

Politically, in 1990, Malaysia was formally ruled by sultans who rotated the kingship. Political parties divided largely along extremely hostile ethnic lines. The Chinese minority dominated the economic realm but, in an unwritten agreement, Muslims controlled the government, the army, and eventually the universities. This uneasy social contract did not bode well for the country's eventual stability.

Yet, Malaysia grew at a rapid economic rate. The real growth of Malaysia was over eight percent annually in the 1960s and 1970s. Even during the world recession of the 1980s, the Malaysia economy prospered at better than 5 percent annually. In 1989, when restrained by a continued decline in oil and tin prices, Malaysia still expanded her economic base by 7 percent.[19]

Commodity exports contributed to this burst in economic activity but, increasingly, manufacturing output—in food processing and electrical products, transport equipment, and steel products—grew at a dramatic pace. Bolstered by investments from Japan, Korea, and Taiwan (seeking to utilize Malaysia's tariff privileges under the Generalized System of Preferences), the manufacturing sector surged forward by 13 percent in 1987, 15 percent in 1988, and 11 percent in 1989.[20] The German-owned Bosch factory in Penang alone exported 1.2 million radio-cassettes annually. Although afflicted by some unemployment (8 percent in 1989), per capita income rose from $500 a year in 1957 to $2,800 in 1989.[21]

Malaysia's government not only sought to increase the nation's wealth but to insure its most equitable distribution. Because of investments in health and educational facilities, Malaysians' physical welfare greatly improved. In measurements of crucial indices of the quality of life (rates of infant mortality, life expectancy, and literacy), Malaysia scored higher than any other Islamic country with a rating of 66. In contrast, the People's Republic of Yemen stagnated at 33, Pakistan scored 38, Syria ranked at 54, and Turkey 55.[22]

Between 1971 and 1990, the government pursued its "New Economic Policy," a highly controversial attempt to increase the share of Malays in the national wealth. In 1971, many Malays (or *bumiputra,* sons of the soil) lived below the official poverty line while the Chinese predominated in the upper income ranks. In the hope of reducing this disparity, the Malay-dominated government created statutory bodies to buy shares in foreign or Chinese-controlled industries, and set "affirmative action" quotas in business and education. The plan increased *bumiputra* participation in corporate ownership from 1.5 percent in 1971 to 20 percent in 1989. A visible Malay middle class of professionals and businessmen also established itself in the cities.[23]

Politically, the Malaysians maintained a relatively free society, but cracks in the generally temperate system had begun to appear in the late 1980s. Just before independence, the Malays founded the United Malays National Organization (Umno) while the Chinese and Indians created their own political groupings. Under the tolerant leadership of Tunko (Prince) Abdul Rahman—a sophisticated, gentle graduate of Cambridge—Umno led the three organizations in seeking independence. In 1955, the Tunku's alliance won 80 percent of the vote in a free election. The Tunku established a multicultural regime, gave amnesty to Communist guerrillas, and fostered a political climate that encouraged compromise. In 1966, the new prime minister survived an attempt by Indonesia to absorb parts of North Borneo that had joined Malaysia. In 1969, the Tunku opposed measures that would make Islam the official religion and Malay the standard language of Malaysia. He failed, and murderous ethnic riots broke out. Although forced to retire, the Tunku continued to oppose divisive measures within Malaysia and to advocate a liberal system.

His eventual successor as prime minister, Datuk Seri Mahathir Mohammad, demanded a stricter work ethic from his people and counseled them to "look east" to Japan and Korea for the most modern technological and management techniques. In 1981, the "look east" policy became official: the Japanese presence in Malaysia brought an upsurge in trade and manufacturing, and Malaysia sent thousands of workers for training in Japan.

Under Mahathir, severe ethnic tensions continued to disturb the Malaysian balance.[24] The government imposed Malay as the medium of instruction in Tamil and Mandarin schools. A move to require a Muslim pledge of allegiance from all school children alarmed the Chinese and Indian minorities. Parti Islam (Pas), a fundamentalist party, tried to establish the reign of Islamic law throughout the country. Pas also advised its members to kill even their own parents if they did not avoid modern inventions such as television. Native minorities in Sabah and Sarawak, rather primitive provinces within the federation, demonstrated for their rights. Malay students in universities demanded that everyone must adapt Islamic garb and that walls should be erected in classrooms to divide males and females.

Invoking fears of ethnic violence, Mahathir struck back indiscriminately in 1987 and 1988. He closed newspapers (including one owned by the Tunku) on grounds that they incited disturbances. Using an old British preventive detention law, Mahathir jailed a mélange of opponents. Without trial, he detained among others nine leaders of Pas and ten members of the parliamentary opposition including Lim Kit Siang, its elected leader.

Even when suffering from political repression and ethnic dissent, Malaysia continued to make great economic progress. An abundance of resources alone did not explain Malaysia's economic advance since equally rich areas, such as the Philippines and Burma, faltered in exploiting their own wealth. Conversely, neighboring Singapore, without resources, progressed even more dramatically than did Malaysia. Observers attributed the success of Malaysia, unique in the Islamic world, to several factors:

—An outward-looking economic policy encouraged foreign investment and promoted unusual advances in industrial activity.

—Various governments encouraged the private sector, imposed relatively low taxes, sought to diversify trading partners and products, and trimmed expenditures to meet income.

—Efforts to improve education and health, particularly among the previously underprivileged Malays, created a new middle class and an impressive group of industrial workers.

—The Chinese minority contributed an energetic entrepreneurial and commercial spirit to Malaysia. Without them, P. T. Bauer has argued, Malaysia would still be an unexplored rain forest.[25]

—The Japanese influence in example and ideas, capital and technology allowed Malaysia to "look east" successfully. (The northeastern states, relatively uninfluenced by cultures other than Islam, remained stagnant and provided converts for fanatical movements such as Pas).

In an atmosphere of ethnic hostility and government repression, it remained questionable whether sustained economic growth could be maintained in an unstable political climate. As M.I.T. political scientist Lucian Pye pointed out in 1985 about the Chinese-Malay tension, "these cultures present numerous points of conflict that make Chinese and Malays scornful of each other. . . . Politically the situation is explosive because the concepts of power and of the proper use of authority are antithetical."[26]

Three decades of substantial economic advance offered hope, however, that Malaysia would continue to prosper as a secular society. Its future depended upon the emergence of another generation of leaders who, like the Tunku, would maintain the fragile political stability that is prerequisite to economic progress.

Thailand: "A Moving Equilibrium"

Surrounded by Indo-Chinese dictatorships and socialist Burma, Thailand once seemed a prime candidate for economic stagnation and revolutionary instability. In 1978, some Western political scientists predicted that a decline into disaster "may already be inevitable"[27] since Thailand had to counter military incursions and, simultaneously, to absorb refugees who spilled over her borders.

Although Thailand was a proud kingdom that had never succumbed to colonization, the nation had a chequered history of internal coups.[28] In the 1930s, a series of military rulers allied the nation with fascist Japan. Between 1945 and 1948, a chaotic civilian government ruled briefly, until the military once again assumed power. More coups—in 1957, 1971, 1972, 1976, and 1980 burst out in a bewildering progression until General Prem Tinsulaound restored a semblance of parliamentary government. He, too, faced challenges from "Young Turks" in 1981 and 1985. Prem, like other military rulers, held power by dispensing favors to officers who came from his own class in the military academy.

On the surface, Thailand's modern history seemed a political cauldron boiling over into anarchy. Yet, the appearance of turmoil obscured a basic tranquility: the revered monarchs continued on their thrones and exercised a moderating influence, the economy steadily advanced, the press freely and often wryly commented on the political circus—and triumphant generals seldom executed the losers in the political game.

The truth is that a "moving equilibrium" of balanced forces—the king, the aristocrats, the army, political parties, students, an intelligentsia, the civil service, and businessmen—had created a tolerant, stable society. Over the years, Thailand (literally, "the land of the free") had consistently "delivered the central 'goods' of modern nationhood: sovereign independence, economic growth, economic diversification, social peace for most Thais most of the time, far more freedom than is typical of Third World countries, and increasing political participation."[29] The country's continuity in basic institutions resulted in "a period of Thai peace, freedom, and growth—all rare in the modern Third World."[30]

In 1988, Thailand's real economic growth jumped by 8 percent and industrial exports surged by 40 percent.[31] This remarkable advance was in sharp contrast to Burma, Thailand's geographical and cultural twin. Thailand and Burma had almost identical resources; both were agrarian and tropical countries; both were pervaded with Buddhism; and, originally, both had semidivine monarchs. Yet, in the late twentieth century, Burma retrogressed economically while Thailand blossomed.

Several elements in their premodern histories and cultures may have shaped their responses to the demands of modernization:

The Burmese suffered from a "ubiquitous fear of losing power."[32] They succumbed to colonization but deeply resented Western intrusion. Thai kings adroitly escaped colonization by playing the English against the French. Nonetheless, the Thai monarchs recognized the utility of Western knowledge and technology. They welcomed foreign advisors from England, Denmark, America, France, and Prussia.[33] Thus, Thailand entered the modern world while Burma, after independence, went into isolation.

In contrast to the Burmese, the Thais had introduced a graceful system for rotating their elites early in their history. The descendants of the higher nobility lost a grade in the hierarchy every generation until, by the fifth generation, all had become commoners once again.[34] In its own way, the system opened the door of "equal opportunity" for ambitious people in the lower ranks.

Unlike the Burmese, the Thais imposed two constraints on their rulers. Every superior in a particular hierarchy had to exhibit *metta* (kindness and compassion) to inferiors and to manifest *karuma* (a willingness to help others and to guide them constructively).[35] In turn, subordinates were expected to respond with *kamlungjie,* "that absolutely essential sense of will, of the vitality and energy necessary for all manner of activities."[36] Thus, Thai culture encouraged mutual compassion and reciprocal services. Such traits, under the right conditions, could help to maintain political civility and to ease the tensions involved in economic modernization.

These cultural and historical characteristics of Thailand may well have contributed to the smoothness of Thai managerial relations, to the relatively bloodless political coups, and to the people's ability to adapt economically useful elements from other cultures.

Based on a gentle, compromising culture, Thailand's economy had undergone "a quiet, unpublicized revolution" by the late 1980s.[37] Industrial exports surpassed the country's traditionally vigorous production of rice, rubber, teak, and sugar. Thailand became a leading exporter of textiles, processed foods, computer disc drives, toys, telephone equipment and even $1 billion worth annually of polished jewels.[38] From the late 1970s to the mid-1980s, Thailand faced the same problems that bankrupted much of the developing world but this resilient society overcame them.[39] By the late 1980s the Thai economy grew at twice the historic rate of the West.[40]

Like the Meiji Japanese, the Thais' economic progress was gradual, first stressing agriculture, then light industry, and later some heavy industry. The keynotes of economic policy included diversification, an outward orientation, and (except for the early 1970s) conservative financing. Taxes and import duties were kept low. Relatively, the Thais maintained a free enterprise economy and, by 1989, had begun to privatize previously state-owned companies.

Until the late 1980s, Thailand was fortunate in having a land surplus and avoiding the problem of land tenancy that hampered the Philippines.

In addition, Thai rulers cultivated Chinese businessmen who faced severe discrimination in countries like Malaysia.

A rigorously free press served as a watchdog over the government and, even when the military dominated, helped to give economic development priority over military spending.

The Thai economy became broadly diversified from an initial dependence on rice and the export of such minerals as tungsten and tin. In the 1980s, the government managed to cut its trade deficit, broaden its markets, hold down inflation, and open extensive oil explorations in the Gulf of Thailand.[41]

For all of its progress, Thailand still faced severe problems. The country's infrastructure, particularly the transportation system, did not keep pace with its fast growth. Urban prosperity—where people earned eight times more than in rural areas—attracted an unmanageable migration. The cities particularly lured young girls (some 100,000 to 400,000 of them) into prostitution and turned Bangkok into the "sex capitol" of Asia. Thai factory workers earned only one-third the wages paid in Korea, Hong Kong, or Taiwan. In spite of an injection of skilled technocrats, corruption prevailed in the traditional civil service. Politically, except for a deep respect for the monarchy, Thais failed to develop a general consensus about the country's future.[42]

Warning signals abounded and clearly Thailand had not achieved the degree of equity exhibited by the NICs during their periods of greatest growth. Nonetheless, the diversification of the economy, the abundance of its resources, and the "moving equilibrium" of its polity suggested that Thailand could survive the threat of world recession and continue to be regarded as the linchpin of the region.[43]

Indonesia: A Potential Giant

Indonesia, a new nation scattered over 13,700 islands, has vast assets, but they had yet to be fully exploited in the twentieth century. The shimmering landscape provided an abundance of oil, gas, coal, minerals, timber, rubber, rice, and untilled rich soil. The country's 175 million people constituted the world's fifth most populous country and the largest Islamic realm. Indonesians had established an impressive petrochemical industry, a nuclear capacity, and their own aircraft industry. Japan foresaw great potential in Indonesia and by 1989 had pumped more capital into the nation than any other Southeast Asian region. Indonesia was described as "the Pacific Basin country with the most potential to become a regional and even a world industrial power."[44]

Nonetheless, by most standards, Indonesia remained an underdeveloped country balanced on the edge of subsistence. In comparison to Thais in 1988, for example, Indonesians had a lower per capita income ($350 annually vs. $612), lived fewer years (58 vs. 63), had more infant deaths

(88 vs. 57 per 1,000 annually), and spent far less of their public budget on education (9% vs. 25%).[45] Similarly, Malaysians who shared the same ethnic stock and religion as most Indonesians outscored them on every measure of physical welfare.[46]

The reasons behind Indonesia's failure to fulfill her promise lay in a history that had produced fragmentation and violence, mismanagement and fanaticism.

For centuries, Arab, Portuguese, and Dutch invaders had squabbled over Indonesia's islands. By 1910, the Dutch managed to extend their domination from a base in Java to most of Sumatra, the Celebes, Borneo, and Irian. The Dutch ruled "indirectly," depending on traditional sultans to carry out their directions. As one result, most Indonesians retained parochial loyalties and did not develop a national identification. The Dutch made little effort to train people either for self-rule or for participation in a market economy. In 1940, when the population had reached 70 million, only 240 Indonesian students graduated from high school.[47] Consequently, Islamic culture, as well as the mystical spiritualism of Java, remained relatively intact and, as Pye noted, "There was no room for the transitional man, the man who sought to become Westernized without necessarily losing all of his traditional values."[48]

With a doctrine of "divide and rule," the Dutch encouraged a fragmentation of power among the Indonesians. Economically, the Dutch allowed Chinese immigrants to work as tax collectors or to enter business, but discouraged Indonesians—leaving behind a lasting distrust of the Chinese.

Politically, the colonialists established a series of competing native rulers, each with his own court and clients. Unfortunately, even after independence, this divisive legacy affected the country.[49] The city of Bandung, for example, housed the governor of West Java, the regent of Bandung, the mayor of Bandung, and the army commander of West Java— each with independent staffs, indistinct powers, and overlapping functions. In the postcolonial era, this fragmentation too often resulted in an inability to reach decisions, as well as pervasive bribery of the competing government officials.

The Japanese invasion of Indonesia in the 1940s destroyed the myth of Dutch invincibility and encouraged nationalist sentiment. The Japanese trained Indonesians in military crafts, as a buffer against the Dutch, and encouraged political puppets—notably Sukarno—to assume active rules under the Japanese regime. With the Japanese defeat, the Dutch initially used Japanese troops to "maintain control" and, for four bitter years, tried to reassert their hegemony. Wearied by fruitless combat and drained financially, the Dutch signed the Hague Agreement of 1949. Among other provisions, the treaty legalized fifteen separate states (in addition to the Republic of Indonesia), imposed huge debts on the new country, and required the maintenance of the Dutch civil service. In 1957, with disastrous economic effects, Indonesia abrogated the treaty, nationalized Dutch property, and expelled 46,000 Hollanders.

Stripped of administrators, technicians, and managers, Indonesia tried to rebuild a shattered economy and create a stable political system. The experiment failed. After meeting for three years, an elected assembly charged with drafting a constitution could agree only on a national flag. Sukarno, a charismatic leader, dismissed the assembly and instituted "guided democracy." He immediately faced various rebellions. *Darul Islam* tried to establish a purified Islamic state in rural Java; its members beheaded opponents and carved a crescent on their chests. The *Permesta* movement fought for greater autonomy for the outer islands from Javanese who were often regarded as neocolonialists. On Sumatra, a third insurrection sought to restore true democracy to Indonesia.[50] Aided by a Japanese-trained army, Sukarno temporarily crushed the revolutionaries and proceeded to create his own brand of socialism.

Sukarno's type of socialism resulted in the nationalization of Indonesia's huge plantations and its meager industrial base. More often than not, as I observed the situation, Sukarno handed over the enterprises to ill-equipped cronies and loyal army officers. Under Sukarno's rule, rubber production dropped 25 percent, coffee by 50 percent, tobacco 60, sugar 66, and copra by 75 percent. Prices rose by 500 percent a year. Chinese entrepreneurs suffered from repression. Bribes lined the pockets of those in Sukarno's favor.

Meanwhile, Sukarno spent money on monuments, luxury hotels, and circuses. As one example: the army commandeered the Bank of Indonesia's fleet of trucks to carry spectators to the flamboyant Asian Games. Bereft of personnel who normally rode the trucks to work, the fiscal system of Indonesia collapsed—but the Games went on. As "guided democracy" squandered the country's assets, discontented officers, some peasants, and the country's small group of industrial workers plotted Sukarno's overthrow.[51]

An incorruptible group of Communists organized the industrial workers of Java and many of the peasants on Sumatra for revolution. They had ready converts since twenty years of independence had meant a drop in the average laborer's wage by 40 percent.[52] In 1965, the Communists attempted revolution.[53] Assassins killed six army generals who supported Sukarno but, strangely, did not harm General Suharto, a high commander. Between 1965 and 1966, the army under Suharto retaliated by killing some 500,000 people. In 1966, Suharto quietly deposed Sukarno and had himself inaugurated as president in 1968.

Politically, Hamish McDonald observed, "the years under the Suharto government held a special dimension of hardship and fear."[54] Suharto arrested 750,000 people and detained them without trial; in 1983, 43,000 had not regained their civil rights.[55] In 1986, twenty years after the coup, Suharto had nine Communists executed.[56] With grim consistency, Suharto suppressed various critical newspapers, imprisoned Muslim protestors, suspended human rights lawyers, and lobbied to secure the dominance of *Golkar* (the government-controlled party) over the nation.[57] Little changed between the regimes of Sukarno and Suharto: an army bloated with corruption held a fragmented Indonesia together, fundamentalists in Muslim ranks continued to agitate for an Islamic state, a single leader proclaimed a uniquely "Indonesian" ideology to perpetuate his power.

The economy, however, began to prosper. More than Sukarno, Suharto insured a degree of stability, advocated a pragmatic approach to world economic problems, and depended upon economic technocrats rather than ideologues to manage economic affairs.

During the late 1960s, the country regained lost momentum, particularly because of an upsurge in world oil prices. The development budget swelled and a great deal of it was spent on previously neglected agriculture. Most significantly, Indonesia moved out of its status as the world's largest importer of rice and became self-sufficient.

In the 1970s, under the guidance of "the Berkeley Mafia," a group of market-oriented economists, the GNP may have grown as much as 10 percent a year. The relatively austere policies of this group reduced inflation, cut down on prestige spending, and increased investments from foreign sources.

The technocrats also implemented a politically sensitive "transmigration" program aimed at relieving Java's intense overpopulation problem. The Suharto government provided subsidies for migrants from Java (2,000 people per square mile) to less populated islands such as West Irian (8.5 people per square mile). Some 3.5 million people moved and brought schools, clinics, and a pioneer spirit to thinly populated territories.[58]

In other parts of Indonesia, farmers planted more tree crops (such as rubber) than in any other country of the world. Indonesians doubled their production of soybeans between 1970 and 1980.[59] Fledgling industries, particularly small-scale factories, blossomed, and Indonesia became the only nation in the region to develop its own helicopter industry. Much of this progress depended upon oil revenues.

By the 1980s, the oil boom collapsed and prices for Indonesian oil dropped in half. Indonesia entered a necessary period of austerity. Living standards in 1988 dropped back to the 1970 level, the country had to repay a massive foreign debt ($42.6 billion) run up during the spendthrift days of Sukarno, and expenditures for new development had to be cut.[60]

Most seriously, almost two million people entered the work force every year with little prospect of decent employment.[61] Corruption continued unabated as army wives and children served as conduits for illicit monies.[62] Only the development of agriculture, labor-intensive industries serving the rural sector, and regional, small-scale industries designed for the ASEAN region could absorb the new labor.

The man-made obstacles facing Indonesia in the 1990s and beyond are formidable. A feudal system of land ownership still concentrates property in few hands. The birth rate continues to soar while interest in Javanese "transmigration" has soured. Hostility to five million Chinese hampers the expression of their business talents. State-owned industries stagnate. (*Petramina,* a state petrochemical complex run by a General Sutowo, collapsed in 1975 and left the nation with an outstanding debt of $10.5 billion which is still being paid.) Foreign investment in agro-business lags since aliens are not allowed to control plantations. An autarkic strategy of industrial development fostered by Sukarno drives up the prices of such basic products as cement to double the cost of imports.[63]

Fortunately, the obstacles to Indonesia's development cannot be traced to natural deprivation. Sensible policies could—in theory—place the nation back on the path to affluence. If Suharto or his successors have the will, remedies to Indonesia's laggard performance are apparent: most generally, Indonesia has a unique opportunity to follow the East Asian model of development for it has the resources and a fresh flow of Asian capital. Implementing the East Asian policy means that the government must institute land reforms to encourage peasant initiatives, capital investment, and labor-intensive industrialization. It requires that the planners abandon state-owned industries to private competition and, for the immediate future, suppress dreams of creating high-technology, capital-intensive enterprises. Honest elements within the elite have to slash governmental corruption by severe methods, as Singapore has done. Turning outwards also demands that restrictions on foreign investment should be lifted and that the government invest public monies in education, building the basic infrastructure, and ending the population explosion. Can a military elite, itself the beneficiary of public largesse, bring about these reforms?

Although cynics might deny it, there were hopeful signs that public-spirited members of the elite could follow such a scenario. Government economists had already adopted the necessary measures of fiscal austerity. Indonesia's private sector, particularly its Chinese entrepreneurs, exhibited extraordinary vigor in spite of discrimination. Indonesia's export-oriented industries, except for state oil enterprises, matured and showed flexibility in meeting the demands of the world market. Foreign investors, particularly the Japanese, had confidence in Indonesia's future. And the majority of Indonesia's peasants had demonstrated their ingenuity in increasing export crops and achieving self-sufficiency in vital produce such as rice and soybeans.

Both the material and human potential were enormous. The barriers, however, were obviously great and ominous. Above all, the strains of modernization in a theoretically, if fairly tolerant Islamic nation had created an urban population "who at a moment's notice can shed their inherent timidity and burst into rage."[64] Nonetheless, as one astute observer argued, "For every argument supporting the theory that Indonesia will achieve the industrial miracles of neighboring Singapore or of Japan, an equally cogent case can be made that the divergent and violent forces within the society will sabotage . . . hard-won unity at some point."[65]

The Southeast Asian Panorama

In spite of immense resources, Southeast Asian countries sometimes stumbled in economic disarray in the latter part of the twentieth century. At times, the region's leaders—Malaysia, Thailand, and Indonesia—matched or even surpassed the previous growth rate of East Asia. Yet none of them had managed to spread the benefits of development to all of their people.

Even in Malaysia, a leader in trying to achieve growth with equity, women in 1989 worked ten hours a day in factories for less than $100 a month. They often lived separated from their families. They had no

pensions, no unions, no job security, and meager medical care for industry–related ailments.[66]

Several elements in the Southeast Asian situation, however, offered a
degree of promise that some nations could join the ranks of more advanced
East Asian regions after the turn of the century.

First, investment by East Asian states in Southeast Asia mounted to a
high level. Indeed, Louis Kraar estimated in 1989 that Japanese investments alone would double the industrial production of Southeast Asia by
1993—barring a world economic disaster.[67] Investments by South Korea
and Taiwan in Southeast Asia continued to grow. By 1989, Japan imported
more goods from Asian than from U.S. manufacturers.[68] As James Abegglen, the business economist, observed in 1989, "The economic growth
advantage of East and Southeast Asia over the rest of the world is
widening."[69]

Second, Southeast Asia, with a combined population of 412 million
people in 1988, formed a gigantic market of its own. As Abegglen noted in
1989,

> There is increased discussion of an Asian (perhaps yen-dominated) trading bloc.
> . . . An Asian bloc will not emerge by choice. An Asian bloc will emerge
> because the nations of the area are driven to it by increased protectionism in the
> West against Asian goods. . . . The international corporations of the world
> would do well to urgently reassess their long-range plans for East and Southeast
> Asia in light of the many and rapid changes now underway throughout the
> area.[70]

With proper foresight, the various economies of the region could com-
plement each other in agriculture, industrial production, financing, and
expertise. Rather than competing in car production, for example, one
country could provide the steel, another the rubber, and a third the
managerial expertise for a giant industry. Hong Kong might finance the
venture while Japan furnishes the engineering. Such cooperation depends
upon the collaboration of already advanced countries and the continued
evolution of ASEAN (the political alliance of Thailand, Malaysia, Singapore, Brunei, Indonesia, and the Philippines). Although the history of
ASEAN recorded many failures in attempts to cooperate, some observers
argued in 1987 that "a concordance system has emerged in the region,
where conflict is about how to co-operate, rather than whether to do so."[71]
In the 1980s, as increasing intra-area trade flowed, the vulnerability of the
region to an economic downturn in the rest of the world decreased.[72]

Third, many statesmen in Southeast Asia, particularly among Thais and Malaysians, had come to realize the truth of labor leader Dennis Mac-Shane's observation that "the price Asia has to pay for rapid and wealth-generating industrialization is the arrival of an industrial working class. . . . The price of economic growth and free trade sooner or later is free trade unions and free citizens. It is a price worth paying."[73]

Notes

1. Robin Broad and John Cavanaugh, "No More NICs," *Foreign Policy* (Fall 1988).
2. Ibid., 85.
3. Ibid., 95.
4. Ibid., 103.
5. Japanese Ministry of Finance, 1988.
6. Ibid.
7. Rod Chapman, "Indonesia," in Michael Smith et al., *Asia's New Industrial World* (London: Methuen, 1985), 128.
8. Ibid., 124.
9. Ibid.
10. Peter Janssen, "The Not-So-Simple Art of Creating Wealth in Thailand," *Billion* (Feb. 1989).
11. *Asia 1988 Yearbook,* Hong Kong, 1987.
12. Ibid., 256.
13. Ibid., 109. The Burmese political system—one that has emphasized autocracy, absolute dependence on the ruler, isolation from the outer world, and an unwillingness to make hard decisions—has been well described by Lucian Pye, *Politics, Personality and Nation Building* (New Haven: Yale University Press, 1962) and in Maung Maung Shi, *Burmese Political Values* (New York: Praeger, 1983).
14. David Aikman, *Pacific Rim* (Boston: Little Brown, 1986), 129.
15. Bernardo Villegas, quoted in ibid., 129. The problems of administering the Philippines' system of politics are well delineated by Pye, *Politics.*
16. Ibid., 129.
17. *Asia 1988 Yearbook,* see note 11, 219.
18. See Barbara Watson Andaya and Leonrd Y. Andaya, *A History of Malaysia* (London: Macmillan, 1982).
19. See Tunku Abdul Rahman, *Contemporary Issues in Malaysian Politics* (Petalung Selangor, Malaysia: Pelunduk Publications, 1984).
20. "Faster Than Forecast," *Far Eastern Economic Review,* 16 Feb. 1989, 62.
21. Ibid.
22. Clark Kerr, *The Future of Industrial Societies* (Cambridge: Harvard University Press, 1983).
23. See Lucian Pye, *Asian Power and Politics* (Cambridge: The Belknap Press of Harvard University Press, 1985), 262; and Suhaini Azman, "The Balance of Wealth," *Far Eastern Economic Review,* 2 Feb. 1989, 30. Opponents of the NEP, including middle-class Malays, argued that the program encouraged the

flight of Chinese capital, made Malays too dependent on the government, and prolonged racial identifications.

24. See Milton J. Esman, *Administration and Development in Malaysia* (Ithaca: Cornell University Press, 1972); Walker Connor, "Ethnology and the Peace of Southeast Asia," *World Politics* 22 (October 1969); Donald Horowitz, *Ethnic Groups in Conflict* (Berkeley: University of California Press, 1985); Karl Von Vorys, *Democracy Without Consensus* (Princeton: Princeton University Press, 1975).
25. Peter Bauer, *Rhetoric and Reality* (Cambridge: Harvard University Press, 1984).
26. Pye, *Asian Power and Politics*, 250.
27. William Bardley, David Morell, David Szanton, and Stephen Young, *Thailand, Domino by Default?* (Athens, Ohio: Ohio University Center for International Studies, Southeast Asia Series no. 46, 1978), 38.
28. See Ian Borown, *The Elite and the Economy in Siam, circa 1890–1920* (Singapore: Oxford University Press, 1988).
29. William H. Overholt, "Thailand: A Moving Equilibrium," *Pacific Review* 1, no. 1 (1988): 7.
30. Ibid.; also see Borown, *Economy in Siam*.
31. *Newsweek*, 11 July 1988.
32. Pye, *Asian Power and Politics*, 99.
33. Walter F. Vella, *The Impact of the West on Government in Thailand* (Berkeley: University of California Press, 1955).
34. Mary Haas, "The Declining Descent Rule for Rank in Thailand," *American Anthropologist* 53 (Oct.–Dec. 1951).
35. Herbert Rubin, "Will and Awe: Illustrations of Thai Villagers' Dependence upon Officials," *Journal of Asian Studies* 32 (May 1972) and Lucian Hanks, "Merit and Power in the Thai Social Order," *American Anthropologist* 64 (1962).
36. Pye, *Asian Power and Politics*, 109.
37. Phisit Pakkasen, deputy director of the National Economic and Social Development Board, quoted in *Newsweek*, 11 July 1988, 52.
38. Ruangthong Chaiprosop, "Thailand," *Southeast Asian Affairs: 1988* (Singapore: Institute of Southeast Asian Studies, 1988).
39. Overholt, "Thailand," 14.
40. Ibid.
41. Aikman, *Pacific Rim*, 170.
42. See Chai Anan Samudavanija, "Political Institutionalization in Thailand" in Robert Scalapino et al., eds., *Asian Political Institutionalization* (Berkeley: Institute of East Asian Studies, University of California, 1986).
43. Aikmen, *Pacific Rim*.
44. Chapman, "Indonesia," 96.
45. *Asia 1988 Yearbook*, note 11.
46. Ibid.
47. Jeanne Mintz, *Indonesia* (Princeton: D. Van Nostrand, 1961).
48. Lucian Pye, "Southeast Asia," in *The Politics of Developing Areas*, Gabriel Almond and James Coleman, eds. (Princeton: Princeton University Press, 1960), 49.
49. See Guy Parker, "The Military in Indonesia" in John Johnson, ed., *The Role of the Military in Underdeveloped Countries* (Princeton: Princeton University Press, 1962).

50. See James Mossman, *Rebels in Paradise* (London: Jonathan Cape, 1961).
51. See Parker, "Military in Indonesia."
52. Hamish McDonald, *Suharto's Indonesia* (Victoria, Australia: Fontana Books, 1981).
53. The truth may never be known in this case. Rumors had it that either Sukarno or Suharto had actually provoked or staged the coup. See ibid. Sukarno might have done it for propaganda reasons while Suharto may have used the coup as an excuse for seizing power.
54. McDonald, *Suharto's Indonesia*, 216.
55. Amnesty International, *Amnesty International Report*, London, 1984.
56. *Asia 1988 Yearbook*, see note 11.
57. Ibid.
58. "Indonesia," *The Economist*, 15 Aug. 1987.
59. Ibid.
60. Ibid.
61. See Chapman, "Indonesia."
62. Ibid.
63. "Indonesia," *The Economist*, 15 Aug. 1987.
64. Pye, *Asian Power and Politics*, 275. Also see Karl Jackson, *Traditional Authority, Islam, and Religion* (Berkeley: University of California Press, 1980), and Clifford Geertz, *The Religion of Java* (New York: Basic Books, 1960).
65. Chapman, "Indonesia," 95.
66. Dennis MacShane, "Paying the Price," *Far Eastern Economic Review*, 23 Feb. 1989.
67. Louis Kraar, "Is Japanese Investment Healthy for the U.S. and Asia?" Japan Society, New York, 22 Feb. 1989.
68. James Abegglen, "The Fast Pace of Asian Change," *Tokyo Business Today* (Jan. 1989): 6.
69. Ibid.
70. Ibid.
71. Donald Crone, "The ASEAN Summit of 1987," *Southeast Asian Affairs 1988* (Singapore: Institute of Southeast Asian Studies, 1988), 33. Also see Michael Antolik, "The Cautious Consolidation of ASEAN, *Contemporary Southeast Asia* 4 (Dec. 1982).
72. Abegglen, *Fast Pace,* 6.
73. MacShane, "Paying," 74, 75.

5

Tier Four: China

When China awakes, she will shake the world.
—Napoleon

The fate of the 1,100 million people of the Chinese mainland may well determine the course of the Pacific century. The facts are obvious if the future is obscure. This stumbling giant has emerged from its cocoon of isolation into a period of stunning, if unstable economic progress. Between 1978 and 1988, China's economy experienced an annual average growth rate of eight percent a year,[1] millions of people escaped the pit of absolute poverty, and experts forecast that China's growth in GDP will continue at the rate of 6.6 to 8 percent annually through the year 2,000, unless political tribulations cripple production.[2]

Peasants, some 80 percent of the population, benefited the most from this great advance and, as economist Albert Keidel commented in 1988, many Chinese believed that "an explosion of rural nonfarm growth . . . will eventually surround and capture the urban enclaves just as Maoist guerrilla strategy says it should."[3]

The biggest developer in the world expected to increase per capita income from $250 a year in 1986[4] to at least $1,000 a year in 2,000.[5] Economists estimated that China's exports of everything from coal to surgical gloves would increase by nine percent annually through 2,000.[6] Merely between 1979 and 1986, American imports from China increased from $592 million to $5.2 billion, leaving America with an annual deficit in 1986 of over $2 billion.[7]

The opening of China had the greatest significance for its premier investors along the Pacific Rim: Japan, Hong Kong, Korea, and Taiwan. As a market, a supplier of raw materials, and as a source of inexpensive

75

labor, China could serve as the kingpin of the area and a cushion against creeping protectionism and imminent recession in America and Europe.

On a subjective level, every Chinese with whom I talked before the disastrous events of 1989 believed that China had entered a new and progressive era. One student from Fudan commented, "People are falling over each other to get Japanese motorcycles, Western clothes, fast food. Millions are learning English. The 'open door' can never be closed again." More mundanely, a Chinese peasant in Sichuan said, "We have four times the money than in the old times. I eat pork and chicken all the time. I will soon have a refrigerator." Among those who studied abroad, a government official in Shanghai optimistically typified reactions among the elite: "With the development of economic pluralism, political pluralism inevitably follows. We will never retun to a monolithic autocracy. Gaps between the coastal regions and the interior will open up, inflation will eat up the salaried cadres, and workers in bankrupt industries will protest but these are growing pains that we can handle when the majority of people are satisfied and hopeful."

Until 1989, most outside observers agreed with the prevailing optimism within China. In 1986, China scholar Dwight Perkins pointedly described China as "Asia's next economic giant," a new partner to (and copier of) Japan and the NICs.[8] In 1987, economist Alvin Rabushka also foresaw a "new China" consciously emulating the market policies and export drive of Taiwan and Hong Kong.[9] And in 1988, Keidel argued that "China's experience in the past ten years indicates that by the end of the century all of China will have joined the process of East Asian 'miracle growth'. . . . The sweep of economic reform has already been so broad that no existing or likely leadership coalition could rebuild the old order."[10]

And yet, some apprehensive journalists focused their attention on discontent among Communist cadres, shortages of raw materials, periodic swings in government policies, growing inequalities, and the revolt of 1989. These objective difficulties, as well as spasmodic official outbursts against "consumerism" and "bourgeois pollution," led observers to question whether the changes in China would survive its xenophobia and onslaughts from its ingrained fiefdoms of Party power. In 1989, journalist Robert Delfs warned that "record levels of inflation, grossly overheated industrial growth, worsening grain shortages and swelling public discontent over official corruption and abuse of power" might undermine China's reforms.[11]

On 20 March 1989, Prime Minister Li Peng, a conservative reformer but not a hardline Maoist type, announced a series of policies designed to moderate the growth of the economy. The supposedly temporary restraints attempted to reimpose central planning, affirmed a government monopoly over raw materials, cut back on public credit to cooperatives and private industries, and strengthened price controls. Li described these policies as short-term measures designed "to put an end to the present chaos."[12] Significantly, Li offered further support to China's peasants; nonetheless, Beijing students and workers erupted in 1989.

What path would China eventually follow? Any prophecy about China's future—a daring enterprise under any circumstances—required a degree of understanding of its immediate past.

Maoist China

In 1949, Mao Zedong overthrew the discredited and corrupt regime of Chiang Kai-shek, distributed land to starving peasants, and launched an initially promising experiment in industrialization.[13] His land reforms eliminated a significant barrier to economic growth, the big land-holding class (including Deng Xiaoping's parents), but Mao eventually replaced the landowners with oppressive collectives. Aided by the Soviet Union between 1949 and 1957, China's energy and steel production increased by almost 25 percent annually while farm produce went up some four percent each year during the same period.[14]

Mao killed millions of people who opposed his efforts at land expropriation and thought control,[15] but millions of other peasants voluntarily donated their labor to build roads, dams, and irrigation canals in an eager search for a new society.[16] Although Mao executed people at the rate of 22,500 each month in the 1950s (according to Zhou En-lai's later estimate), he could not achieve the nation's total dedication to economic advance for which he had hoped.

Enthusiastically abetted by the latter-day reformer, Deng, Mao attempted to galvanize his "empire of the blue ants" by squashing all individuality and freedom of thought. Between 1957 and 1959, Mao launched his "Great Leap Forward," a brutal effort to bring China up to Great Britain's economic level. The dictator ordered 90 percent of the Chinese population to join supposedly self-reliant communes. Each commune held eight thousand families under a tight grip and was ordered to produce all of its own goods, including grain and steel. The results were disastrous: peasants tore up forests and lands that used to produce goods for the market in a frantic but futile effort to meet grain quotas; "backyard" steel furnaces gobbled up the nation's iron scrap uselessly; big industries stagnated; and Russia withdrew her aid when Krushchev denounced China's leaders as "madmen."[17] As famine threatened the nation, Mao temporarily relented and later admitted, "The chaos caused was on a grand scale."[18]

Disappointed by his subjects' lack of ideological fervor, Mao initiated the Cultural Revolution between 1964 and 1966. The attack by young, fevered Red Guards on the Party bureaucracy and intellectuals decimated the ranks of scientists and technicians, closed down libraries, and led to the killing, imprisonment, or crippling of some eleven million people. Altogether, according to the *People's Daily's* eventual estimate, the Red Guards humiliated, tried, or killed a total of 100 million people in a frenzied, anti-foreign attempt to eliminate "bourgeois" influences.[19] By exiling students to the countryside in order to "learn from the peasants," the Cultural Revolution doomed 100 million young people to illiteracy and a total lack of technical training.[20]

Among the purge victims, Deng Xiaoping, once a high Party official, was twice banned by Mao. Because of his modulated criticism of the regime, Red Guards reviled Deng as a "demon" and a "freak." The diminutive old man went to the countryside, shoveled manure, worked on a lathe, and waited on tables in a Party canteen.[21] The Red Guards shoved Deng's favorite son from a balcony, condemning him to paralysis.

This paroxysm of ideology crippled China's economy and turned the nation into a shrill, implacable place until Mao's death in 1976. Briefly, the "gang of four," a group of radicals led by Mao's actress-wife, tried to prolong the Cultural Revolution but forces of reform, led by Deng, swept aside the old guard. As historian Paul Johnson described the era, "Mao's reign was a lurid melodrama, sometimes degenerating into farce but always, in the deepest sense, a tragedy: for what he caused to be enacted was not theatre but a gigantic series of experiments on hundreds of millions of real, living, suffering people."[22]

Reform in China

Backed by the army, the intelligentsia, and a major segment of the Party, Deng and other reformers began to transform China in 1978. They retained a socialist label for the nation but thoroughly condemned the past under Mao. "We have repudiated the Cultural Revolution in its entirety,"

Deng said in 1984, and Hu Yaobang, once secretary general of the Party, declared in 1985, "We have wasted twenty years because of radical leftist nonsense."[23]

To rectify the past, the reformers unleashed the peasants from communes, initially freed many enterprises from stifling central planning, welcomed contacts with the West and Japan, pruned millions of people from the army and the bureaucracy, encouraged entrepreneurial experiments, and cautiously modified the Party dictatorship.[24] With the supreme goal of modernizing China, Deng instituted a "responsibility system" that allowed peasants to benefit directly from their work, welcomed capital and technology from abroad, and encouraged a more benign rule that allowed individuals to exploit their abilities and (within limits) to express their opinions.

The immediate result was unquestioned progress for China and, most importantly, its beleaguered peasants. Between 1979 and 1984, rural per capita incomes more than doubled and, by 1985, "peasants in China had doubled their wheat production through increasing productivity per square inch of their tiny plots by an annual average of 12 percent."[25] Although China still imported grain in 1989 as its population grew, the number of chronically malnourished people dropped from 280 million in 1978 to almost zero in 1989.[26]

Nonetheless, with all of its progress—indeed, to some degree, precisely because of its advances—China was still embattled as it entered the 1990s. Achievements in four segments of the society—agriculture, rural industry, urban areas, and coastal enterprise zones—brought with them grave socio-economic risks.

Agricultural Advance and Obstacles

China's peasants eagerly embraced the new regime's incongruous slogan: "To Get Rich is Glorious." Deng and the ex-governor of Sichuan, Zhao Ziyang, dismantled the cumbersome commune system and allowed peasants to produce anything they wished for premium prices, once they had met a minimum state quota of grain. Farmers could also pool their capital to buy tractors or other agricultural implements and they could hire up to two hundred employees. Peasants leased their land for fifteen years from the state and were allowed to pass it on to their heirs.[27]

The first effects of these reforms were stunning. Starvation and malnutrition in China came to an end. Peasants went on a spending orgy, buying color televisions sets, washing machines, refrigerators, and most importantly, houses. Between 1979 and 1984, about half of all peasant houses in China went up in new construction.[28] In some fortunate provinces such as Guangdong where rice could be cropped three times a year, peasant incomes increased ten times between 1979 and 1986.[29]

In one Guangdong village which I visited, the material gains of rural reform were obvious. Typical peasant families lived in new, well-scrubbed concrete houses. They grew traditional crops but were free to sell extra products—pigs, chickens, even flowers—in urban markets. New shops with lacquered shelves had sprung up in the village, huge cassette recorders blared out Hong Kong love songs, motorbikes puttered about, and young dandies played billiards in outdoor cafes.

Clumsy government policies, however, hindered rural growth. Aggravated by drought, bad harvests between 1984 and 1988 forced some peasant households to purchase rice at high market prices in order to meet grain quotas imposed on their village by the government.[30] Other farmers in 1989 slaughtered pigs and chickens earlier than usual in order to garner bumper profits, but the practice doomed consumers to later shortages. A lack of inputs such as insecticides and fertilizers produced in inefficient state-run industries caused severe problems. As a provincial Party secretary, Han Peixin, told the *World Economic Herald* (once China's freest and best newspaper), "When the county cadre goes to the countryside, the peasants won't sell. . . . So he slaps himself in the ear and blames himself for the fact that the fertilizer, insecticides and plastic sheets . . . never actually arrived. Then he slaps himself in the face again, begging the peasants to hand over the grain."[31]

In spite of these difficulties, China's agriculture advanced splendidly after the Dengist reforms. In a country where arable land amounted to one-tenth of a hectare per person, such remarkable growth had its natural limits. As economist Qian Jiaju noted, "We have almost reached the maximum benefits that accrue to the right policies. Any leap forward will have to come from science and technology."[32] Improvements were possible since China still lagged behind Taiwan in yield per acre, but advanced techniques, in turn, required new seeds, better irrigation systems, and additional machinery. An infusion of new technology, however, made peasant labor redundant and demanded the development of new rural industries to absorb surplus population in productive activities. Whether China's private and semi-public sector could rise to this challenge remains in doubt.

Advances and Obstacles in Rural Industry

Small-scale industries initiated by private owners, villages, or "collectives" (cooperatives) responded to market demands and emerged as the most dynamic sector of the economy between 1978 and 1988. Rural industries increased their output ninefold over the decade and accounted for more than 25 percent of China's total industrial production. As market-oriented, unsubsidized, and cost-effective units, rural industries absorbed 88 million people and accounted for more rural productivity than agriculture itself.[33] Between 1984 and 1987, rural industries grew by almost 38 percent a year, four times the rate of state industries.[34] By the year 2,000, some Chinese predict that village industries would employ half of China's industrial workers.[35] Such growth created new markets for urban industries as well as new pressures on the government to provide the credit, transportation, and basic supplies required to sustain the evolution.[36]

One village in Sichuan, Longzhao, typified the changes wrought by the growth in rural industry. While 80 percent of the villagers tilled rice fields in 1977, the majority had switched into small industries by 1987. In one instance, 110 women formed a "collective," a group-owned enterprise, to mend clothing. They eventually managed to purchase sixty sewing machines and witnessed a growth of per capita income from $10 a month to $40 a month. Other cooperatives, ranging in size from a handful of people to several hundred, issued "internal shares" (stocks) to their members and paid "bonuses" (dividends) each year. The collectives produced soft drinks, refined edible oil, and made simple farm machinery. Many of the men in the village joined in construction teams that built everything from private homes to hotels in nearby urban centers.

According to the manager of one collective in Longzhao, the combined income of a family where the wife worked in the sewing factory and the husband labored on a construction team reached $670 a year in 1986. Released from the back-breaking toil of the rice paddies, the family could afford to purchase a three-room, Tudor-looking duplex, two bicycles, and a small refrigerator.

The rural industries had several advantages. They gave profitable work to the more than 100 million people who were still underemployed in agriculture. They provided immediate consumer goods, from mixed fodder to a potent rice wine that the villagers enjoy. They required little capital and, as small units, were relatively risk-free and flexible. Unlike state-owned heavy industries, the cooperatives secured an efficient pace of productivity from their members. In a crisis, a collective that lost money disbanded and everyone lost. In contrast, a state-owned firm, however inefficient, merely received a government subsidy to hide its losses and retain its workers.

The greater efficiency and sharp growth of rural industries in China, Nicholas Kristoff noted, meant that "as in Britain, 200 years ago, the revolution begins in small towns."[37] The head of one large collective, Xian Bin, remarked in 1989, "more and more collectives will appear, because at collectives those who work harder will get a bigger bonus."[38]

Nevertheless, the government still monopolized basic supplies of capital and resources. It could dampen if not halt the advance of collectives. In 1989, China's prime minister Li Peng, disturbed by the "overheating" of the economy, announced a retrenchment that cut off injections of credit and raw materials into rural industries. Some Chinese officials estimated that one-third of rural industries might have to close because of these restrictions.[39] By 1990, five percent of China's rural industries had, in fact, collapsed.

The dramatic progress of light industries had undoubtedly contributed to the "overheating" of the economy. State-controlled industries failed to keep up with the demand of rural enterprises. Supplies of electricity, for example, grew by an average of only six percent annually between 1981 and 1987, not enough to keep pace with light industrial growth. Between 1980 and 1988, railroads expanded at a yearly pace of only 0.88 percent and roads at a laggardly 1.10 percent.[40] Naturally, such gaps in essential services hindered the delivery of new products.

The government's response to these imbalances in early 1990—cutting off credit to light industries, restrictions on supplies of raw materials, and a tightening of central planning—was understandable, but it made little sense in the long run for it inevitably slowed rural industrial growth. Two measures particularly hampered the village enterprises:

The imposition of credit controls slashed lending to rural enterprises by 50 percent from 1989 to 1990.[41] While some rural companies had "reached the point where many could survive even protracted denial of access to the state banking system," fledgling enterprises were put in serious jeopardy.[42]

An announced government cutback in construction projects also hit hard at rural endeavors since twelve million peasants belonged to construction teams. The government expected to reduce construction by 30 percent in

1989 and by 40 percent in 1990.[43] Remaining investment would go to state-run companies, and some four million ex-peasants would have to go back to agriculture.

The Chinese changes in policy in 1990, similar to temporary oscillations in 1985, might well retard the growth of rural industries for a decade. Nonetheless, the gains already made in this sector, the absolute need to transform peasants from paddy coolies into industrial workers, and sheer population pressure made it probable that progress would eventually continue.

Only a very unlikely revolution aimed at the ex-peasants themselves could totally undo the developments in China's rural industries. No leadership group in China anticipated or sought such an outcome. In any case, mass political opposition in the provinces rendered it impossible. Consequently, pressures mounted for reforms in urban production, prices, and management to meet new rural demands.

Advances and Obstacles in Urban Areas

Deng's bold experiments in economic reform also affected China's cities and major industries, but the initiatives often met with less success and enthusiasm than in the countryside. Between 1979 and 1985, Deng partially decentralized control over China's 390,000 primarily state-owned urban industries. With some latitude, companies could retain profits for their own use rather than returning them to central control. As a result, urban industrial production jumped some 12 percent a year between 1983 and 1987. In 1988, it reached an unsustainable peak of 17.5 percent annually.[44] Because inflation in the cities had climbed to 19 percent annually in 1988, the government decided to slow down the heavy industrial economy to a rate of 8 to 10 percent annually—still an extraordinarily rapid pace of advance for urban industries.[45]

The expansion of China's heavy industry owed a great deal to an increase in *director control*.[46] Implemented on a nationwide scale in 1986, the new system transferred power and responsibilities from Party secretaries to enterprise managers. Legally, the enterprise director became the boss and, theoretically, his firm could go bankrupt if it did not operate on a profitable basis. Accounting changes made visible the amounts of revenue earned by a firm and the degree to which the state had to subsidize its activities.[47] As a consequence of these new policies, Keidel observed in 1988 that "Director control makes sure that someone cares about costs and revenues. . . . Directors will want to buy cheap and sell dear and will do so in black markets and free markets if state markets are inadequate.''[48] In practice, different provinces varied widely in implementing the new approach since the bankruptcy provision carried with it the political danger of creating a mass of unemployed urban workers.

One exemplar of the proposed changes was the Zigong steel casing plant where the reforms were first initiated. Between 1979 and 1980, the government freed the plant from Party control and gave direct responsibility to the company's director, Wang Zizhen. Most importantly, Wang was allowed to "break the iron rice bowl"—that is, to abrogate a system where workers were retained forever and paid equally regardless of their efficiency or laziness. With the introduction of wage incentives, production of steel casings jumped from 1500 units a year in 1979 to 10,000 in 1984. The wages for workers doubled every year. Wang, a Party member, said that "We tell workers to love their country and factory and to work hard." But, he added, "We also teach them that they should become wealthy."[49]

Following the Zigong model, the city of Guangzhou (Canton) proved a particularly congenial place for reform. It blossomed with thousands of private enterprises, while older firms such as the Yu Hua Industrial Co. became major exporters. Ou Jiangquan, manager of the plant, said in 1988, "It's not easy for state-run enterprises to compete against us. They have to carry out reforms, or they will have no way out."[50]

The expansion of thriving Guangzhou was impressive. Industrial output increased by 18 percent in 1987 and another 11 percent in 1988. The Dongping street market displayed stalls spilling over with food—vegetables, fruits, and pork (pork had been rationed in cities such as Beijing and Shanghai, but Guangzhou officials allowed its cost to rise to free-market prices). To the shock of my children who were accompanying me, even puppies and kittens were on sale as delicacies. Privately owned stores had an abundance of clothes, SONY cassette recorders, and Casio calculators.

Guangzhou's economists projected that the city (and its surrounding province of Guangdong) would join the ranks of the NICs by the turn of the century and its GNP should grow to $4,000 a year in 2010, not far from Taiwan's level in 1990. As a leader in economic reform, Guangzhou released 80 percent of its commodities from state price-fixing. The private sector employed one million people as the state sector constantly shrank.[51] An infusion of capital and subcontracts from Hong Kong served to stimulate the protean economy. In 1988, Hong Kong contributed 90 percent of Guangdong's foreign investment and absorbed 60 percent of its exports.[52]

The relative prosperity of Guangzhou created its own problems. Traffic clogged the streets, and more than one million people suffered from a drastic housing shortage. A typical family of five had to accommodate themselves in one room, share a kitchen with another family, and use a communal toilet. They could afford more comfortable lodgings, but none were available. Moreover, millions of youths tried to enter Guangzhou from the more backward province of Hunan, Mao's birthplace. Hunan's officials had not adjusted to price reforms and their state-owned industries languished. In consequence, a flood of economic refugees sought relief in Guangzhou. In 1989, officials tried to seal off the city from migrants and reassert the power of the central government.

Other problems stemmed from the "overheating" of urban economies. One major bottleneck for urban advance, as well as for rural industries, was the shortage of energy supplies. Raw materials for urban industries were also hard to obtain; Gangzhou's enterpreneurs tried to solve this issue by buying factories and mines in the northern provinces. Inefficient state-owned industries continued to eat up large shares of available supplies of energy and materials causing the newer urban ventures to suffer. In a city such as Guangzhou, the renewed imposition of government controls caused resentment. "We are on the verge of a major take-off," Zheng Yanchao, a professor at Guangdon's Academy of Social Sciences, said in 1988, "but the central government is restraining us."[53] In spite of temporary readjustments, it seemed that "urban industrial reforms have proceeded so far and are continuing to evolve so rapidly that stagnation is not an option."[54] Nonetheless, by 1990, both native entrepreneurs and foreign investors feared that Beijing's policies might produce "stagflation."

Advances and Obstacles in the Coastal Regions

One of Deng's more ambitious experiments was the establishment of three "Special Economic Zones" (SEZs) in 1979: Shenzhen on the border with Hong Kong, Zuhai and Shantou in Guangdong, and Xiamen in Fujian Province. The zones offered special tax advantages to foreign investors, a relaxation in bureaucratic rules, and a new infrastructure. Deng hoped that foreign capital and technology would pour in from the outside world, eventually invigorating the entire economy. Joined later by fourteen other coastal areas, the SEZs were supposed to function as a conduit of foreign technology, managerial skills, and commercial services to China's interior cities and, eventually, to her most remote areas.

Shenzhen, the largest of these zones, became China's "boom" city. In 1979, Shenzhen was a 126-square-mile marsh of paddy fields and fishing villages holding only 30,000 people. Within a few years after being designated as an SEZ, Shenzhen's population went up eleven times, skyscrapers housed seven hundred new businesses, and thirty-story apartment blocks had replaced the fishing villages. A fifty-four-story International Trade Center, China's tallest building, dominated the horizon. When I first crossed the boundary into Shenzhen, the youth clad in jeans and gold chains, the sparkling new buildings, and the thickets of high-rise apartments seemed no different from Hong Kong's. Indeed, Hong Kong and Macao contributed 90 percent of foreign investment to Shenzhen, and 270,000 people streamed in each week from Hong Kong to visit such exotic attractions as Sea World and Honey Lake amusement park (complete with a double-loop roller coaster).

The new streets of Shenzhen, some no more elegant than mud paths, were thronged with thousands of day visitors from the interior who sought out bargains in Yamaha motorbikes, cartons of American cigarettes, or French brandy. The younger generation was particularly lured to Shenzhen because the zone provided ample living quarters, abundant consumer goods, and higher wages. Salaries for industrial workers averaged $79 a month, twice the pay in China's other cities. In 1984, Deng declared, "The development and experience of Shenzhen have proved the correctness of the policy of establishing special economic zones."[55]

Yet, all had not gone well in the SEZs. They had largely failed to attract high-technology industries, as Deng had hoped, and instead produced clothing, electronic wares, plastics, and other assembly-line goods. The managers of some zone enterprises engaged in currency speculation and corrupt practices such as the importation of luxury goods to be resold at high prices in the interior. Conservatives in the ranks of the Party complained that the zones were a "brain drain" on the rest of the country and a source of spiritual contamination. Indeed, in 1986, the government built a barbed-wire fence topped with arc lamps to keep out a growing tide of illegal migrants along Shenzhen's fifty-three-mile border with the rest of China.

Foreign investors, in turn, complained that the SEZs were not really free of bureaucratic controls and that decisions made in a Shenzhen could be overturned abruptly by Beijing. In addition, they said, the government's urgent need for foreign exchange compelled investors to produce for a (perhaps nonexistent) foreign market rather than for China itself. In addition, foreigners complained of China's lack of consistent laws governing such matters as the property market and the banking system.

These uncertainties prompted Deng to comment in 1985 that Shenzhen was "an experiment which could fall."[56] In spite of this caution, three facts about the SEZs stood out:

First, the government exempted the SEZs from the austerity policies of 1989–1990. There was no practical way for the officialdom to stem the tide of investment from overseas Chinese.

Second, China took the necessary steps to encourage even more foreign investment in the SEZs. In 1988, for example, Shenzhen's authorities announced that ten areas of Hong Kong law would be adapted in a wholesale fashion to Shenzhen.[57] In spite of the difficulties of transporting (and interpreting) Hong Kong's common law into China's planned economy and anarchic legal system,[58] this change promised to facilitate the flow of foreign capital and technology to the SEZs.[59] Moreover, the government encouraged industries in the SEZs to "climb the export ladder" by increasingly offering sophisticated goods such as automotive parts to the world market.[60]

Third, projections of China's future export growth of manufactured goods (excluding foods, commodities, and fuels) were encouraging, particularly for the SEZs that specialized in manufactured exports. With labor costs low by the standards of industrialized nations (although extraordinarily high by Chinese measures), the SEZs had a good chance of making significant inroads into the world economy. Based on 1980 dollars, the World Bank predicted a rise in machines and machine-goods exports of 9.7 percent every year through 2000.[61] More modest but still exceptional forecasts ranged from 7.6 percent to 3.3 percent annually through 2000.[62] Thus, the concept of the Special Economic Zones, epitomized in Shenzhen, was a signal of China's commitment to an "open door" policy. The door could be closed only at the risk of a major economic retrogression.

The Population Issue

In fact, the Chinese leadership could not afford to end its ambitious, if beleaguered attempts to open the economy, revitalize rural and urban industries, and grant attractive incentives to the rural sector. The pressure of a huge and still expanding population demanded the continuation of economic development including, at the minimum, increasing supplies of food. The only other option was a return to starvation and insurrection—an outcome that neither conservatives nor liberals in China wanted.

In 1979, the reformers had reversed Mao's sporadically pro-natalist policies and discouraged families from having more than one child. Some provinces offered financial rewards to couples who agreed to be sterilized after their first child, others imposed fines and, in some remote areas, forced abortions were reported.[63] In spite of these efforts, China's population grew by 22 million in 1986 and 23 million in 1987. Official estimates put the rate of population growth at a moderate 1.3 in 1988 but certain groups, such as migrants from one province to another, were often uncounted. The number of children per household averaged 2.3 in 1989.[64] While population growth seemed to have slowed in the cities, rural areas often ignored birth control. Foreign and Chinese experts expect this growth to taper off by 1995.[65] Until then, China has to maintain the pace of economic growth and even import food. Otherwise, the six million people who will be seeking new jobs every year after 1990 could turn into rebels.[66]

The Political Factor

Contrary to Marx, political machinations in China have been the key to advancing or retarding the economy. Clearly, China faces massive problems as it entered the 1990s—capping population pressures, controlling inflation, ensuring rural productivity, building an infrastructure, expanding transport and energy supplies, paring the bureaucracy, curbing corruption, and above all, shifting from a tightly closed economy to one that is open to the outside world and promotes change.

In China, permeated by a socialist ideology, all of these were political issues: Who owns a factory? Should state industries be allowed to wither away? How rich should certain peasants become? What recompense should workers in a bankrupt industry receive? How much freedom should be given to intellectuals and scientists in their pursuit of new ideas and innovations? As Deborah Diamond-Kim, an economic journalist, observed in 1988, "Every market-oriented move in China portends a change in the balance of power, inevitably diminishing the Communist party's authority while giving more control to technocrats."[67]

In fact, Deng's political initiatives launched "one of the greatest experiments of all previous economic history."[68] The unleashing of economic growth pitted segments of the Party and the army at odds with new interest groups including "rich" peasants, cooperative managers, technocrats, students, and younger party members, all of whom had much to gain by forwarding the reform process. Most importantly, China's peasants had no tangible reason for desiring a retreat to Maoist times. Thus, "even as they taste a measure of the good life after three decades of tumult and austerity, China's citizens are daily making it more difficult for their leaders to turn the clock back on their economics-first policies."[69] Moreover, the technicians for the process of modernization and had to grant them freedom of thought in their own domains. Liberalization in technical and economic activities had a creeping tendency to invade the political realm. And, as China tried to adapt the economic techniques of capitalism, it was "no coincidence that those societies that served as models of modernity for the Chinese today are the same liberal democracies that have carefully nurtured and zealously guarded independent thought."[70]

Although "commodity socialism" remained the announced government goal, Marxist-Leninism no longer served as China's unerring compass. In 1984, Shanghai's *Social Sciences* first criticized *Das Kapital*, *The Red Flag* warned that China must "search for truth on its own," and the *People's Daily* argued that "We cannot depend on the works of Marx and Lenin to solve [all of] our modern questions."[71]

Deng himself called Party bureaucracy "the most serious problem for our nation"[72] and announced that "Writers and artists must have freedom. . . . No interference in this regard is permitted."[73]

Nonetheless, Deng was no liberal democrat. He had, after all, bitterly oppposed freedom of thought under Mao;[74] he was intolerant of a multi-party system;[75] and he imprisoned dissenters who regarded democracy as prerequisite to solving China's problems.[76] The ambiguities of the Party line encouraged schisms within the Party itself.

Four political groups, all confined within the Party framework, juggled for the power to determine China's fate after the death of Deng:

A dwindling number of "Maoist hard-liners" complained of "spiritual pollution," growing inequalities, corruption, and the abandonment of Marxist-Leninism.[77] Although the leaders of this faction were old, they gained strength from some peasants who were jealous of the riches earned by some of their neighbors and from elements in the lower levels of the Party hierarchy who could not engage legally in profit-making activities and suffered galling restrictions on their power. These salaried cadres had to bear the burden of increasing food prices and other forms of inflation while everywhere around them, from enterprising peasants to workers increased their incomes.

A second element in the Party, led by Li Peng, supported the reform movement but longed for more order and more central planning. They suspected foreign influences and opposed any further decentralization of power. This group received cynical support from middle-level cadres who "double-dipped."[78] Because of their bureaucratic positions, such officials could exploit two aspects of the Dengist regime: They maintained a degree of power and, simultaneously, used their influence in a corrupt fashion to re-sell imports or raw materials to growing rural industries.

A third sector within the Party, headed by the deposed Zhao Ziyang and the late Hu Yaobang, could be termed pragmatic liberals. They still gave lip service to socialist ideals but had taken the lead in decentralizing the economy, giving freer rein to intellectual life, pruning the bureaucracy, and welcoming foreign ideas. They won the allegiance of newly emerging interest groups who had benefited from the reforms. Intellectuals, students, and technocrats (particularly those who had studied abroad) backed this group of leaders. In 1990, they were in temporary retreat.

A radical minority of dissenters, such as prominent astrophysicist Fang Lizhi and writer Wei Jingsheng, demanded the extension of full civil rights, complete democracy, academic freedom, and freedom of speech. In 1979, Wei wrote in the underground journal *Tansuo:* "Furthering reforms wtihin the social system and moving Chinese politics toward democracy are the prerequisites necessary to solve all the social and economic problems which confront China today."[79] Wei went to jail for his opinions but reemerged in 1989, unrepentant about his "crimes." Fang, a Party member, even dared to criticize socialism itself. In one speech in Shanghai, he declared, "I am here to tell you that the socialist movement from Marx and Lenin to Stalin and Mao Zedung has been a failure. . . . We must remold our society by absorbing influences from all cultures."[80] Fang's oratory won the allegiance of many students and intellectuals. In 1986, student demonstrations for greater democracy engulfed more than 150 universities. Although more widespread than the "Democracy Wall Movement" of 1978–1979, the student demonstrators met with only mild rebukes, and even Fang merely lost his Party membership. In 1989, however, more widespread student protests resulted in the tragedies of Tinnamen Square. Fang retired to exile in the United States embasssy.

Such developments hardly marked a sudden change in China's autocratic tradition or even the evolutionary trends of a Taiwan or a Korea. Nonetheless, they did suggest to China observer Orville Schell in 1988 that "the idea of a hard-line, never mind an outright Maoist revival, had come to seem an increasingly remote possibility."[81] China was caught in an unresolvable contradiction: "If China was to modernize, it desperately needed to rally to its cause those students, intellectuals and technocrats who had been alienated from the Party for so much of the revolution." Schell went on to say that opening China to the outside world was critical to success but "the dilemma . . . was that along with foreign languages, technology, science, capital, and management techniques came foreign political ideas and values that by their nature challenged the hegemony of one-party rule."[82]

The Party leadership knew that "they were riding a tiger and have to keep moving"[83] but, as the official Party publication *Red Flag* noted, "the problems of reform can be resolved only by more reform."[84] The pace of economic change, whether "overheated" or moderate, the creation of new interest groups, and the freeing of the intelligentsia can not easily be reversed. In the long run, these trends portend an opening of the political order that China has never before experienced.

The tragic events of 1989 both illustrated the opening of China and supported the predictions of the brilliant historian of revolution, Crane Brinton.[85] He observed that mass demonstrations, civil wars, and revolutions explode when a people has experienced economic progress and then must face a relatively minor worsening in their conditions. This was exactly the case in China. After a decade of economic advance, China suddenly encountered shortages, corruption, inflation, and continuing restrictions on political freedom. "Ironically," Bette Bao Lord, the Chinese writer, observed, "Deng Xiaoping himself sowed the seed of discontent. The students matured in his era—when Marxism was muted, when the door was open to the world, when seeking truth from reality was the norm."[86]

By firing on their own people, elements in the Communist party, like the ancien régime in France, lost their last remnants of legitimacy. Since the brutalities of the Cultural Revolution, the Party had been unable to maintain absolute control of the country. As one first-hand observer noted in June 1989, "If the proximate cause of the rebellion was festering discontent, the underlying reason was that the Communist party had long been losing its grip on the country. . . . The love, fear and awe that the Communist party once aroused have collapsed into something closer to disdain or even contempt."[87] Suggesting that China might once again close its doors, one "reformist" colleague of mine telexed me from Beijing in

May 1989, saying "You must postpone your visit. The unrest is severe. Poor Deng. He deserves no blame."

Whether a Robespierre or a Napoleon, a Lenin or a Kádár replaces the old regime, it is clear that the economic reform process could not be stopped—although it could be slowed. Whoever governs the country, economic stability has to remain their major concern. Too much power has already been granted to the peasants, to particular economic zones, and to rural enterprises to allow any central government to reassert effective central planning. Without legitimacy or unified army support, the Beijing rulers are forced to solicit the help of local authorities and peasants to keep the economy going.

In 1989, Deng resigned his last formal post as chairman of the Central Military Commission and handed the powerful post over to Jiang Zemin. Significantly, Jiang was known as an economic moderate. The Party's Central Committee reaffirmed the importance of the special economic zones, de-emphasized a crackdown on the private sector, and stressed the importance of agricultural production. The committee left the position of Zhao Ziyang open. Zhao had refused to suppress the pro-democracy protests but still retained his Party membership.

Clearly, as Napoleon observed about a once dormant China, her emergence from stagnation would change the balance of world power.[88] The scope and rapid pace of reform during the last decade warrant Deng's description of it as a "second revolution." China has indeed stirred, and no one predicts that it will slumber again.

Notes

1. Albert Keidel, "China's Economy in the Year 2000" in David Lampton and Katherine Keyser, *China's Global Presence* (Washington, D.C.: American Enterprise Institute, 1988).
2. World Bank, *China: Long Term Issues and Options,* Washington, D.C., 1985, and Rock Creek Research, *China Economic Trends,* Washington, D.C., 1986.
3. Keidel, "China's Economy," 75.
4. *Asia 1988 Yearbook,* Hong Kong, 1989.
5. World Bank, *Issues and Options.*
6. Laurence Lau, "An Economic Model of China," (Stanford, CA: Stanford University, 1985).
7. U.S. Department of Commerce, Bureau of the Census, *Highlights of U.S. Export and Import Trade.* Washington, D.C. FT 990, 1987.
8. Dwight Perkins, *China: Asia's Next Economic Giant* (Seattle: University of Washington Press, 1986).

9. Alvin Rabushka, *The New China* (Boulder: Pacific Research Institute for Public Policy, Westview Press, 1986).
10. Keidel, "China's Economy," 67.
11. Robert Delfs, "The Perils of Progress," *The Far Eastern Economic Review*, 2 March 1989.
12. Li Peng, quoted in *New York Times*, 21 March 1989.
13. Among the better descriptions of this early period, see Felix Greene, *Awakened China* (Garden City, N.Y.: Doubleday, 1961); George Paloozi-Horvath, *Mao Tse-Tung* (Garden City, N.Y.: Doubleday, 1963); Sripati Chandra-Sehkar, *Red China* (New York: Praeger, 1961); Michael Edwards, *Asia in the Balance* (Baltimore: Penguin Books, 1962); Choh-Ming Li, *The Economic Development of Communist China* (Berkeley: University of California Press, 1963); Tibor Mende, *China and Her Shadow* (Bombay: Asia Publishing House, 1961); W. R. Geddes, *Peasant Life in Communist China* (Ithaca: The Society for Applied Anthropology, monograph no. 6, 1963).
14. Wilfred Malenbaum and Wolfgang Stopler, "Political Ideology and Economic Progress: The Basic Question," *World Politics* 12, no. 3 (April 1960).
15. See William Hinton, *Fanshen* (New York: Random House, 1966).
16. See Chandra-Sehkar, *Red China*.
17. See John Frasier, *The Chinese* (New York: Summit Books, 1970); Fox Butterfield, *China* (London: Hadden and Stoughton, 1982).
18. Mao Zedung, quoted in Bill Brugger, *China: Liberation and Transformation* (Princeton: Princeton University Press, 1981), 174.
19. See Roderick MacFarquhar, *The Origins of the Cultural Revolution* (New York: Oxford University Press, 1983).
20. Butterfield, *China*, 42.
21. See Uli Franz, *Deng Xiaoping* (Boston: Harcourt Brace, 1988).
22. Paul Johnson, *Modern Times* (New York: Harper and Row, 1983), 548.
23. *Asiaweek*, 19 Oct. 1984, 37.
24. For excellent accounts of Dengist reforms, see Orville Schell, *To Get Rich Is Glorious* (New York: Pantheon Books, 1983); Perry Peck, ed, *Roses and Thorns* (Berkeley: University of California Press, 1983); Roger Garside, *China After Mao* (New York: McGraw Hill, 1981); David Bonavia, *The Chinese*, (New York: Lippincott, 1980); Orville Schell, *Discos and Democracy* (New York: Pantheon, 1988); Harry Harding, *China's Second Revolution* (Washington, D.C.: Brookings Institutions, 1987); Perkings, *China;* Rabushka, *New China;* A. Doak Barnett and Ralph N. Clough, eds., *Modernizing China* (Boulder: Westview Press, 1985); Stephen Feuchtwang, ed., *The Chinese Economy* (Boulder: Westview Press, 1988); Andrew J. Nathan, *Chinese Democracy* Berkeley: University of California Press, 1985); Lucian Pye, "On Chinese Pragmatism in the 1980's," *China Quarterly*, no. 106, 1986.
25. *The Economist*, 2 Feb. 1985, 11.
26. *New York Times*, 24 March 1989, A2.
27. See David Aikman, *Pacific Rim* (Boston: Little, Brown, 1986).
28. Ibid., 55.
29. Ibid.
30. Robert Delfs, "Perils of Progress," 47.
31. Han Peixin in *World Economic Herald*, quoted in ibid.
32. Qian Jiaju, quoted in *Asiaweek*, 19 Oct. 1984, 41.
33. Delfs, "Perils of Progress," 47.

34. Ibid.
35. Nieu Ruofeng, "Industries Top Farms in Rural Output Value," *China Daily*, 14 Nov. 1986.
36. Vincent Nee, "Privatization Market Reforms in State Socialism," Eastern Sociological Association, 16 March 1989. Nee found that transportation was the single most important factor affecting village economic growth.
37. Nicholas D. Kristof, "State's Share of Business Falls in China," *New York Times*, 21 March 1989.
38. Xian Bin, quoted in ibid.
39. China News Agency press release, 21 March 1989.
40. Louise de Rosario, "Growth Faces Many Hurdles," *Far Eastern Economic Review*, 2 March 1989.
41. Wang Jingshi, Agricultural Bank of China, 1989.
42. Delfs, "Perils of Progress," 48.
43. Ministry of Construction, December 1988.
44. China's State Statistical Bureau, Beijing, October 1988.
45. Ibid.
46. Keidel, "China's Economy," 76.
47. See "China's Haywire Profits: Sharp Differences Underscore Price Problems," *China Economic Letter*, 23 Feb. 1987.
48. Keidel, "China's Economy," 77.
49. Wang Zizhen, quoted in Christopher Wren, "Zigong Plant Is Industrial Model," *International Herald Tribune*, 1 Aug. 1984.
50. Ou Jiangquan, quoted by Howard G. Chua-Eoan, "One for the Money, One Goes Slow," *Time*, 11 April 1988, 38.
51. Louise do Rosario, "Asia's Fifth Dragon," *Far Eastern Economic Review*, 8 Dec. 1988, 61.
52. Ibid.
53. Zheng Yanchao, quoted in "The Envy of China," *Far Eastern Economic Review*, 8 Dec. 1988, 61.
54. Keidel, "China's Economy," 77.
55. Deng Xiaoping, quoted in Aiken, *Pacific Rim*, 90.
56. Deng Xiaoping, quoted in ibid.
57. Edward Epstein, "Transplant Plan Turns Marxism Upside Down," *Far Eastern Economic Review*, 2 March 1989, 66.
58. See Ibid.
59. Some observers, such as Epstein, ibid., seriously questioned the feasibility of importing a new legal system. The fact remained, however, that Japan, Korea, Taiwan, and, to some degree, China, had done it once before by originally borrowing civic and private law from Germany.
60. "Year 2000 Targets Appear Conservative," *China Economic Letter*, 30 June 1986.
61. World Bank, *Issues and Options*.
62. Lau, "Economic Model," Rock Creek Research, *Economic Trends*.
63. Steven W. Mosher, *Broken Earth* (New York: The Free Press, 1983).
64. Asia 1988 Yearbook, see n. 4.
65. See "China's Economy," *The Economist*, 1 Aug. 1987.
66. Uli franz, *Deng Xiaoping*, 204.
67. Deborah Diamond-Kim, *The China Business Review* (July–August 1988): 56.
68. Uli Franz, *Deng Xiaoping*, 307.

69. *Asiaweek,* 19 Oct. 1984.
70. Kent Morrison, "Intellectuals Given More Rein in China," *The Straits Times,* 14 Sept. 1984.
71. *Social Sciences* (July 1984); *The Red Flag,* 21 Aug. 1984; *The People's Daily,* as amended, 8 Dec. 1984.
72. Deng Xiaoping, quoted in *Asiaweek,* 19 Oct. 1984, 38.
73. Deng Xiaoping, quoted in Liang Heng and Judith Shapiro, *Intellectual Freedom in China after Mao* (New York: Fund for Free Expression, 1984).
74. Uli Franz, *Deng Xiaoping,* 146.
75. Amnesty International, *China: Violations of Human Rights* (London: Amnesty International Publications, 1985).
76. Ibid.
77. Schell, *Discos,* 184.
78. See Nee, "Market Reforms in Socialism."
79. Wei Jingsheng, "Democracy or a New Dictatorship" in Amnesty International, *Violations,* 79.
80. Fang Luzhi, quoted in Schell, *Discos,* 219.
81. Schell, *Discos,* 380.
82. Schell, *Discos,* 265.
83. Adam Pilarski in Lampton and Keyser, *China's Presence,* 81.
84. Ibid.; *The Red Flag,* 81.
85. Crane Brinton, *The Anatomy of Revolution* (New York: Prentice Hall, 1952).
86. Bette Bao Lord, "China's Next Long March," *New York Times,* 4 June 1989, E31.
87. Nicholas D. Kristof, "China Erupts," *New York Times,* 4 June 1989, 29.
88. Napoleon, quoted in Harry Harding, *Second Revolution,* 239.

6

The Reasons for Asian Achievements

*Their success was almost entirely due to good
policies and the abilities of the people—scarcely
at all to favorable circumstances or a good start.*
—Ian M.D. Little, 1982

In 1990, China and Hong Kong planned to complete a six-lane road linking Guangzhou, Shenzhen, Macao, and Hong Kong. The superhighway will enable motorists to cover the 120-kilometer drive between the four major centers of the Pearl River delta in one hour. (When I first entered China from Hong Kong in 1985, even a speedy hydrofoil required three hours for the journey.)

As Frank Ching, a Hong Kong journalist, observed, "The new road is both a symbol of, and impetus to, economic cooperation and integration that only a few years ago would have been regarded as unthinkable."[1] Its significance extends far beyond transportation. Economically, if China recovers from chaos, the new highway represents a type of economic cooperation that was common in Asia: the privately owned Hong Kong company of Hopewell Holdings and the Guangdoing provincial government joined together in pioneering the venture. Politically, the road epitomizes the growth in precarious collaboration between previously distinct parts of Asia since Britain will return a reluctant Hong Kong to China in 1997 and Portugal will relinquish control over Macao in 1999.

The unification of the Pearl River delta, two hopeful observers noted, heralds the possible development of a "world class high-technology corridor from Hong Kong to Canton."[2] Stephen Cheong, a Hong Kong lawyer, foresaw a fruitful interaction between the Crown Colony and China: "For thirty years, we have developed and absorbed modern technology while China was cut off. Now we have the educated people, the technicians and the managers to tap China's resources and markets. This is our future role."[3] From a different and perhaps overly optimistic perspective, Wang Guorin, a Communist cadre, agreed: "We will start with just the assembly, the simple part. Then we will move on. We are building the firm foundation for a major electronic industry here. . . . We will make the leap in a very short time."[4] With the explosion of Tiananmen Square, construction of the highway temporarily stopped.

Nonetheless, as the Pacific century dawned, the possibilities of potential cooperation among all of the Asian countries increased. Japan became the major trading partner of China, Indonesia, and Thailand. Hong Kong imported more goods from China than any other country. Malaysia emerged as the prime partner for Singapore.[5] In 1985, the United States ranked in first place as a recipient of exports from the Pacific Rim countries, but its proportional share of trade steadily dropped. Concurrently, Japan solidified its position as the premier exporter to South Korea, Taiwan, Indonesia, Thailand, and Singapore.[6]

Since Japanese capital naturally followed its trade, *Fortune* editor Louis Kraar suggested in 1989 that "Japanese investment is changing the face of Asia."[7] Indeed, the Pacific Rim Consulting Group predicted that "the industrial capacity that Japan will add to Southeast Asia through investment will equal the entire [1989] output of the group."[8] Old complaints in other Asian countries about Japanese trade barriers disappeared as Japan opened factories in Thailand, Singapore, Taiwan, and Malaysia. These, in turn, sold back much of their production to Japan.

Japan's net acquisition of equities in Singapore soared fifteen times in 1988 alone and doubled in Hong Kong. Simultaneously, Japanese equity acquisitions in the United States dropped in 1988 by 87 percent.[9] Japanese investors had followed a careful strategy of buying equity in stages: first, in the United States, second in Europe, and third, in Asia itself.

Meanwhile, the reunification of China and Taiwan, perhaps in a loose confederation of a "Greater China" (including Hong Kong and Macao) became a possibility for the next century—if China overcame anarchy. In the last decade of the twentieth century, the flow of trade and capital, the natural linkage between Taiwan's managerial talents and the mainland's resources and labor, a tide of visitors, Taiwan's interest in developing the nearby island of Hainan, and a common heritage—all make this scenario politically plausible in the long run.[10] A "Greater China" would immediately have more foreign exchange reserves than Japan and, by 1995, an economy that would rank it as the world's fourth largest industrial power, displacing Germany.[11]

Thus, as the year 2000 approaches, the Pacific Rim countries are moving hesitantly toward closer integration and into a position to form their own economic "bloc." With two-thirds of the world's people, the Pacific Rim could well dominate the world economy.

Even in the event of a world recession, as historian Paul Kennedy has acknowledged, it seems reasonable to expect that the rise of the Pacific "is likely to continue, simply because the development is so broad-based."[12] The industrial power of Japan and the NICs combines nicely with the resources and markets of China, Malaysia, Indonesia, and Thailand. Economist S. B. Lindner noted that it is very likely that the Pacific region will equal the GDP of the United States or Europe by the year 2000—even if the growth-rate differentials are much smaller than over the last thirty years.[13] Thus, one economic expert confidently predicted, "The center of world economic growth is shifting rapidly towards Asia and the Pacific, as the Pacific takes its place as one of the key centers of economic power."[14]

Three aspects of the East Asian achievement have been apparent:

- Unlike most of the "third world," the more successful Pacific regions had virtually no resources other than their human capital.
- The East Asian areas expanded their economies at a rate unprecedented in world history.
- Most importantly, as I have emphasized, many of the Asian regions invigorated their economies while decreasing the gap between the rich and poor. They achieved growth with equity—a remarkable increase in productivity as well as an improvement in the health, education, life expectancy, and general economic welfare or their peoples.[15]

Inevitably, the great and small powers of the world must respond to this phenomenon. The United States and Western Europe have to question whether and how their prosperity can be maintained in the face of shifting patterns of global production. The Soviet Union and Eastern Europe should ponder whether their troubled economic systems might benefit from the Asian example. For the developing countries still caught in the quagmire of poverty, the startling ascendence of Asia raises two central questions: Is there an East Asian model of development? Can it be adapted?

Wisdom in these matters lies in the recognition that none of the more fashionable schools of thought—whether derived from Karl Marx or Adam Smith, from Max Weber or "dependency" and "world systems" theorists—helps to explain this unparalleled event.

The Poverty of Theory

"Modern East Asia is a junkyard for Western theories of economic development and political modernization," political scientist Chalmers Johnson has rightly observed, "and it is wise to remind ourselves of the area's profound exceptionalism."[16]

Marxism, as the prime example, explained nothing about the Asian miracle. Johnson observed that "Marx's great scheme of a progression from primitive communism to slave society and then on to feudalism, capitalism, socialism, and communism cracked on its obvious irrelevance to the history of classical Asia." In turn, this "suggests that Marx's analysis of the role of classes in development and revolution is equally overgeneralized."[17]

Almost every basic prediction from the Marxist model foundered on the realities of contemporary Asia. The secular rate of capitalist profit has not dropped in Asia or elsewhere—thus, invalidating the basic premise of Marxist theory.[18] Extraction of surplus value in labor-intensive industries resulted in growing equality between the classes in most of Asia, rather than polarization.[19] The expansion of state capitalism eventuated in greater wealth for the poor, not, as Marx anticipated, in greater "immiseration."[20] Collaboration between the state and capitalists circumvented the periodic crises which Marx once described as inevitable and increasingly severe.[21] In short, any Asian who still clung to the tattered banners of Marxism did so out of faith in a civic religion rather than as a result of empirical observation.[22]

In everyday practice, the Marxist orthodoxy proved an extraordinarily unreliable guide to actual events in the Pacific Basin.

The industrial proletariat failed to provide even a semblance of leadership for socialist revolution. Instead, the real leaders of reform or revolution came from the ranks of aristocrats or bourgeoisie. Singapore produced Lee Kuan Yew, a Cambridge scholar; Korea had its Park Chung-Hee, a graduate of the nation's military academy; Taiwan followed the dynastic guidance of Chiang Kai-shek; Hong Kong thrived under British colonial officers and Chinese entrepreneurs; Thailand and Malaysia moved forward under their kings and sultans; and the Chinese put their faith first in Mao (a descendant of China's "kulaks") and then in Zhou and Deng (both worldly, French-educated members of the land-owning class.) Changes came from above and were not dictated by class position. Even the revolutionary events in the China of 1989 were led by students who were often the sons of the party elite.

Again, contrary to Marxist doctrine, the political realm in each case took precedence over the economy. Political decisions by an elite, rather than changes in the mode of production, served as the critical impetus for progress. On a mass level, Mao despaired of the Shanghai industrial proletariat and instead put his faith in the enthusiasm of peasants whom Marx had once derided as products of "rural idiocy."

Thus, the real agents of productive change in Asia differed substantially from the Marxist model. Newly rich peasants in Taiwan, entrepreneurs (aided by MITI) in Japan, the PAP elite in Singapore, even generals in Thailand took the lead in improving the welfare of the masses.

Where Marxist ideologues actually tried out Marxist prescriptions, they proved a disastrous failure. Pol Pot's drive to impose collectivization on his people resulted in a bloody civil war. Mao's attempt to emulate the Soviet model of heavy industrialization and forced "communalization" of agriculture represented the most grievous mistake in twentieth-century history. Only abrupt changes in policy by men like Deng saved these countries from disaster.

In other Asian regions, people came to realize that "it is possible for economic growth to be compatible with an improved distribution of income during every phase of the transition from colonialism to a modern developed economy."[23] Since Marxism had failed to explain the Asian situation, S.N.G. Davies, the Hong Kong scholar, argued that "capitalism and socialism did not have the standard Western meanings in East Asian ideological debate."[24] Perhaps, Davies argued, "the Japanese and other East Asian societies are creating a completely new form of polity and economy."[25] Whatever the future, Peter Berger cogently stated, "East Asia, to put it bluntly, is bad news for Marxists."[26]

Weberian theories did not fare any better in the Asian context. In his *The Religion of China,* Max Weber originally argued that Confucianism blocked the development of capitalism in Asia.[27] Weber believed that Confucian values failed to provide the dynamic motivation for capitalistic endeavors. Supposedly, the Confucian disdain for the merchant, its dislike for formal law, and its belief that "a cultured man is not a tool" hindered economic development. According to Chia-Chu Hou's interpretation of

Weber, "As Confucian ethics reduced tension with the world to an absolute minimum, this world was the best of all possible worlds, man was disposed to be ethically good, and economic achievement deserved less attention."[28]

The subsequent development of neo-Confucian societies such as Japan, the NICs, and the Chinese segments of Indonesia, Thailand, and Malaysia took place under the auspices of a form of capitalism that confounded Weber's thesis.[29] Indeed, a spate of authors set Weber on his head and contended that Confucianism spurred economic development. While ignoring the fact that traditional Chinese culture could not wholly be identified with Confucian culture, Herman Kahn first asserted in 1979 that neo-Confucianism served to stimulate modernization.[30] That opinion met with equally vigorous exceptions.[31]

"Dependency theory" and "World Systems theory," advocated by neo-Marxists such as Samir Amin and Immanuel Wallerstein, encountered particular difficulties in explaining the Asian scene. In different ways, these theories posited that "third world" poverty emerged from exploitation by a "core" of capitalist nations. Capitalist powers allegedly consigned the rest of the world to a "periphery" whose labor and resources served only to increase the wealth of the "core." Supposedly, the only escape for the peripheral nations was, at the minimum, self-sufficient industrialization and, at the maximum, a socialist revolution that would cut all ties with the capitalist world.[32]

The Asian explosion flatly contradicted these positions. Japan decisively moved into the "core" and, indeed came to dominate it—an outcome that the various dependency theorists did not and could not logically predict. Moreover, Japan and the other successful regions followed the exact obverse of the policies advocated by dependency theorists: they adapted an outward-looking, export-oriented strategy that linked them more closely with the old capitalist "core" and placed them squarely in the world market. "In fact," Peter Bauer has noted, "commercial contacts with the West have been the prime instruments of material progress in the Third World."[33]

The degree of Asian "dependence" on the outside world differed dramatically: In 1988, for example, total imports and exports for Japan amounted to 17 percent of the GNP, a rather small proportion of its economy. In China, the export-import share of GNP rose to 33 percent, in Korea to 70 percent, and in Taiwan to an astounding 88 percent.[34] Whatever the degree of interaction with the world economy, it was clear, as Johnson observed, that "so-called *dependencia* and World Systems theories foundered on the economic performances of South Korea, Taiwan, Hong Kong and Singapore."[35]

If the neo-Marxist theories failed to enlighten Asian leaders concerning the process of development, widespread praise for free market capitalism as the source of progress seemed less than adequate. Economist Alvin Rabushka, for example, attributed rapid economic advance in Taiwan and Hong Kong, as well as Dengist China, primarily to the play of market forces.[36] Bauer argued powerfully against central planning and socialism, maintaining that the experience of Japan, Hong Kong, Malaysia, the Philippines, Korea, and Taiwan contradicted the advice offered by social democratic economists such as Gunnar Myrdal or the prescriptions of a hard-line Marxist such as Paul Baran.[37]

Yet, Berger, an advocate of capitalism, noted that "East Asia is not very comforting to ideologists who still adhere to some laissez-faire notions to the effect that state interventionism is bad for economic development. All of these societies are characterized by massive state interventions in economic life. They are heavily *dirigiste* and have been so from the beginnings of their respective modernization process."[38]

The truth is that collaboration between governments and industry, rather than laissez-faire economics, dominated East Asia, even in the extreme case of Hong Kong. As Vogel noted, MITI planners played a major role in Japan.[39] Singapore used its Central Provident Fund to manipulate the economy.[40] Taiwan's government, although engaged in "privatization," still owned large segments of the economy.[41]

Nonetheless, the thrust of the East Asian initiative was capitalist in its general contours. The East Asian governments usually intervened in their economies in order to promote the accumulation of private capital, to attract foreign capital, to build export industries, to curb trade unions, and to provide a basic infrastructure—from schools to dams to roads—as an essential undergirding for development. They were, in Johnson's phrase, "capitalist development states" (CDS) that were far removed from the command economies created by Lenin, Stalin, and Mao.[42]

What, then, produced the miracle of Asian growth? I would suggest that a set of common policies imposed on a receptive culture and an amenable social structure by a determined political elite played the central role. Although a favorable combination of external factors aided Asian development, the credit should go to rational policies implemented by an extraordinarily competent group of political leaders.

The Role of Culture

East Asia has in common a largely Oriental population influenced by a strong Chinese cultural strain. Even in those Asian nations that have not quite lived up to their potential such as Malaysia, Thailand, and Indonesia, a minority of Chinese entrepreneurs have taken the lead in economic activity. In other countries, such as Brazil, small groups of Japanese migrants have played a disproportionate role in economic development.

In Malaysia, Bauer has pointed out, the original Chinese migrants worked harder, were more proficient at even humble tasks than Malays, and earned more money. The Chinese, for example, tapped much more rubber from the same forests but used the same tools as did Malays.[43] In consequence, he has argued, the contemporary Chinese have achieved a dominant role in the economy.

In the case of Singapore, Berger has suggested, "It is inherently implausible to believe that Singapore would be what it is today if it were populated, not by a majority of ethnic Chinese, but by Brazilians or Bengalis—or, for that matter, by a majority of ethnic Malays."[44]

Similarly, Ronald Dore cites as the premier ingredient in the "Japanese recipe" the unsubtle fact that "the Japanese work hard."[45] In addition, the homogeneity of the Japanese population has been described as a factor promoting both political and economic consensus.

Clearly, elements in the folk cultures of Japan, China, and Korea stress pragmatism, hard work, discipline, and an active rather than contemplative way of life.[46] Chie Nakane has argued convincingly that the two prime values of Japanese culture, "groupism" and hierarchy, have been transmitted from the *ie,* or household, to modern business organizations.[47] A pronounced tendency to save, an obvious prerequisite for capital investment, has also been described as a cultural tendency based on familial obligations. (Such an assertion ignores the fact that savings in Taiwan and Korea fluctuated greatly in response to government policies).

In many ways, the traits described as essential to Asian success involve worldly asceticism and stand in sharp contrast to other traditions such as the fatalism of Hinduism and the other-worldliness of Buddhism.

Nonetheless, I would hesitate to attribute the recent economic dynamism of the Pacific region solely or even mainly to cultural factors or to a rather vague Chinese of Japanese "work ethic."

For many centuries, these same traditions were associated with stagnation. The Chinese, for example, have always worked hard and saved for the future but their efforts brought few material benefits. Under Mao, many Chinese donated their labor as a substitute for capital, but the Cultural Revolution crippled the economy. Only major changes in policy in 1978 rescued the Chinese from an enduring "culture of poverty." Subsequent changes in 1989 may have returned them temporarily to privation.

The case of Taiwan also contradicts the theory that "Chinese character" accounted for the country's economic history. In the 1950s, Taiwan, like the mainland, launched an import substitution policy, suppressed dissent, and invested grandly in military preparations. Like China, Taiwan stumbled along until the 1960s when economist K. Y. Yin guided the country on a new path. Stimulated by the creation of free economic zones and an export-oriented policy, Taiwan surged far ahead of mainland China in economic development. The Taiwanese succeeded because "they invented ways to stimulate exports and to derive the benefits of world price competition, while still shielding sections of the domestic economy."[48]

Further, Pacific countries that have a meager Chinese heritage but followed similar economic policies made strides comparable to the original achievements of Japan and the NICs. As I have noted, Thailand's economy in 1988, for example, grew at the rate of 9 percent annually while exports of industrial goods surged by 40 percent. But Thailand's dominant culture is Buddhism, an unlikely spiritual source for economic innovation.

In every case, as Gustav Papanek has pointed out, economic growth in the successful regions occurred *only after* the countries adapted new economic strategies: "Culture was invariant, economic policies changed, and, almost simultaneously, economic performance changed."[49] Papanek emphasized a high rate of investment, good returns to private investors, managerial efficiency, the utilization of abundant labor, and government intervention to correct distortions in free market economies as the key policies.

It would seem reasonable, then, to assume that socio-economic strategies combined with political stability have played a more decisive role than culture in promoting modernization. At most, Berger argues cautiously, certain cultural attributes—an emphasis on "activism, rational innovativeness, and self-discipline—have given the East Asian regions a comparative advantage in the modernization process."[50]

One specific variant of the culturalists' argument is to credit East Asian success to the Confucian ethic. With the rise of the Asian countries, some social scientists cited elements of Confucianism, such as its reverence for education, as a prime reason for East Asia's growth. Michio Morishima, for example, argues that Confucianism played a crucial role in Japanese development.[51] Berger contended that "a vulgar Confucianism" emphasizing respect for authority, education, and diligence provided a necessary background—a "genuine, dynamic trigger"—for East Asian development.[52] Some enthusiasts, such as an editorialist in Taiwan's *China News* even argued that "It was thrift, frugality, hard work, and dedication to the principles of Confucius . . . that create the material wealth and economic strength which now allows people to feel relatively secure in their future."[53]

In making such comparative estimates, it is wise to remember that regions uninfluenced by the Confucian ethic (or its Protestant, Jewish, or Sikh "functional equivalents") have achieved similar advances. Confucian countries, such as Taiwan and Korea, initially followed policies that inhibited economic growth. After specific reforms, they moved forward dramatically. Again, these facts point to the importance of social, economic, and political strategies as the true initiators of change.

Moreover, those who would credit Confucian virtues with the success of East Asia ignore a great diversity in cultures. As Roy Hofheinz and Kent Calder point out in discussing the Confucian contribution to the "East Asian Edge": "We might just as easily term the European tradition 'Platonic' or 'Aristotelian.'. . . In fact, many of the philosophical underpinnings of modern East Asia lie with non-Confucian doctrines such as Legalism or Taoism."[54]

Further, as Hiroshi Takeuchi has argued, even the same Chinese characters expressing the philosophy of Confucianism have been differently interpreted in China, Korea, and Japan: "The character which signifies both 'soldier' and 'scholar' is highly valued . . . but with quite different meanings. In Japan, it generally means *Samurai,* including his *Bushido,* while in Korea, it means *scholar.*"[55] Takeuchi maintains that this transformation in meaning has made Japan a relatively militaristic nation and has excluded scholars from the corporate or political worlds. In Korea, on the other hand, it is common for university professors to advise corporations or become cabinet ministers.[56]

Faced with such diversity, it would seem reasonable to grant only a modest amount of credit to some of the cultural influences of Confucianism. (Other inheritances, such as the Korean tradition that elder sons must always take over from their fathers as presidents of companies, may be actively harmful.) On balance, as Papanek avers, "the principal element in economic success was the strategy adopted, which should be readily reproducible elsewhere."[57]

The Role of Social Structure

Some, although not all, of the Asian states enjoyed social advantages and benefited from historical circumstances that may have eased their transition into modern economies.

Unlike parts of Latin America, for example, many of the successful Asian states did not have to contend with an entrenched "feudal" elite. In Japan, the early Meiji reforms and the later MacArthur initiatives radically undermined large landowners. The Communist revolution in China, whatever its other faults, swept away a feudal system of land ownership. Similarly, on Taiwan, the KMT could ignore the interests of big Formosan landlords and institute major reforms.

In addition, the Asian nations generally did not have a tradition of tribal land ownership as do many parts of Africa. Whatever its virtues, such a communal tradition often hampers individual initiative and agricultural innovation. Consequently, the institution of "household" or "plantation" farming for profit proceeded more easily in Japan, Taiwan, Korea, Malaysia, and China than it could in some African regions.

On a different level, the absence of well-developed industrial labor movements may well have aided Japan, Taiwan, Korea, Hong Kong, and Singapore during their initial stages of economic expansion. Weak or co-opted Asian trade unions were in no position to pose unrealistic wage demands on economies that counted on labor-intensive industries as the engine of growth. The immediate human costs of this lack of union support were enormous but the eventual gains were also great.[58]

Asian governments also initiated a series of policies that encouraged whatever entrepreneurial talent was latent in their societies. In Japan, MITI cushioned the blows that fell on budding export-oriented industrialists. In Singapore, the PAP government provided incentives for outward-looking entrepreneurs. Taiwan and Korea found "a balance in the 1950s between providing enough protection to native industries to give managers and workers experience, but not so much as to stymie their desire and ability to compete."[59] The post-Mao reforms in China gave incentives to peasants to branch out into highly successful rural industries. Han Seung Soo has contended that a series of social dislocations caused this sudden explosion of entrepreneurial energies in Asia: "population migration, disintegration of ruling classes, atomization of economic oligarchies backed by the colonial power—these necessitated a new spirit of enterprise and daring."[60]

In sharp contrast to Han, other observers argued that a general social consensus within East Asian societies has provided a sure foundation for economic progress. Davies, for example, has put forward a position shared by many Asian leaders that "the stricter disciplines of family and social life, the greater respect for order and authority, the absence of an assertive individualism—these and many other features of Asian life are held to represent the proper basis for the efficient operation of a modern state and a 'capitalist' economy."[61]

In the great panorama of the Asian experiment, exceptions to almost any sociological generalization abound:

If one assumes greater social cohesion in the Orient than in other parts of the world, why would this ancient order suddenly precipitate unprecedented economic growth from the 1950s to the 1990s? How would this attribute account for the achievements of Singapore and Malaysia, countries that were split by conflict?

If, on the other hand, one argues that disruption of the old social order contributes to entrepreneurial drive, how does one explain Thailand—a country where the monarchy, the aristocracy, and the military have ruled tranquilly—and yet the economy boomed in the 1980s?

If one contends that the lack of a powerful trade union movement is critical in the initial stages of growth, what promoted the unexpected take off of some Asian nations during the 1960s? Since the exploitation of labor has been a perennial characteristic of Asia (as well as most of the rest of the world), what made the difference?

Or, if one asserts that the destruction of a feudal land-owning class is necessary for economic growth, how does one explain the cases of Thailand and Malaysia where aristocrats and sultans still rule?

The truth is that the social advantages and constraints on economic progress have differed from region to region, but the magnificent achievements of Northeast and Southeast Asia cannot be denied.[62] The reasons for their advance lie far more in the exercise of wise political policies than in their traditional social structures.

Political Structures and Policies

In Asia, for good or evil, political decisions proved to have had more impact on development than socio-cultural factors, the objective economic situation, or natural resources. Dwight Perkins, for example, points to "political stability under an independent sovereign government" combined with modest income differentials as essential to East Asia's economic successes.[63] Johnson believes that a determined political elite willing to force economic priorities on a nation was crucial.[64] Hofheinz and Calder go farther and argue that "the economic performance of East Asia rests heavily on political conditions so unique as to be unreproducible."[65]

With certain exceptions during particular historical periods, the high-growth economies have exhibited marked similarities in political policies. Some of these characteristics may not be easily translatable elsewhere. Other policies, with necessary cultural adaptations, seem adaptable in certain developing countries. The following are the major features of the East Asian political system:

First, since the late 1950s, Japan, Singapore, Hong Kong, Taiwan, and Korea have been politically stable. Since the 1960s, Malaysia and Thailand have in their own peculiar ways maintained political balance. In some cases, such as Korea and Taiwan until the 1980s, governments achieved political tranquility only at the price of heavy repression of the opposition. In others, such as Singapore and Malaysia until the 1980s, mildly authoritarian governments kept a steady hand on the economy but tolerated dissent. In Japan, a fully democratic society allowed political opposition, a free press, and vociferous protests.[66] Nonetheless, the same political party remained in power. Regardless of the forms of political participation, the reigning elite in all areas held onto office and allowed some degree of discussion, dissent, and protest. And they all stressed economic development as the prime goal of their regimes.

Whatever its faults, such a political system allows for economic predictability, encourages policies aimed at economic growth, and adheres to international law and financial obligations.

Second, the East Asian governments have generally managed to maintain balanced budgets since the 1960s, thus aiding in the control of inflation. In response to the oil crises of the 1970s and 1980s, some nations experienced inflationary spirals, but these were rather easily controlled by cautious fiscal policies. Korea, in particular, went through severe inflation and, in addition, amassed a large foreign debt, but the economy's growth allowed the nation to meet her foreign obligations.

Third, the East Asian governments have spent lavishly in building an infrastructure and an educational system that contribute directly to economic development. They have generally economized, however, in providing direct social welfare benefits, housing subsidies, and social security for their populations. Economic growth has come first; social welfare, a distant second. Because of the general rise in incomes, this policy did not interfere with a spectacular advance in the educational level and health of the various Asian populations. Nonetheless, it meant that Japan will have to correct an abysmal housing shortage in the 1990s, that Taiwan must address the problems caused by urban pollution, and that Malaysia will have to alleviate the miserable work conditions of its increasingly vocal industrial workers.

Fourth, unlike the usual pattern traced by the "Kuznets curve," some East Asian governments have consciously attempted to narrow the gap between classes as economic progress has occurred. In countries such as Singapore, Taiwan and, to a lesser extent, Korea and Japan, careful fiscal and income policies and a steady demand for previously unskilled labor allowed the economy to expand while the income of the masses increased. Since their peoples have received an increasingly "fair share" in the economy, the political stability of some Asian governments has been reinforced.[67]

Fifth, the East Asian governments have engaged in planning their economies by removing distortions in the free-market system, particularly in the export sector. Thus, in Japan, government taxes have been heaviest on domestic consumer-oriented industries, and MITI has targeted certain export industries for special aid to meet foreign competition. With variations, the same pattern has been repeated in Korea, Taiwan, and even in the supposedly laissez-faire, but finely managed, Hong Kong. In post-Mao China, "commodity socialism" retained a degree of state ownership over the means of production but, in fact, the government between 1978 and 1989 encouraged the leasing of land to independent peasants, the creation of rural industries owned by "cooperatives," and the introduction of foreign-owned industries in the coastal zones.

Sixth, East Asian governments invested heavily in education and often adjusted admissions to higher education in accord with the future needs of the economy. Educational policy most often reflected a political decision to use education as a "tool" rather than as an end in itself.

Seventh, perhaps underlying these approaches and contributing to the stability of these regimes, there may be a core of paternalistic authoritarianism that motivated and sustained the various elites. As Pye has described the essence of the East Asian political model, "Authority is expected to combine, with grace and benevolence, both elitism and sympathy. . . . The culture reveres hierarchy . . . but they also expect rulers to be concerned about the livelihood of the masses."[68]

Johnson maintains that the Asian political regimes have followed an "unbalanced" strategy of development: economic advance came first at the expense of "social development" (such as unemployment insurance) or "political development" (increases in access to forums where binding decisions for the society as a whole are made).[69] When a CDS progresses to a high level of industrialization, Johnson argues, "the resulting high levels of pluralism will create a crisis of stability that *can* lead to democracy."[70] But, he rightly adds, "there is nothing predetermined about the outcome of the crisis of imbalance."[71] Indeed, as I have noted, the 1980s marked the transition of previously authoritarian regimes such as Korea, Taiwan, and Thailand in a liberal, even democratic direction while leaders in Singapore and Malaysia drifted toward more austere controls over their populations. And China erupted into anarchy.

It is also clear that the mere imposition of an authoritarian regime, however dedicated and ruthless, can lead to economic blunders and disasters. The experience of Mao and Chiang on mainland China testifies to this fact. For economic success to result, the political elite must implement wise socio-economic policies. Here, I believe, is the real key to contemporary Asian achievements.

Common Socio-Economic Policies

Regardless of their political heritage, the flourishing Asian societies have followed a common set of socio-economic policies that have infused their peoples with new dynamism:

Land reform came as a first step in Japan, Taiwan, and Korea.[72] Post-Mao China also offered peasants the incentives to produce abundantly for their home markets. Usually, the governments of these nations provided technical assistance, credit, and improved seeds to promote agricultural expansion. The reforms generally increased the ownership and motivation of peasants without (except in the case of Japan) artificial subsidies. Malaysia and even Indonesia followed similar policies.[73] An initial concentration on agricultural reform had several advantages: it provided food for urban workers, it opened up some export markets, it supplied capital for the building of new industries, and it exposed peasants to the operation of the market system.

Labor-intensive industrialization allowed these originally poor countries to use their most abundant resource, unskilled labor, in the first stages of economic growth. For varying, but relatively short periods of time, the NICs all depended on labor-intensive activities that required little capital, skills, or technology. Postwar Japan, financed by Postal Savings, the largest bank in the world, launched immediately into large-scale but labor-intensive enterprises. Malaysia, Thailand, and Indonesia took the same labor-intensive path in the 1980s and benefited from infusions of Japanese capital.

Obviously, such a policy places tremendous burdens on the workers and allows more advanced industrial countries to seek out opportunities for the use of low-wage workers. This approach did not represent true exploitation of the poor, however, since the ancient alternative was idleness and starvation. Moreover, as Papanek has remarked, "one crucial consequence of the strategy pursued by the East Asian countries was that the poor also benefited from rapid growth and that there was, in general, no worsening of income inequalities."[74]

As vocational education spread—notably in Singapore, Taiwan, and Korea—previously illiterate workers gained the knowledge that allowed for an upgrading of industries and, consequently, of wages.[75] Thus, the wages of Korean textile workers (adjusted for inflation) surged from $32 a month in the 1950s to $242 in the 1980s; wages of construction workers in Japan jumped from $41 a month to $1,280 a month; and the earnings of manufacturing labor in Hong Kong went from 64 cents a day in the 1950s to $11.50 a day in the 1980s.[76]

Singapore and Taiwan followed a deliberate policy of encouraging foreign investments while Korea widely engaged in joint ventures with foreign companies. Such efforts relieved entrepreneurs and enterprises of some of the initial risks of entering the world market.[77]

The East Asian countries largely avoided the more common economic mistakes in developing countries that adapted an import substitution policy such as the subsidization of inefficient state-owned companies, the early launching of huge capital-intensive industries, the construction of prestigious but wasteful projects, or the granting to a particular company of exclusive protection from competition.

Since the 1960s, the successful regions have had consistently *high rates of investment and high returns on investment*. East Asian countries have benefited from an extraordinary level of either compulsory or voluntary savings (at least 25 percent more than other developing countries).[78] Investment of these savings, particularly in labor-intensive industries, brought large returns to entrepreneurs who were virtually guaranteed against nationalization of their enterprises. In the 1950s and 1960s, Japan and Hong Kong depended upon internal savings (encouraged by high bank interest rates) and the willingness of their people to give up quick profits for long-term growth. Taiwan and Korea encouraged domestic savings but depended more on foreign aid or foreign loans. Singapore relied on private foreign capital as well as its Central Provident Fund.

As a beneficient cycle began, high investment led to rapid growth which, in turn, encouraged further investment. In all of the countries, tax schemes strongly encouraged (or compelled) a high rate of savings and investment.

The more successful Asian regions strongly encouraged a *meritocracy* in both business and government. In contrast to many developing countries, the richer Asian nations have generally turned away from personalistic, family-based, ethnic, or political criteria as their standard for appointment or advancement. Instead, they have emphasized educational attainment, examination results, and actual performance on the job as a prime standard for moving young people into the elite civil service and first-ranked corporations.[79] Taiwan has admitted Formosans to its highest levels; Japan depends on university achievements in hiring "the best and the brightest"; and Singapore sorts out people of different abilities from the primary levels on.[80]

The high growth regions have followed conscious policies of *population control*, thus lessening the pressure of their peoples upon sometimes limited food supplies. Japan and Singapore have reached a zero population growth;[81] Taiwan and Thailand have drastically reduced their birth rates; and Hong Kong, after many years of tolerance, has tried to close its doors on refugees. After a vigorous campaign, urban Chinese have also cut their population growth, although newly "rich" rural Chinese show signs of returning to relatively large families.

Although political orators sometimes praised the "uniqueness" of their societies, the East Asian nations (with the possible exception of China) have been notably successful in *absorbing alien economic and cultural intrusions*. Unlike many developing countries that have pursued economic policies aimed at self-sufficiency, or political policies designed to promote cultural authenticity, or social goals geared to the exclusion of foreign peoples or ideas, most of the Asian regions have been generally receptive to outside influences. More recently, Singapore opened its doors to multinationals, post-Mao China welcomed joint ventures, and Korea imported Japanese technology. Other Pacific countries, such as Malaysia and Thailand, consciously began "to look East" to Japan and Korea for capital, technology, and ideas.[82] Thousands of Chinese, Taiwanese, and Korean students have poured into the United States, Japan, and West Germany. This welcoming of foreign influences has caused anxiety in the home countries and prompted political mutterings about preserving or restoring the authentic culture. In China, conservatives have complained about "spiritual pollution." Usually, however, rhetoric has not interfered with reality: Singaporean children are, for example, taught a Confucian course in school, but they must master English as a basic language of commerce.

Taken together, these common policies—land reform; government-guided free enterprises with an original emphasis on labor-intensive and export-oriented industries; a high rate of savings and private profit; a decrease in real poverty; an emphasis on meritocracy; population control; an acceptance of alien capital, technology and ideas; political stability; expenditures for a productive infrastructure; and an impetus for educa-tion—provide a model of socio-economic strategies that has proven suc-cessful in achieving growth, equity, and the general welfare.

As a result of these strategies, the ICOR scores of East Asian nations (the rate of growth extracted per unit of investment) have been highly favorable. Reliable estimates suggest that half of the astounding rate of East Asian growth is due to the greater efficiency enabled by these policies rather than to higher capital investment.[83] For poorer countries, once as desperate as East Asia, this is an example of policies that should not be ignored.

There are, of course, detractors of the East Asian model who attribute its efficacy merely to fortunate timing, foreign aid, and devious policies. Those who deride the applicability of the model should perhaps consider it again.

The Influence of External Factors

Some scholars attempt to explain the success of East Asia by referring to external factors beyond the control of policymakers in the region, such as the circumstances of their initial contact with the world market, foreign aid, historical "shocks" that galvanized their economies, or to the laxity of industrialized countries in destroying trade barriers erected by the Asian governments. In a sense, such theories reduce the complex story of East Asian expansion to mere good fortune.

In the 1960s, when some Pacific countries first penetrated the world market, there was an abundance of foreign capital in the world and fewer trade barriers. Consequently, so the argument goes, well-made labor-intensive goods could find a niche in foreign markets, particularly the United States. Without such an unusual opportunity, some maintain, a country such as Taiwan could not have sustained its achievements.[84]

Certainly, too, nations like Japan, Korea, and Taiwan temporarily bene-fited from injections of American aid which enabled them to reform their agriculture and to build new industries from scratch. In the case of Japan, the Korean War necessitated a major influx of American monies to support the military effort. In Taiwan between 1951 and 1965, American assistance comprised more than 30 percent of domestic investment each year and helped to build efficient electrical, transportation, and communications systems.[85] United States aid to Korea in the 1950s kept the war-ravaged economy from foundering. Clearly, all of these economies were "under pressure to perform," and abundant American assistance proved of crucial value.[86]

Alterations in the world economy since that period have led some analysts to claim that there will be "no more NICs."[87] Robin Broad and John Cavanagh, for example, have argued that "far-reaching changes in the global economy—from synthetic substitutes for commodity exports to unsustainable levels of external debt—have created a glut economy offer-ing little room for entrants."[88]

Such a position overlooks the fact that the original NICs did not make their fortunes from the export of commodities, that Japan has emerged as a major actor in the reduction of world debt, and huge new entries in the world market such as China and Indonesia do not suffer from a "glut" in demand.

Moreover, various counterarguments suggest that the East Asian coun-tries did not occupy a peculiarity unique position at the time of their initial surge forward or that their "good luck" has continued to assist their growth.

Japan, the NICs, Thailand, and Malaysia have prospered in spite of the twists and turns of the world economy, the oil shocks, the debt crisis, the end of American aid, and the partial closing of European and American markets. They have done so by flexibly exploiting their comparative advantages, opening new markets in the Pacific and beyond, moving quickly into high-tech industries, investing in Western countries and in Southeast Asia to avoid trade barriers, encouraging domestic demand (in

Japan) and, in some cases, inviting foreign capital investments on attractive terms.

These are rational policies that have allowed the East Asian nations to respond with alacrity to mini-recessions and changes in world supply and demand. There seems no reason to assume a priori that they could not be followed by other nations. Thus, it may be that Japan in 1953, Singapore in 1965, and Thailand in 1985 temporarily prospered from their comparative advantages at those times, but their achievements since then have demonstrated that they do not depend on the vagaries of the world economy or the generosity of other areas.

Although both Korea and Taiwan could be considered as "success stories" of American aid, economic assistance ended long ago and before the real expansion of these countries. (Conversely, America has poured aid into its three major recipients—Israel, Pakistan, and Egypt—without noticeable economic improvements in those areas.)

Japan, Taiwan, and Korea still have an umbrella of American military assistance, but the importance of that aid to their economies may well be questioned. Taiwan and Korea spend as much of their GNP on military activities as do America or Europe; Japan spends much less. And yet, the Asian regions have all grown dramatically in economic terms.

Lucian Pye has proposed another version that stresses external factors: the East Asian nations prospered because they suffered from "second shocks"—threats from the outside world that "shattered the traditional Confucian sense of cultural superiority and made genuine learning from the outside world possible."[89] Pye notes the impact of World War II on Japan, the Koumingtang's retreat to Taiwan, the Korean War—perhaps even China's disastrous Cultural Revolution—as events that forced the various elites to ensure their legitimacy through outstanding economic advances.

Certainly, the elites of East Asia once had to face the possibility that their regimes would collapse. Sometimes, as in contemporary Malaysia and Singapore, the ruling class has even invented the current "threat."

Nonetheless, two facts stand out: many of the East Asian economies, particularly Japan, have continued to advance although the elites and their peoples no longer perceive any real threat to their stability. Clearly, too, other countries throughout the world have experienced "second shocks"—repeated defeats of Arabs at the hands of Israel, the Nigerian civil war, bloody revolutions in Zaire—without any improvement in their government's policies or the progress of their economies. If the "shock theory" has validity, it is not universal.

Still other observers attribute Asian success to an uncanny ability to manipulate world markets, keep out foreign goods, and squash competitors. It is a comfortable American and European belief that East Asian countries have competed unfairly by erecting protectionist barriers against foreign encroachments. Supposedly, their companies are encouraged to dump goods on the world market and infringe on patents by copying foreign manufacturers. The actual record on these matters is decidedly mixed.

Japan and some other East Asian countries do protect some of their industries, particularly the infant ones, and their agriculture from European or American competition. Protectionism most often takes the form of applying worrisome inspection procedures, taxes, and bureaucratic delays to the entrance of new products rather than direct tariffs.[90] Taiwanese companies have been fairly accused of pirating technology from foreign sources. The Asian governments also help to ease the transition of their own new companies into the world economy and aid certain uncompetitive industries out of both domestic and world competition. Mechanisms such as the reevaluation of currency abet the process.[91]

The East Asian societies cannot, however be accused of direct protectionism. The Japanese have, after all, imposed voluntary quotes on some of their exports and opened their markets to competition from the NICs. Products that have a certain "chachet" in Japan—Mercedes, BMWs, French perfumes—enjoy a good market. Only the American products, with their reputation for shoddiness, do not sell well.

Moreover, certain Asian economies such as Singapore and Hong Kong have advanced with great speed and exported their products without ever being accused of protectionism.

In Japan and the smaller Asian economies, government officials fully realize that a protectionist policy would merely provoke more intense retaliation from Europe and America. Rather than blaming protectionist policies, it is more disquieting but more realistic, as Ezra Vogel has suggested, "to admit that the Japanese have beaten us in economic competition because of their superior planning, organization, and effort."[92]

"Dumping"—the practice of selling below costs abroad in order to ensure a greater share of eventual sales—has undoubtedly occurred, particularly in new high-tech industries such as semiconductors.[93] In Japan, the policy was encouraged in a business and governmental climate that treasured long-term economic gains over immediate profits. Such an approach cannot work indefinitely, Vogel observes, since businessmen would hardly "remain so zealous in selling goods to America if they were basically selling below cost."[94]

It would be comfortable for some Western businessmen, but illusory, to assume that unfair practices or external circumstances played the major role in explaining Asian achievements. Too many exceptions undermine such generalizations:

Singapore received no American aid and was cut off from British assistance; and yet, the "Lion City" roared.

After suffering from decades of American boycott, post-Mao China blossomed for a decade.

Late entries into the world arena, such as Thailand, are doing well—not least because they benefit from the experience, example, and investments of other Asian regions.

Areas such as Hong Kong never had any restrictions on trade and yet the colony's infant industries prospered and her bankers now pour money into other Asian enterprises.

Thus, it would be extremely difficult to explain the advance of these areas as due to external practices or any barriers they construct against Western trade.

In sum, it is irresponsible to belittle the Asian achievement by crediting it to favorable circumstances, foreign assistance, an ineffable Confucian spirit, or a social structure free of conflict. Indeed, Asia faced more obstacles to development—war, civil war, and a lack of resources—than most areas that have yet to achieve the Asian level of affluence.

Favorable circumstances were neither the sufficient nor the necessary cause for the Asian advance. Rather, common political, economic, and social policies make up the Asian model of development.

An "Asian" Model of Development

Two general elements in the Asian drama—most prominently in Japan, Korea, Singapore, Hong Kong, and Taiwan; and less brilliantly, but still significantly in Indonesia, Malaysia, and Thailand—accounted for the region's rapid development:

First, a determined, stable, and highly competent political elite adapted a set of policies that generally included land reform, greater incentives for peasants, a broadening of education, a determination to achieve growth with equity, and wage restraints in labor-intensive industries. In varying degrees, an initially authoritarian government overcame stubborn opposition and allowed a degree of dissent from their policies.

Second, the political rulers pursued particular economic policies that could, in theory, be adapted anywhere—an "outward" orientation, an encouragement of foreign investment (in some cases), an emphasis on labor-intensive industrialization, a strong stress on domestic savings, the removal of obstacles to small- and medium-sized free enterprises, a cautious fiscal policy, and an allowance for market forces to determine prices and wages.

Unleashing the energies of Asia's peoples and propelling many of them into a more affluent stage of history creates a whole new set of possibilities in the world. The opening of the Pacific offers advantages to both industrialized and developing nations—huge markets in Asia, sources of investment, a supply of foreign aid and technical advice and, most importantly, a proven model of development. The "other Pacific Rim"—North and Latin America, the Soviet Union and Australia—must pay attention to the beacon shining from Asia.

Notes

1. Frank Ching, "The Emergence of Greater China," *Billion* (January 1989): 28.
2. Joel Kotkin and Yoriko Kishimoto, *The Third Century* (New York: Crown Publishers, 1988), 41.
3. Stephen Cheong, quoted in ibid., 40.
4. Wang Guorin, quoted in ibid., 41.
5. Wong Kwei Cheong, "The Singapore Experience of Economic Growth," Taipei, Huang-Chou Institution for Economic Research, 17 Nov. 1988, 3.
6. Ibid.
7. Louis Kraar, "Is Japanese Investment Healthy for the U.S. and Asia?" (New York: Japan Society, 27 Feb. 1989).
8. Cited in ibid.
9. Japan Securities Dealers Association, press release, April 1987.
10. Ching, "Emergence of China."
11. Ibid., 30.
12. Paul Kennedy, *The Rise and Fall of Great Powers* (New York: Random House, 1987), 441.
13. S. B. Linder, *The Pacific Century* (Stanford: Stanford University Press, 1986), 13–14.
14. P. Drysdale, "The Pacific Basin and Its Economic Vitality" in J. W. Morely, ed., *The Pacific Basin* (Princeton: Princeton University Press, 1986), 11.
15. Yan-Peng Chi, "Towards a Theoretical Explanation of Taiwan's Development with Decreasing Inequality," Taipei, Chung-Hua Institute of Economic Research, 16 Nov. 1988.

16. Chalmers Johnson, "South Korean Democratization," *The Pacific Review* 2, no. 1 (1989).
17. Ibid.
18. See Thomas Sowell, *Marxism* (New York: William Morrow, 1985).
19. Chi-ming Hou, "Relevance of the Taiwan Model of Development," Taipei, Chung Hua Institution of Economics, 16 Nov. 1988.
20. See Clinton Rossiter, *Marxism* (New York: Harcourt Brace, 1960).
21. See Betram Wolfe, "The Prophet and his Prophecies," *Problems of Communism* 7, no. 6 (1958), and Robert Heilbroner, *Marxism: For and Against* (New York: W. W. Norton, 1980).
22. See Timothy Luke, Civil Religion and Secularization," *Sociological Forum* 2, no. 1 (Winter 1987), and Christal Lane, *The Rites of Rulers* (Cambridge: Cambridge University Press, 1981).
23. See Shirley Kuo et al., *The Taiwan Success Story* (Boulder, CO: Westview Press, 1981), 143.
24. S.N.G. Davies, "The Capitalism/Socialism Debate in East Asia," *Society* (March/April 1989): 29.
25. Ibid., 34.
26. Peter Berger, *The Capitalist Revolution* (New York: Basic Books, 1986), 157.
27. Max Weber, *The Religion of China,* trans. by Hans H. Gerth (Glencoe, IL.: Free Press, 1951), chap. 8. "Confucianism and Protestantism". Also see Andreas E. Buss, ed., *Max Weber in Asian Studies* (Leiden: E. J. Bull, 1986).
28. Chia-Chu Hou, "Public and Private Ethics on Economic Development—with Special Reference to Confucianism," Chung-Hua Institute for Economic Research, Taipei, 17 Nov. 1988, 9.
29. See Winston Davis, "Religion and Development: Weber and the East Asian Experience," in Myron Weiner and Samuel P. Huntington, eds., *Understanding Political Development* (Boston: Little, Brown, 1987).
30. Herman Kahn, *World Economic Development* (Boulder, CO: Westview Press, 1979).
31. Davis, "Religion and Development."
32. See Immanuel Wallerstein, "The Rise and Demise of the World Capitalist System," *Comparative Studies of Society and History* no. 4 (1974).
33. Peter Bauer, *Rhetoric and Reality* (Cambridge: Harvard University Press, 1984).
34. "Asian Interdependence," World Bank, 1989.
35. Johnson, "Democratization," 1. Also see Kim Yong-Dong, "Socio-Cultural Aspects of Political Democratization in East Asia," Washington, American Enterprise Institute, May 18–19, 1988; and Thomas Gadd, *State and Society in Taiwan Miracle* (Armonk, NY: M. E. Sharpe, 1980).
36. Alvin Rabushka, *The New China* (Pacific Research Institute for Public Policy, Boulder, CO: Westview Press, 1987).
37. Bauer, *Rhetoric,* 28.
38. Berger, *Capitalist Revolution,* 157.
39. Ezra Vogel, *Japan as Number One* (Cambridge: Harvard University Press, 1979).
40. See You Poh Seng and Lim Chong Yah, eds., *Singapore: 25 Years of Development* (Singapore: Times Press, 1985).
41. Nan Yang Xing Zhou and Lianhe Zaboado, *Singapore,* n. 40.
42. Chi-ming Hou, "Relevance of Taiwan Model." Johnson, *Politics and Productivity: How Japan's Development Strategy Works* (Cambridge: Ballinger, 1989).

43. Bauer, *Rhetoric*.
44. Berger, *Capitalist Revolution,* 166.
45. Ronald Dore, *Taking Japan Seriously* (Stanford: Stanford University Press, 1987).
46. Michio Morishima, *Why Has Japan Succeeded?* (Stanford: Stanford University Press, 1987).
47. Chie Nakane, *Japanese Society* (Berkeley: University of California Press, 1972).
48. Arthur N. Waldron, "Taiwan Economy May Be Blueprint for China's Growth," *International Herald Tribune,* 10 Nov. 1984.
49. Gustav Papanek, "The New Asian Capitalism: An Economic Portrait," in *In Search of An East Asian Development Model,* ed. by Peter Berger and Shin-Huang Hsiao (New Brunswick and Oxford: Transaction Books, 1986), 76.
50. Peter Berger, "An East Asian Development Model: Empirical Explorations," in Berger and Hsiao, ibid., 20.
51. Morishima, *Why Japan*.
52. Berger, *Capitalist Revolution,* 166.
53. Editorial, *China News,* Taipei, 16 Nov. 1988.
54. Roy Hofheinz and Kent E. Calder, *The East Asia Edge* (New York: Basic Books, 1982), 41.
55. Hiroshi Takeuchi, Address at Japan Society, New York, 6 June 1988, p. 3.
56. Ibid.
57. Papanek, "New Asian Capitalism," 77.
58. Han Seung Soo, quoted in *Far Eastern Economic Review,* 20 Dec. 1984, 105. I do not want to argue that effective labor unions only develop at later stages of industrialization. In some areas of the world, such as Scandinavia, unions formed and played an important cooperative role in the early stages of economic growth. In other societies, such as Ireland, strong unions appeared in a predominantly agrarian society that had a surplus of labor. Copied from the British model, these unions prematurely demanded higher wages from a society that could not afford them and inhibited the industrialization of Ireland.
59. Deborah Diamond-Kim, *The China Business Review* (July 1–August 1988), 55.
60. Han Seung Soo, *Far Eastern Economic Review,* 20 Dec. 1984, 105.
61. Davies, *"Capitalism/Socialism Debate, 33.*
62. *Diamond-Kim, The China Business Review,* July–August 1988, 56. Thus, as one commentator put it in 1988, "Unlike Chinese managers today, NIC entrepreneus did not have to grapple with Party officials or government bureaucrats for control over their own enterprises, or face a long-term struggle simply to fire redundant or incompetent labor. That makes China's achievements all the more astounding."
63. Dwight Perkins, *China: Asia's Next Economic Giant* (Seattle: University of Washington Press, 1986).
64. Johnson, "Democratization," 5.
65. Hofheinz and Calder, *East Asia Edge,* 11.
66. Some critics of Japan, such as Karel van Wolferen, contend that the Japanese system is a sham democracy (Karl van Wolferen, *The Enigma of Japanese Power* [New York: Alfred Knopf, 1989]). Yet the vigor of Japan's press in exposing scandals, the disproportionate influence of its peasants, and the vehemence of student dissent testify to a high degree of liberty.
67. Post-Mao China still struggles with this problem. As "rich" peasants increase

their ranks, urban workers pay higher food prices. As coastal zones leap ahead, the relatively impoverished interior provinces grow restive. In a society officially governed by an egalitarian ideology, such disparities create grave political difficulties.

68. "Political Portrait," Lucian Pye, *Asian Power and Politics* (Cambridge: Harvard University Press, 1985), 84.
69. Johnson, "Democratization."
70. Ibid., 5.
71. Ibid., 6.
72. See Ann Tutwiler, Barbara Elliott, and George Rossmiller, "Economic Development and Land Reform: Japan, Taiwan and South Korea," Washington, D.C. National Center for Food and Agricultural Policy, 1988; and Rong-I Wu, "The Distinctive Features of Taiwan's Development," in Berger and Hsiao, *In Search of Model.*
73. Singapore and Hong Kong, because of their limited size, did not depend on agricultural changes for their growth but instead leapt immediately into the stage of labor-intensive industrialization. Until 1989, Thailand counted on urban industrialization and, relatively, neglected agriculture—a policy that the nation may live to regret.
74. Papanek, "New Asian Capitalism."
75. Papanek, ibid., 54.
76. See, for example, Chi-ming Hou, "Relevance of the Taiwan Model of Development," Taipei, Chung-Hua Institute for Economic Research, 17 Nov. 1988.
77. Prestowitz, *Trading Places.*
78. See, for example, Shirley W. Y Kuo, "Development of the Taiwan Economy," Taipei, Chung-Hua Institution for Economic Research, 14 Nov. 1988; Dore, *Taking Seriously;* Vogel, *Number One.*
80. No region is totally free of corruption or the influence of "pull." Japan has had its scandals, Indonesia is rife with corruption, and even in Singapore it seems likely that Lee's son (an exceptionally able man) will eventually follow his father as prime minister. As in many places, nepotism is an ancient Asian tradition, but several efforts have been made in all of the Pacific Rim societies to transform them into meritocracies.
81. In 1990, in a strange swing in policy due to his genetic theories, Singapore's Lee began to advocate a pro-natality policy, particularly for college graduates.
82. See William McCord and Arline McCord, *Paths to Progress* (New York: W. W. Norton, 1986).
83. Papanek, "New Asian Capitalism," 42.
84. See Yun Peng Chi, "Towards a Theoretical Explanation," 19–20.
85. See Kuo, "Taiwan Economy," 43; Also see John C. H. Fei, Gustav Ranis, and Shirely W. Y. Kuo, *Growth and Structural Change in Taiwan* (Ithaca: Cornell University Press, 1979).
86. Lucian Pye, "The New Asian Capitalism: A Political Portrait," in Berger and Hsiao, *In Search of Model,* 89.
87. Robin Broad and John Cavanaugh, "No More NICS," *Foreign Policy* (Fall 1988): 81.
88. Ibid.
89. Pye, "Political Portrait."
90. Vogel, *Number One,* 226.

91. Prestowitz, *Trading Places*.
92. Vogel, *Number One*, 226.
93. Prestowitz, *Trading Places*.
94. Vogel, *Number One*, 226.

Part II

IMPLICATIONS OF THE PACIFIC RENAISSANCE

As a new millenium approaches, the world is experiencing a sudden tilt in economic and perhaps ultimately political power away from the Atlantic region.
—David Tinnin, 1989

Introduction

In 1989, Hong Kong investors bought the entire site of Canada's Exposition.[1] One hundred billion dollars of Asian trade passed through California.[2] And Japan purchased more than 30 percent of America's treasury bonds, the basis of the nations's economy.[3]

Meanwhile, in Beijing, one million protestors marched for democracy in Tiananmen Square and erected a replica of the Statue of Liberty. They requested simple liberties already enjoyed in the West. Temporarily, the octogenarians in control of China crushed the dissidents, but few would predict that China's crisis was solved. Mikhail Gorbachev, an honored visitor at the time, publicly admitted that communism was at "a very serious turning point."[4]

Clearly, the "other Rim" of the Pacific, particularly the Soviet Union and the United States, could not ignore the Pacific. Economically, politically, and strategically, the new Asia intruded on capitalist nations, the "socialist bloc," and the Third World with unprecedented urgency.

Politely and prudently—or, at times, violently and ruthlessly—Asia exerted her power throughout the world.

In 1985, when Japan doubled the value of the yen, Japanese investors bought American real estate at bargain prices while the American trade deficit fell only marginally. Meanwhile, Japan's major brokerages (Nomura, Daiwa, Nikko, and Yamaichi) secured a large segment of American industrial assets.[5]

By 1989, Japan had accumulated 20 percent of California's financial equities, employed 250,000 Americans, and contributed 11 percent to the United Nation's annual budget.[6] Japan bought half of the bonds issued by the World Bank and was the only nation to offer underwriting funds for debt-ridden Latin American countries.[7]

If trends in the early 1990s continued, the Asia-Pacific region alone could supply all of the world's demand for autos, computers, robots, and clothing by the year 2000—a prospect that appalled American and European manufacturers.[8]

Japanese takeovers of Australian companies increased sixteen times between 1984 and 1988.[9] Because of liberal citizenship policies, 26,000 Hong Kong executives migrated to Canada in 1988 alone.[10] This drain of talent particularly enriched British Columbia, but many of the Cantonese-speaking emigrés returned to China temporarily as middle managers under contract.[11]

To bridge the gap between America and the Pacific Basin, ex-Secretary of the Treasury William Simon put together a great ocean-spanning banking system based in Hawaii.[12] Simon, an ardent capitalist, foresaw a boom in the countries of the Pacific Rim. "I'm building Noble House," he said in 1987, "I won't live to see it, but my sons will."[13]

Australia, an historically anti-Asian nation oriented to Great Britain, welcomed new migrants, particularly 78,000 people from Vietnam. "Every day, it becomes clearer to met that Australia's future lies in Asia," political analyst Greg Sheridan wrote in 1988.[14] And Australian jouranlist Russell Spurr noted that "money and immigrants from the Far East are forcing changes on a 'whites-only continent.' "[15]

Across the Pacific, a devalued peso attracted Asian investments in Mexico while Japan's financial aid helped to ease Mexico's debt crisis. In Chile, ignoring the military dictatorship, Shirley Christian commented in 1988 that the nation's "fast-growning, free-market economy increasingly looks across the Pacific—to Asia, Australia, and New Zealand for trade and investments."[16] In Costa Rica, Singaporean concerns bought up the largest resorts. Although not on a huge scale, it became increasingly evident that Asia and Latin America were forming a new economic alliance.

The two "super-powers," the Soviet Union and the United States, had perhaps the greatest stake in the Asian-Pacific resurgence.

As a major importer from Asia, with military outposts scattered from Japan to the Philippines (including secret observation posts in Northern China), America evinced a strong interest in the Asian renaissance and a degree of anxiety that Asian competition might weaken American preeminence. Indeed, a spate of books warned of the new Asian strength and encouraged America to adopt Oriental business practices or to respond to them in an effective matter.[17]

Bordering on China, Japan, and North Korea, the Soviet Union also had an intense geopolitical concern with the region's development and politics. Governed by an elite that hungered for economic growth, Soviet leaders looked to Japan and South Korea for capital and technology. China beckoned with its resources and labor but threatened the Soviet Union with an unstable government which conceivably might unleash its nuclear weapons.

In spite of grave uncertainties, no responsible Soviet or American leader could neglect the Asian-Pacific arc. Whether they wished it or not, both Americans and Russians had an engagement in Asia.

Notes

1. Timothy Egan, "Prosperity from Asia Has West In Conflict," *New York Times,* 9 May 1989, A14.
2. "Flows of Trade," California Department of Commerce, 1989.
3. Daniel Burstein, *Yen!* (New York: Simon and Schuster, 1989).
4. *New York Times,* 18 May 1989.
5. Burstein, *Yen!*
6. Robert Manning, "Unwelcome But Unstoppable," *Far Eastern Economic Review,* 16 March 1989, 75.
7. "From Superrich to Superpower," *Time,* 4 July 1988.
8. David B. Tinnin, "The Dawning of the Pacific Century," *Billion,* inaugural issue (1989): 20.
9. "Rapid Increase in Japanese Overseas M and A," *Tokyo Business Today* (January 1989).
10. Elizabeth M. Fowler, "Hong Kong Brain Aids Canada," *New York Times,* 4 Jan. 1989, D10.
11. Ibid.
12. L. J. Davis, "William Simons's Pacific Overtures," *New York Times,* 27 December 1987.
13. Ibid., 16.
14. Greg Sheridan, quoted in Russell Spurr, "Australia Goes Asian," *New York Times,* 14 Dec. 1988, 47.
15. "World Business," *The Economist,* 18 May 1985.
16. Shirley Christian, "Chile's Growning Trans-Pacific Ties," *New York Times,* 9 July 1988.
17. The concern of this book is not with the issue of whether America could or should adapt Asian, especially Japanese, approaches to management, industrial relations, or business-government interactions. For interesting treatises on this subject, see Ezra Vogel, *Japan As Number One* (Cambridge: Harvard University Press, 1979) as the most authoritative argument that America should adapt some aspects of Japan's producers. In a more popular vein, William G. Ouchi in *Theory Z* (Reading, MA: Addison-Wesley Co., 1981) contended that trust, subtlety, and intimacy underlay Japanese success. Johannes Hirschmeier and Tsuneko Yui wrote in *The Development Of Japanese Business* (Cambridge:

Harvard University Press, 1975) that Japan represented an original model of economic development. Ronald Dore, ed., *Aspects of Social Change in Modern Japan* (Princeton: Princeton University Press, 1973) took a balanced view of the many factors that contributed to the "Asian Miracle." Nick Lyons in *The SONY Vision* (New York: Crown Publishers, 1976) found that the Sony Corporation, operating under primitive conditions, offered an example of marketing and engineering genius. Ronald Dore, in *Taking Japan Seriously* (Stanford: Stanford University Press, 1987) suggested that Europe had lessons to learn from Japan. In *Trading Places* (New York: Basic Books, 1988), Clyde Prestowitz cited some of the political-economic reasons why Japan out-paced America. Jared Taylor, in *Shadows of the Rising Sun* (New York: Quill, 1983) warned against attributing Asian success to the "Japanese spirit."

7

Impact on the Super Powers

The great Pacific Basin with all its nations and all its potential for growth and development—this is the future.

—Ronald Reagan
Washington, 1984

I am convinced that we are at a very serious turning point in the development of world socialism.

—Mikhail Gorbachev
Beijing, 1989

The Soviet Union and the Pacific Rim

While standing beside a primitive railroad track that stretched into the wall-like jungle of Tanzania, I listened as a Russian engineer scoffed at the project. "It'll go nowhere," he said. "The Chinese will never complete it and, even if they did, they couldn't run it." That was in the 1960s.

Pressed by Chinese advisors, the workers finished the railroad and it remained as one, if not the only, tangible achievement of the Tanazanian socialist revolution. The Russian had seriously underestimated Chinese skills, a mistake that he would not have made at the end of the century.

My grandfather, William Cochrane Maxwell, knew this even in the 1920s when he built the first railroad in Manchuria joining China and the Soviet Union. Now, both sides use it to deliver resources to factories and goods for urban markets. The Soviet Union wanted Chinese cooperation, even in an era of anarchy, and indeed the rulers of the Soviet Union desired collaborative endeavors with the entire Pacific Rim. Alexander Solitsky, a

131

prominent Soviet specialist on the Far East, noted in 1989 that "Moscow is coming to realize the simple truth that solid and mutually beneficial business contracts are preferable and more reliable than lofty words about friendship and common class interests."[1]

Such an attitude would have been unspeakable in 1960 during Mao's "great leap forward." The Soviet Union cut off economic aid and withdrew 1,390 technicians working in China. In 1969, Soviet and Chinese troops clashed along their joint border. In the early 1970s, Mao even warned the Northern Chinese to dig deep into the earth and to store everything. His purpose was to protect them from a possible Soviet nuclear attack. In fact, at the time, Moscow maintained fifty-six divisions surrounding Northern China while China kept twenty-eight divisions on its border.

Yet, in 1989, in spite of turmoil in China, a meeting in Beijing renewed a formal normalization of state and party relations between Beijing and Moscow. Although each side maintained their battle formations, the bitter feud seemed to have ended after three decades of hostility. With young Chinese marching in Tiananmen Square in May 1989, Mikhail Gorbachev dared to say that he "valued their position."[2] Chinese hard-liners crushed the potential rebellion, but Gorbachev apparently recognized the similarities between events in China and his own glasnost policy in the Soviet Union. Chinese leaders of the time did not publicly rebuke him.

The apparent reconciliation between the two great nations began in July 1986 when Gorbachev made an historic declaration in Vladivostock, a naval port lying a mere twenty miles from China and eighty miles from Korea. He said that Moscow would accept Beijing's definition of the Sino-Soviet border and that his country would withdraw troops from Mongolia. In 1987, he did pull back some mechanized divisions from the Chinese border, and in 1988 he took steps to resolve the Cambodian conflict that disturbed China as well as ASEAN nations.

The Vladivostock initiative included a declaration that "the Soviet Union is also an Asian and Pacific country."[3] Gorbachev replaced second-rank Soviet diplomats in China and Japan, offered to cooperate in an Asian nuclear-free zone and, in 1987, dispatched his foreign minister on state visits to Indonesia, Thailand, and Australia—a journey portending a new Soviet approach to the entire Pacific. Gorbachev strongly hinted at improved Soviet-Japanese relations[4] and acknowledged, too, that the United States "is a great Pacific power, without whom it is impossible to resolve the problem of security and cooperation in the Pacific Ocean."[5] On 16

September 1988, the Soviets offered to place a disputed radar installation in Siberia under international control for the peaceful exploration of space.[6]

The Soviet Union had solid reasons for making these concessions. By 1987, Japan had already become the top supplier to Russia of construction machinery and seamless steel pipes. Russia had expressed a distinct interest in such Japanese products as machine tools and chemical plants.

Korea and Taiwan investigated possibilities of investing in the Soviet Far East while Soviet traders tried to expand exports to China. (In 1989, China took only 3 percent of her imports from the Soviet Union, a sharp drop from 16 percent in 1914).

Although the economic dealings of the Soviet Union with the Pacific Basin faced various political obstacles—China's turmoil, North Korea's hostility to South Korea, Japan's demand for the Kurile islands, and possible American sanctions—the economic repercussions of Vladivostock had many effects. Some might have seemed minor or temporary, but they indicated a revision in Soviet policy.

In 1988, for example, Chinese peasants crossed the border into the Soviet Union at Suifenhe, accompanied by interpreters and greeted by a brass band. The seventy-six peasants were to demonstrate new farming techniques to Siberian peasants for six months. The Soviets had apparently recognized the achievements of Chinese agriculture and wished to learn about them. Soviet officials in another area of Siberia agreed to supply hydroelectric power in exchange for Chinese food. Russians also welcomed Chinese laborers to cut timber in Siberia. Local merchants in Heilongjiang and the Soviet Union's Maritime Province received permission to conduct direct cross-border trade. Concurrently, the nuclear shelters that Mao had once ordered built in Harbin were converted into hotels and shopping centers.

On a broader level, Mikhail Gorbachev indicated in Krasnoyarsk that Russia's Pacific neighbors could have a significant role in developing Russia's far east and suggested the founding of joint industrial ventures. He also offered to close Soviet naval facilities at Vietnam's Cam Ranh Bay if America would withdraw from its military installations in the Philippines. America refused but internal Philippine reaction was positive.

The Soviet relationship with China took the form of barter trade at the borders—the relatively minor direct exchange of goods and services in adjoining provinces. Russia, for her part, wanted food, labor, and basic consumer goods from China. The Chinese primarily wanted Russian assistance in modernizing factories that were built in the 1950s. Both sides wanted barter trade since it relieved their foreign debts and saved hard-currency reserves. As a result, Sino-Soviet trade increased modestly from $2.6 billion in 1987 to $3.1 billion in 1989.[7] Whether the growth in trade would continue depended upon the state of the Chinese border economy.

In other parts of the Pacific region, Hungary opened a permanent diplomatic mission in South Korea—much to the dismay of North Korea. And Soviet officials devised more and more links with South Korea, explicitly recognizing that Korea was in a process of "world development which we can neither stop, hinder, or change. . . . Without this, it is impossible to create economic security"[8] North Korea itself welcomed the head of the Hyundai Corporation for discussions of industrial development while Thailand explored new exports to the Soviet Union. In addition, Russia gained unprecedented fishing rights in the islands of Micronesia. In his 1989 summit meeting in Beijing, Gorbachev expressed his eagerness to improve relations with Japan, a probable development in the 1990s.

The trend toward greater Pacific cooperation had many reasons to flourish. On the most elementary level, China needed Russian help in updating its industries; the Soviet Union required Chinese grain exports and labor; Japan, Korea, and Taiwan could supply the capital and technology to invigorate Siberia. In turn, they could import the Soviet's far east resources. There was no question that geopolitical reasons dictated a closer relationship. Unfortunately, there was also no question that political upheavals, particularly in China, could disrupt the most rational and equitable forms of cooperation.

Nonetheless, Y. M. Primako, director of Moscow's Institute of World Economics, acknowledged that "the Far East [Siberia] is an integral part of our total national economy. But we also realize that this area must be integrated into the international division of labor in the Pacific."[9]

The possibility of a Soviet economic reconciliation with Asia had strategic implications that no one could predict. Already, by 1987, the Soviet Union had acquired a major naval presence in the Pacific[10] and potentially threatened Japan with attack.[11] Pressed by the United States to rearm, Japan had the capacity with her existing forces to block the strategic straits of Tsushima, Soya, and Sugaru.[12] In a wild scenario, the Chinese *Red Flag* said that Russia might create a sea route that would link its Pacific and Black Sea fleets and could effectively block all trade routes in the Pacific.[13]

I believe that these more or less paranoid fantasies can be ignored. The overriding reality is that the Soviet Union needs the Far East to develop its Siberian hinterland, that major parts of the Pacific Rim could use Soviet resources, and that Japan and Taiwan are major exporters of capital and technology.[14] The time of gun boat diplomacy has long passed.[15] Furthermore, the unfolding drama within the Soviet bloc led to the possibility of a realignment among Western Europe, Eastern Europe, and Asia. The collapse of the walls around Eastern Europe led Japanese, Taiwanese, and Koreans to glimpse the Soviet bloc as a huge territory for investment. The East European nations offered a heavy industrial base, a solid infrastructure, and a relatively educated but cheap labor force.

In essence, the opening of Eastern Europe provided an attractive alternative for developed Asian nations to the morass of China and, possibly, to Southeast Asian investments. Similarly, West European nations might well neglect Southeast Asian opportunities when given a chance to invest in bordering East European countries. Thus, the opening of the East European bloc might well work to the detriment of the less developed Asian regions, while inviting a closer alignment between the Soviet bloc and developed Asian countries.

North America and the Pacific Rim

On 7 December 1941, my brother, Don McCord, flew a B-17 from California to Pearl Harbor. Under radio silence, he had no idea that Japan had launched its "day of infamy." Against the advice of senior military leaders,[16] Japan decided to attack the United States in a desperate effort to retain control over China and gain access to Southeast Asian resources. On that day, my brother had good luck and shot down a Zero with his pistol. On 7 August 1942, he was killed somewhere in the Pacific. With the American fleet gone and most of Southeast Asia in the hands of the Japanese, few Americans could confidently predict, at that time, whether the United States would prevail.

On 2 September 1945, after Japan had been devastated by bombing, the Japanese finally surrendered to General Douglas MacArthur aboard the battleship *Missouri*. The flag of Commodore Perry, who had opened Japan to the West ninety years before, covered the rear turret of the battleship. The ceremony symbolized Japanese humiliation under drizzly grey skies. Most experts, as I have noted, prophesied in 1945 that Japan would have a very modest future, if the nation survived the immediate threat of starvation. Japan's former colonies—Korea, Singapore, Malaysia, Hong Kong,

Taiwan, and Indonesia—seemed destined, at best, to a bare subsistence level of existence.

And yet, less than a half century later, Japan and her Pacific neighbors made all radios, black and white television sets, office machinery, high-fidelity audio equipment, and most of the calculators and many of the automobiles purchased by the American consumer.[17] The rest of Asia devoured Japanese capital and technology.

Even the Brooklyn Navy Yard, which had built the surrender vessel *Missouri*, had disappeared in the face of Japanese and Korean competition. Clearly Japan dominated Asia, but the region gained much of its export income from a dormant America burdened by a huge foreign debt. Certain journalists who remembered the past viewed this reversal in roles as a new "danger from Japan."[18]

Some government officials, such as Malcolm Baldridge, once an American secretary of commerce, declared that "Japanese export policy has as its objectives not participation in, but dominance of world markets."[19] Commentator Gore Vidal warned that the combined force of a technologically advanced Asia would mean that "the long feared Asiatic colossus takes its turn as world leader." For Vidal, the only way to escape Asiatic dominance would be for America, Europe, and the Soviet Union to form an alliance. Otherwise, he argued, America would be merely one subject "in a highly centralized Asiatic world."[20]

Clearly, America and Europe can no longer dominate Asia as they once did. Although the influences spread both ways, it is evident that Asian power has drastically increased in North America. Two examples, British Columbia and California, particularly illustrate the potency of a new Asia.

In Canada, the increasing Asian presence produced both affluence and alarm. In Vancouver, Japanese investors bought the largest paper mill and several banks. Hong Kong buyers purchased a prime resort site for a price well in excess of other offers. The cost of salmon and timber, two abundant products of the region, surged because of Asian demand. The Asian population of British Columbia tripled between 1970 and 1989, bringing with it an influx of capital and talent. Real estate prices also jumped, particularly because of buyers from Hong Kong.[21]

In addition, Canada attracted some 26,000 middle-management émigrés from Hong Kong in 1987 alone—a trend that could accelerate if unrest in China continues. While this flow represented a "brain drain" from Hong Kong, the new citizens provided valuable entrepreneurial assets and bilingual access to Chinese and Canadian markets.[22]

Nonetheless, the Asian incoming spawned deep currents of resentment. "Some workers," Timothy Egan commented, "feel they have lost control of their economic destiny to Asian owners. Even as they welcome the new jobs, they are uncertain about their role in a global economy."[23] The *Vancouver Sun* ran a series of articles on the Hong Kong migration that many Asians regarded as insultingly racist.[24] On walls around Vancouver's Asian district, hooligans sprayed graffiti saying "Go Back to Hong Kong."

Reactions to the Asian presence were similarly ambivalent in California, another North American center for Asian investment and migration.

While the Pacific impact affected the American economy and culture as a whole, it was perhaps most evident in California, the sixth largest economy in the world. Perched on the edge of the Pacific, California has the largest and fastest-growing Asian population in the United States. Between 1985 and 1989, the gross state product increased by 40 percent, largely due to the $100 billion of Asian trade that went through California each year. In addition, California contained one-third of America's high-tech companies, many of which had been purchased by or allied with Japanese companies.[25]

The link of California with the Pacific Rim had an ironic, sometimes tragic background. Californians had taken the lead in discriminating against Chinese and Japanese. A 1904 bill excluding all Chinese immigration had strong support in California and resulted in a boycott of American goods in China.[26] Similarly, Japanese migration to America inspired fears among the editors of the *San Francisco Chronicle* of a "yellow peril" and "the complete Orientalizing of the Pacific Coast."[27] The Japanese government officially complained when San Francisco segregated Japanese children in separate schools. Theodore Roosevelt, an admirer of Pacific nations, feared that such provocations might lead to a future war with Japan and fumed to his cabinet members that California "was too small to become a nation, and too large to put into a lunatic asylum."[28] When war did break out in 1941, California played a prominent part in the illegal detention of Japanese Americans.[29]

As the century neared its end, however, the Asian penetration of California profoundly affected its prosperity. The Bank of America, a California institution and once the largest bank in the world, had to depend on the Sumitomo Bank of California for funds. Toyota saved a San Jose automobile plant from bankruptcy. By 1986, Hong Kong investors had already bought $500 million worth of assets in California. The Taiwanese purchased two-thirds of all independent motels in Los Angeles.[30] Asian

Americans made up a disproportionate share of the University of California's elite institutions, prompting demands for the imposition of quotas. Asians in Southern California enjoyed a higher level of prosperity than did any other group.[31] "It's a reality of life," Hansen Lau, a naturalized Chinese commented. "These immigrants are educated. They bring money. They move into the nicest neighborhoods. They are no longer coolies."[32]

A prime symbol of the Asian "invasion" was Monterey Park, a suburb east of Los Angeles that became the first American city dominated by Asians. By 1987, Taiwanese investors had put $500 million into this once quiet town.[33] Monterey Park became a glittering enclave of well-educated Asians. Taiwanese capital created new office buildings, factories, and shops. Nonetheless, prejudice still persisted: the city council at one point unsuccessfully tried to forbid Chinese language signs in the town.

Regardless of lingering racism, the dynamism of Asian migrants was crucial to the California economy. On one level, well-educated Vietnamese and Chinese staffed the high-technology plants of Silicon Valley where ten thousand Chinese engineers worked in 1988.[34] Vietnamese migrants spawned a major expansion in Orange County's high-technology industries.[35]

On a lower level of skill, Asian workers participated heavily in Los Angeles's industries such as garment manufacturing because they were willing to work hard at near minimum wages.[36] Koreans employed their skills to build small businesses such as grocery shops. They pooled their capital into *Kye,* a credit union financed by the immigrants' savings. By the 1980s, Koreans owned seven thousand businesses in Southern California and had the highest self-employment rate of any immigrant group in America.[37] As an entity, Asian Americans were doubling their per capita income each decade.[38]

One of the more striking examples of California's transformation was the increasing Japanese importance in basic transportation, industry, and banking in Los Angeles. Financed by Japanese firms, the ports of Los Angeles and Long Beach emerged as the premier trade centers in America.[39] Japanese firms owned industries ranging from hi-tech firms, to computer industries, to automobile companies (including the headquarters of Honda).[40] Five of the largest Japanese banks established their major branches in Los Angeles.[41] From its previous status as a financial desert, Los Angeles ranked second only to New York as an American banking center.[42]

While California led America in its relation with Asia, all of the United States was affected by the resurgent Pacific Rim.

Ohio housed a Honda plant, Kentucky snared a Toyota motor factory, Indiana secured manufacturing facilities from Fuji Heavy Industries, while Georgia lured a diverse set of 100 Japanese firms. In 1988, ten states had gained $1 billion each in Asian investment.[43] Some companies, such as the Honda and Sony Corporations, began exporting their American products back to Asia.[44]

The new wave of Asian investments in America brought with it not only capital gains but also a way of avoiding American trade barriers. Optimists hoped that the infusion of new capital would rejuvenate depressed states, create new jobs, and diminish trade frictions between America and the Pacific Rim. Pessimists portrayed an America owned by Japan, subservient to her interests, and dominated by Asian powers who could dictate not only international policies but also domestic politics.

Neither scenario seemed particularly convincing. Holland and Great Britain had led Japan in American investment but had yet to create a new atmosphere of international trade, labor relations, or political influence in America. Similarly, except in minor instances, they had not commanded American politics either internally or externally.

Yet, the flow of Asian investments continued at a rate that alarmed American chauvinists. Japanese control over American treasury bonds, as I have noted, created a situation where the foundation of the American economy rested on Japanese goodwill and a continuous flow of money. In 1986, the Japanese purchases of American government and corporate bonds reached $70 billion annually,[45] while Japanese banks lent an average of $300 billion a year for United States assets.[46]

Asia and America became united in unprecedented ways. Yoshitaka Sajima, vice president of Mitsui (USA) observed in 1986, "The U.S. and Japan are not just trading with each other anymore—they're becoming part of each other."[47] Indeed, Normoura Securities alone bought $4.7 billion in American securities and saved New York City from total bankruptcy.[48]

The infusion of Asian funds meant that Tokyo, Hong Kong, or Singapore could call in their loans at a time of American collapse. If Japan and the emergent Asian countries suddenly decided to reverse their capital flow by, for example, directing it totally to Asia, the American economy could well founder.

There were simply not enough funds in the United States Federal

Reserve Bank to pay back the American treasury bonds that were amassed in Asia.[49] That fact should have caused fear in any investor, from Hong Kong to Singapore, about the solidity of the U.S. economy.

Since Japan owned so many American treasury bonds, it meant that Tokyo could recoup its money at any indication of American feebleness.[50]

The fear that Asia had "bought" America created severe threats to intra-Pacific trade. The supposed problem was not only economic but political. Populist politicians in America could use Asia as a "menace" to the American economy and polity. The American Congress passed a bill granting the president authority to bar foreign acquisitions and to prevent America from buying certain Asian products.[51] Unqualified by amendments, any president could impose whatever restrictions he wished on Asian commerce.[52] The foreboding that America would be "sold out" affected both businessmen and scholars.[53]

As it had been in the past, the fear of an Asian dictatorship of the United States was highly exaggerated. Although some American industries might suffer from stiffer competition, America was hardly likely to become "Japan, U.S.A.," as one journal put it.[54] In fact, as I have noted, Europe had far more of America's 1.5 trillion foreign-owned assets than did Asia. Further, Asian-owned equities from the Nissan plant in Tennessee to the Hardee's hamburger chain depended on American labor and the goodwill of American consumers. It was unlikely that Asian owners would alienate such a clientele.

The relation of the United States with Asia was, of course, mutual. On the cultural level, Asian students outnumbered all other foreigners who attended American universities. In 1988 alone, some 27,000 came from Taiwan, 25,000 from China, 21,000 from Korea, 19,000 from Malaysia, and 18,000 from Japan. The closest non-Asian competitor was Canada with 15,000 students.[55] This exposure to American education influenced many of the Asian students. China feared "spiritual pollution" from the West, the Malaysians were concerned about a possible contamination of Islam, and both Hong Kong and Taiwan were worried that too many students would choose to remain in America. Nonetheless, with the possible exception of China, the flow of students continued as education became America's most valued "export."

At the same time, Asian immigration invigorated America. During the 1980s, America took in huge numbers of Asians, more than all other regions in the world combined. The Asian population in America jumped by 142 percent between 1970 and 1980.[56] The immigrants' children did exceptionally well in school, partially because 44 percent of all Asian adult immigrants held college degrees compared to 16 percent fo the general American population.[57]

As Joel Kotkin, an editor, and Yoriko Kishimoto, a trans-Pacific businesswoman, have observed, "Through their explosive growth and tremendous energy, the new arrivals are transforming the United States from a European melting pot into a multinational world nation."[58]

Thus, following the advice of Thomas Jefferson, America has turned East and has an historic opening to the Pacific area. The prophecy of William Sewell, Lincoln's secretary of state in the 1860s, has come true: "The Pacific Ocean, its shores, its islands will become the great theater of events in the world's commerce henceforward."[59]

Notes

1. Alexander Solitsky, "Communist Economic Giants," *Far Eastern Economic Review,* 18 May 1989, 20.
2. Mikhail Gorbachev, quoted in the *New York Times,* 18 May 1989.
3. Mikhail Gorbachev, 28 July 1986, Vladivostock.
4. Robert Manning, "New Soviet Threats in Asia," *New York Times,* 4 July 1987.
5. Mikhail Gorbachev, quoted by Paul Wolfowitz, "Southeast Asia—Deferring Hard Choices," *The National Interest* (Summer 1988): 122.
6. Michael Taubman, *New York Times,* 17 Sept. 1988.
7. Nayan Chandra, "A Dispersion of Power," *Far Eastern Economic Review,* 30 March 1989, 31.
8. Officials quoted in Sophie Quinn-Judge, "Walking a Tightrope Between North and South," *Far Eastern Economic Review,* 8 Dec. 1988, 22.
9. Y. M. Primako, quoted in Sophie Quinn-Judge, "Opening Up the East," *Far Eastern Economic Review,* 20 Oct. 1989, 36.
10. Laszlo Lajos, S. Bartalits, Johannes Wilhelmus, and H. C. M. Schneider, "Soviet Strategy and the Pacific Basin," in *The Pacific Rim and the Western World,* ed. by Philip West and A. M. Alting von Geusawu, Boulder, CO: *Westview Press,* 1987), 43.
11. Ibid., 46.
12. See Joachim Glaubitz, "Japan's Foreign Policy and Security," *Aussenpolik* 35 (1984): 184–6.
13. See Lajos et al., *Pacific Rim* 61.
14. Staffon B. Linder, *The Pacific Century* (Stanford: Stanford University Press, 1986), 82.
15. Ibid.
16. See, for example, Gordon W. Prange, *At Dawn We Slept* (New York: Penguin Books, 1983).
17. Theodore White, "The Danger From Japan," *New York Times,* 28 July 1985, 40.
18. Ibid., 19.
19. Malcolm Baldridge, quoted in ibid., 38.

20. Gore Vidal, "Requiem for the American Empire," *The Nation*, 11 Jan. 1986.
21. Timothy Egan, "Prosperity from Asia has West in Conflict," *New York Times*, 8 May 1989, A19.
22. Elizabeth Fowler, "Hong Kong 'Brain Drain' Aids Canada," *New York Times*, January 1989.
23. Egan, "Prosperity in Asia," A19.
24. *Vancouver Sun*, 8 April 1989.
25. "Flow of Trade," California Department of Commerce, 1989.
26. A. Whitney Griswold, *The Far Eastern Policy of the United States* (New York: Harcourt Brace, 1938).
27. Akira Iriye, *Across the Pacific* (New York: Harcourt, Brace, and World, 1967), 105.
28. Raymond A. Ethus, *Theodore Roosevelt and Japan* (Seattle: University of Washington Press, 1966), 293.
29. Audrie Girdner and Anne Loftis, *The Great Betrayal* (New York: Macmillan, 1969).
30. Joel Kotkin and Yoriko Kishimoto, *The Third Century* (New York: Crown Publishers, 1988), 182.
31. Ibid.
32. Ronald Alsop, "Firms Translate Sales Pitches to Asian Americans," *Markets*, 10 April 1986.
33. Egan, "Prosperity in Asia."
34. Frank Viviano, "Transplanting Silicon Valley," *Image* 21 June 1987.
35. Kotkin and Kishimoto, *Third Century*, 177.
36. See Eugene Carlson, "Regions," *Wall Street Journal*, 10 Sept. 1985.
37. Kotkin and Kishimoto, *Third Century*, 181.
38. "Marketing the New America," *INC.* (August 1987).
39. Steve Kaufman, "Los Angeles, Long Beach Ports Going Full Steam," *Los Angeles Times*, 17 August 1987.
40. "The Sixty-Mile Circle," *Security Pacific Book* (Feb. 1984).
41. Robert Neff, "Los Angeles Becomes the Money Bags of the West," *Los Angeles Times*, 27 Oct. 1986.
42. Joel Kotkin in Mark Gerson, "California: the New Non-Atlantic Melting Pot," *World Paper* (March 1985): 3.
43. United States Commerce Department, 1989.
44. "Japan, U.S.A.," *Business Week*, 14 July 1986.
45. Lynch Capital Markets, 1986.
46. Morgan Guarranty Trust, 1986.
47. Quoted in "Japan, U.S.A."
48. Ibid.
49. Felix Royhatan, address to Japan Society, New York, 9 June 1989.
50. Rich Thomas, "The Selling of America," *New York Times*, 18 Jan. 1989.
51. Rich Thomas, "The Selling America Threat," *Newsweek*, 18 Jan. 1989.
52. Ibid.
53. Ibid; and Martin Tolchin and Susan Tolchin, *Buying Into America* (New York: New York Times Books, 1988).
54. "Japan, U.S.A."
55. *The Chronicle of Higher Education*, 16 Oct. 1988, A30.
56. Kotkin and Kishimoto, *Third Century*, 160.
57. Ibid., 161.
58. Ibid., 167–168.
59. Sewell, quoted in Ibid, 186.

8

Implications for the Third World

*A quiet revolution has begun in the Third World
that is likely to have more dramatic effects on
more human beings than any revolution that has
gone before.*

— Richard Critchfield

Can other developing countries in Latin America, Africa, Central America, South Asia, and the Middle East emulate the East Asian "miracle"? Anyone who has lived in these areas, as I have, would respond with deep skepticism.

It would require a Pangloss to answer such a question with positive certainty. Yet, cautiously, I believe that many of the lessons derived from the Pacific region can go far in enriching the common good of people who live in poverty and stagnation throughout much of the world. Asia offers a model of growth with equity. Some of its policies could be copied in many countries—*if* the political will and power of reasonable people prevailed. That is, of course, a big if since countries like Zaire were left by the colonists with virtually no educated elite; others like Peru suffer from civil war, and still others like Arabia are burdened by a feudal aristocracy.

The common sense policies that might be adapted in the Third World include an assurance of political stability, investment in education, land reform, government-guided free enterprise with an original emphasis on labor-intensive and export-oriented industries, a high rate of investment and private profit with a decrease in real poverty, a dedication to meritocracy, population control, an acceptance of foreign influences, and the flexibility to exploit comparative advantages.[1]

In addition, as Chi-ming Hou has argued, the high-growth nations enacted a taxation system that encouraged savings and a work incentive, minimized monopoly power, and often privatized public enterprises.[2] In

143

explaining the specific example of Taiwan, Hou added, "it would be senseless to assert that the Taiwanese model can be duplicated in totality" but such policies "might be relevant to most if not all developing nations."[3]

These common policies have been followed throughout many parts of Asia, and they work in Confucian, Buddhist, and even Islamic cultures. Why, then, cannot other developing countries follow the same rational policies? The reasons are complex, deeply rooted in the cultures and social structures of particular countries—but not ineradicable.

As I have noted, some of the more popular theories that hold that other countries cannot adapt an Asian model do not stand up under scholarly scrutiny. Theorists who attribute success to an "oriental" culture of asceticism and hard work have ignored the fact that the ancient cultures remained basically the same. Only when policies changed did their economies explode. Those who credited Confucianism with success failed to recognize prolonged failure and the fact that where Buddhism prevailed, such as Thailand, similar policies have achieved the same success.[4] Neither protectionism nor "dumping" account for the Asian achievements.[5]

The timing of entry into the world market played some part in the success of Japan and the NICs, but by 1990 they still prospered and were opening markets to other developing countries. There were signs that Asia itself might form the hugest "common market" in the world. As Japan expert James Abegglen pointed out, "There is increased discussion of an Asian (perhaps yen-dominated) trading bloc. . . . With fast increasing intra-trade flows, the risk to the economies of the area of a U.S. depression will be more manageable."[6]

The problems faced by the developing countries at the end of the century were hardly more formidable than the obstacles that were overcome in Asia during the 1950s. After all, the Asian social system was itself regarded as an intractable barrier to economic advance. And in the 1940s and 1950s all of the newly prospering countries suffered from terrible social and economic dislocations.

Although Japan possessed a trained industrial force willing to work for meagre wages and entrepreneurs eager for profit, military defeat had destroyed Japan's industrial base. American aid did not rebuild it on the scale that the Marshall Plan did in Europe.

Both Japanese occupation and civil war had torn apart China. A corrupt, discredited, and inept Koumingtang ruled Taiwan. Singapore fell victim to ethnic riots, the severing of ties with Malaysia, and "confrontation" with

Indonesia. War ruined Korea. Hong Kong absorbed millions of penniless refugees. Both Malaysia and Indonesia endured bloody revolutions.

Neither Japan nor the NICs had natural resources, sufficient food, or energy supplies. These burdens were as severe as those experienced by developing countries today, but they did not prevent Asia's eventual triumph.

Outstanding, if sometimes austere political leadership, such as Lee Kuan Yew's in Singapore, often made the difference. And usually, politicians followed the sound advice of economic technocrats, such as the MITI experts in Japan or the "Berkeley Mafia" in Indonesia, who introduced the strategies outlined above. As economist Yun-Peng Chu pointed out in the case of Taiwan—a situation replicated in Japan, Hong Kong, Korea, and Dengist China (perhaps until 1989)—"the government had the will and the power to implement economic policies that were judged best for the nation as a whole, and not merely for narrow interest groups."[7] If this had not been the case, these economies, like many in Latin America and Africa, would have become "rent-seeking" societies where only the lucky few became richer.[8]

The grave and formidable obstacles facing any developing nation that might wish to follow the Asian example are obvious and, some would say, insurmountable. Robin Broad and John Cavanagh have argued that there will be "no more NICs" because the Pacific Rim nations have already co-opted the export market, and industrial nations are finding more and more substitutes for basic commodities.[9] Other suggest that American and European protectionism blocks further access to existing markets.[10] Many currently developing countries have incurred huge debts in their pursuit of import-substitution industries which the East Asian states—with the notable exception of Korea—did not.[11] Some experts believe that the debt problems of certain countries such as Brazil, Argentina, and Mexico doom their economies. Minor dictators and feudal elites in many areas hardly provide a receptive or stable environment for reform.[12]

Culturally, many developing countries suffer from caste, linguistic, tribal, and religious divisions that history did not impose on much of East Asia.[13] And, of course, corruption has to risen to historic heights even in a country such as India where the civil service and the judiciary were once viewed as unreachable by bribery.[14] Population prssures, particularly in Latin America and South Asia, are widely cited as obstacles to adapting an Asian strategy.[15] Institutional differences, such as the dominance of the Catholic church in Latin America, are also noted as important obstacles.[16]

Each of these grave problems pose barriers to emulating the East Asian model, but I would argue that they can be—and have been—overcome in some areas of the world.

Lack of An Export Market

One powerful argument is that "outward-oriented" societies will disintegrate in the event of a world recession or the disappearance of a commodity market.

It is, of course, true that a major recession, particularly in the United States, would temporarily damage the Asian economies and particularly those of currently developing countries. Yet, as I have pointed out, Asia is developing its own new and powerful market. And, as Julian Simon has argued in the long range of world history, "The standard of living [of the word] has risen . . . since the beginning of recorded time, . . . and there is no convincing reason why these trends toward a better life should not continue indefinitely."[17]

In fact, the very emergence of affluent Asian societies increases the demand for resources and products from less developed countries.[18] In the long run, a pronounced Asian need for everything from food to mineral resources to oil benefits regions as different as the Middle East, Africa, and Siberia. Exports of virtually anything could continue to be profitable for all concerned, but each developing country must be as versatile as a Singapore or a Japan in recognizing and capitalizing on its comparative advantage at every point in time.

The Threat of Protectionism

Admittedly, political pressures in Europe and America could limit the potentialities of both Asian and currently underdeveloped economies. Italy has erected barriers to the sale of Japanese cars, Japan bars the import of American rice, and the United States even hampers the flow of flowers from Costa Rica. In developing countries, the establishment of "Fortress Europe 1992" could create tri-lateral blocs across the world.[19] Europe could isolate itself. America, allied perhaps with Canada, Mexico, and the Caribbean, could form a market excluding others. Asia could create a third bloc stretching from Melbourne to Sapporo. A tri-lateral system of blocs might exclude Third World nations from membership.

If this threat came true, it would be a sad event for many developing countries. Fortunately, even if a tri-lateral division of the world took place, many areas of the Third World would continue to have unique benefits and some might even improve their position through special arrangements. Motivated by a desire for cheap labor, North America could expand its industrial commitments in Mexico, Central America, and the Caribbean. Francophone Africa would have easier access to larger European markets while members of the British Commonwealth would continue their special relation with Great Britain (and presumably the European bloc). Japan would have a strong motive to expand even further its "co-prosperity sphere" with Thailand, Malaysia, India, China, and Indonesia.[20]

Asian nations, particularly Japan, were already increasing their investment in both Europe and America, as well as the developing countries, to avoid potential trade barriers.[21] Thus, stiffened protectionism, while a major threat, could well be circumvented by countries following the Asian example.

The Debt Burden

Without concerted action by both the rich countries and the poor, the debt crisis could prove a major obstacle for some developing countries— unless, once again, political solutions are found.

In 1988, many developing nations, particularly in Latin America, owed $1.3 trillion, including $350 billion to banks, in unpaid debts to industrialized countries.[22] From 1985 to 1987, interest and principal repayments from Mexico, Argentina, Brazil, and other debt-owing countries exceeded capital inflows by $42 billion.[23] Interest payments alone represented 32 percent of the export income of Brazil, 34 percent in Ecuador, and 41 percent in Argentina.[24] Living standards and wages fell as Latin America tried to repay debts incurred because of an inflated expectation of oil revenues or income from domestic, "inward-oriented" industries. Even after debt relief, many developing countries such as Argentina, Mexico, and Nigeria will still have to deal with interest payments that exceed their net trade earnings.[25]

The International Monetary Fund (IMF) imposed austere restrictions on debtor countries that many regarded as unfair. Mexico complied but without a major increase in her income.

Yet, the options of underdeveloped countries are severely constrained. They could default entirely on their debts at the cost of receiving no further loans for industrialization, replacement of machine parts, medicines, food, or other necessities. That is a recipe for national pride but not national survival.

Conversely, the underdeveloped countries could continue to pay back the interest on their loans at a severe risk to their economies and polities. Within this very limited range, several options seemed possible for the 1990s.

Debt-equity swaps allowed banks to exchange their loans at a big discount, usually of 83 percent, for local currency as reimbursement. This option meant in reality that the banks lost most of their investment and suffered severe losses, but both the debtor nations and the banks gained tangible assets. Mexico, Chile, and Brazil followed this approach although it carried with it the risk that debtor countries would simply print more money, fueling inflation.[26]

Debt-for-debt swaps involved banks in exchanging loans, again at a major discount, for bonds issued in hard currency. Such an approach depreciated the reserves of debtor nations and required a vigorous export-oriented policy. An alternative was to issue government bonds for the full value of the loans but at a much lower, fixed interest rate. This strategy appealed to world banks, particularly if the bonds were insured by world lending agencies such as the IMF or the World Bank.[27]

In 1989, U.S. Treasury Secretary Nicholas Brady, following Japanese proposals, suggested that the IMF and the World Bank guarantee debt-equity swaps. The banks would have to accept much smaller repayments or bonds from a debtor country. Nonetheless, the banks would have a new security backing their interests and developing countries would be relieved of much, although not all, of the debt burden. Japan initially promised $4.5 billion to the world lending agencies, taking the lead among industrialized nations. Because of Japan's special interests, the Philippines was thought to be the first country to benefit from the "Brady initiative," followed by Venezuela and Mexico.[28]

Doubts remain as to whether these new approaches will truly solve the debt crisis. If interest rates rise, for example, the heavy burden on developing countries will drastically increase. Political pressures—particularly in Brazil, Venezuela, Peru, Mexico, and Argentina—could cause a disastrous default and cut off all capital flows to these developing nations.

Nonetheless, the debt burden, while awesome, was perhaps overemphasized. The truth is that foreign capital and aid still flow to developing countries that show signs of stability and progress. Korea was in the front ranks of debtor countries and yet no one questioned that nation's ability to repay the debt. And the fact that Japan emerged as the major world creditor and aid-giver while even Taiwan agreed in 1989 to donate $1 billion a year in aid meant that a fresh source of capital exists for the newly developing regions.

Social Obstacles to Adapting an Asian Model

In contrast to many developing nations, the successful Asian regions often did not suffer from ethnic, religious, caste, tribal, or linguistic differences. Such traditional social divisions have sparked bloody revolts in India,[29] tribal confrontation in Africa,[30] and civil war in Nigeria, Leganon, Sri Lanka, and Zaire.[31] These social tensions make the business of governing a much more tenuous and dangerous enterprise than in a homogenous country such as Japan.

And yet, examples from recent Asian history have indicated that statesmen (or generals) have managed to achieve governmental stability in the face of severe social tensions either by compromise or sheer repression. Singapore managed to survive ethnic riots, partially by mixing ethnic groups in housing estates and partly by giving special privileges (except in the army) to Malays. Malaysia has maintained a finely managed, if tenuous balance between Malays and Chinese. Thailand has successfully repressed many tribal rebellions. Even Suharto's Indonesia has quieted rebellions by Communists, Moluccans, Irians, and Sumatrans. These victories have at times required a great sacrifice in human life while, at other times, wise policies allowed solutions that were—more or less—acceptable to all. The tolerance exhibited by the Tunku of Malaysia could well serve as a model to be followed in other divided nations.

Eradicating traditional hatreds and achieving political stability is, of course, more difficult in countries where people do not share the same language, are illiterate, and cannot understand the reports of even a relatively free press.

In India, for example, a vociferous press tried to inform the people, but in villages in India, only 40 percent of men and 20 percent of women were able to read in 1985. Only 3 percent could understand English, the lingua franca of government and business. In fact, because of uncontrolled population growth, there were 130 million more illiterates than at the time of independence.[32] In an African nation such as Guinea, only 21 percent of adults could read, less than when France granted Guinea her total independence.[33] Under such conditions, the creation of a modern economy or the maintenance of even a vestige of self-government were extremely difficult.

Here again the Asian nations, particularly Singapore and Taiwan, showed the way by making huge investments in education. Moreover, mass education was practical and geared to the countries' needs.[34] Asian leaders accept John Kenneth Galbraith's argument that "education is not something that economic development affords. It is the experience of the older industrial lands that economic development is what education allows."[35] A few non-Asian developing countries, such as Costa Rica, recognized the truth of this observation.

Curbing corruption represented another social challenge to development. Nepotism, favoritism, and the distribution of "tea money," "bakshish," "dash," or "mahmool" infected many developing economies. In some nations, the practice emerged from an honorable tradition of exchanging gifts. Certainly, too, it was hardly an unknown practice in advanced industrial nations—as "Abscam" in America and the downfall of politicians in Japan amply demonstrated.

In China, the practice of *zou-hou-men* ("taking the back door") posed grim political as well as economic risks. Chiang Kai-shek's government fell partially because of pervasive corruption. And in 1989, the massive student rebellion demanded not only political freedom but an end to growing corruption and nepotism.

Clearly, corruption was not an inevitable side effect of development. The more successful Asian regions have more or less efficiently introduced merit as a standard of promotion, and some countries, such as Singapore, virtually eliminated financial temptations. Singaporean policy encouraged high salaries for civil servants and severe penalties for those who violated their trust—a carrot-and-stick approach that could well be emulated in many developing areas.

Other severe social challenges—achieving land reform, curbing urbanization, coping with tides of refugees, and defusing the population crisis— plague the developing areas in the 1990s.[36] In each case, East or Southeast Asia has already offered ways of successfully resolving these problems— if the political will and power existed. The Taiwan model of land reform gives hope to countries, such as many in Latin America and Africa, that suffer from both inequitable and unprofitable land distribution.[37] Singapore presented an admirable solution to urban dilemmas.[38] Hong Kong provided approaches to the refugee problem.[39] And countries as different as Japan and Thailand have invented ways to defuse "the population bomb."[40]

However severe, the solution to developing countries' socio-economic problems remains essentially political at base.

The Political Factor

A dedicated leadership, Chalmers Johnson has argued, is a necessary element in the process of development. He has contended that "determined leadership presupposes the existence of a serious, ruthless, informed elite" willing to impose Draconian measures on a society in order to push forward the progress of the economy.[41] At various points in history, Asia has produced such competent leaders—Lee Kuan Yew in Singapore, Chou-en-lai (and perhaps until 1989) Deng Xiaoping in China, Chiang Ching-kuo of Taiwan, and even Park Chung-Hee of Korea. Sheer ruthlessness has, in itself, produced as many disasters as successes,[42] as Mao, Kim il Sung, and Pol Pot have demonstrated. Even the best of leaders must call upon reserves of talent, capital, and a receptive social environment to achieve results.[43] And, most importantly, an informed leadership should follow the policies initiated in Asia. Thus, no one would deny the role of determined, intelligent, and informed leaders as key actors in development.

Many would question, however, whether other developing areas can develop the dedicated and flexible political leadership that has characterized most of East and Southeast Asia for twenty-five years. If they cannot, the prospects for adapting an Asian model seem dim indeed. Nonetheless, my experience indicates that there are great reservoirs of untapped talent throughout the world—in entrepreneurs and educators, peasant leaders and even in military men. The problem lies in granting them enough freedom to exercise their skills, experience, and knowledge.

One prominent element in East Asia was, for example, the implementation of a land reform policy that gave inventive peasants an incentive for higher production, more investment, and greater diversification. Once those policies were implemented, the economy "took off." But the policy was originally dictated by Americans occupying Japan, the Koumingtang in Taiwan (who had nothing to lose), a military junta in Korea, and by a Dengist politburo in China. In countries such as Brazil where huge landowners, allied with the army, control politics,[44] or in nations such as India where the landholders (and a money-lending class) have a major stake in maintaining the status quo, popular reforms seem unlikely.[45]

Change in such areas depended on various unpredictable or unlikely, but not impossible, events: a successful peasant revolt, a democratic revision of the power structure, defeat in war, or the imposition of rule by an army elite concerned with rural welfare. Even currently ruling governments such as generals in Thailand, some Dengists in China or, for that matter, followers of Gorbachev in the Soviet Union and Eastern Europe have come to realize that their very survival and eventual prosperity depend critically upon a rejuvenation of the rural sector by unleashing and supporting the peasants.

The gradual creation of invigorated peasant societies, intended or not, offers some hope that the problem could be solved nonviolently.[46]

Experiments in such diverse areas as Kerala (India), El Westiani (Egypt), Alipur (India), and Awgu (Nigeria) demonstrated that village economic progress can occur in areas where either land reform has occurred or outside influences have disrupted traditional patterns.[47] In each of these places where I have observed, indigenous movements produced remarkable changes—without alterations in the political structure at the top of their countries.

In Kerala, a local organization (KSSP) established village learning centers and dramatically increased agricultural production, leaving basic ownership of land untouched.[48] In El Westiani, agricultural agents from Cairo initiated a "green revolution" and doubled the village income.[49] In Alipur, the Phillips electronics company established a plant, hired and trained two hundred landless laborers, and indirectly undermined the caste system.[50] In Awgu, a Cornell Ph.D, taught villagers about the market process and led them to build a hospital and a new school. In each case, the peasants were introduced into a wider market system and profited from it. Village life was transformed, "outsiders" generally initiated the change, a sympathetic government buttressed the nonviolent revolution with everything from hybrid seeds to credit opportunities, the thrust toward progress was voluntary, and the peasants enthusiastically entered into the realm of commercial agriculture. These successes demonstrated Nobelist Sir Arthur Lewis's position that "the underdeveloped countries have no shortage of the commercial instincts. . . . Their people demonstrate as great a fondness for trading and taking risks as one can find anywhere."[51] Perhaps other developing nations can provide the conditions for fostering this commercial instinct among their people, as the Asian countries have done.

Another extremely difficult problem, particularly in inflation-prone and debt-ridden countries, is "labor discipline." The East Asian areas grew initially because of low-cost, labor-intensive industries in which workers sweated their lives out and accepted relatively low wages on the world market. Fortunately, that situation changed rapidly in the successful regions, but the first stages of growth in Japan or Korea, a Hong Kong or a Taiwan required that workers restrained their demands for higher wages. That situation has changed for the better in all of the regions. The workers joined in sharing the growing wealth, and the gap between rich and poor narrowed.

In countries like Argentina that have strong labor unions, historically imported from Italy, workers exerted intense pressure to keep wages and benefits high, even though the economy retrogressed.[52] By supporting Peronista movements that catered to the legitimate grievances of the labor movement, politicians put the short-term interests of the workers ahead of their long-term benefits. Inadvertently, they caused a flight in domestic capital, frightened off foreign investment, and precipitated inflation.[53] From its status as the tenth largest economy in the world in 1910, Argentina gradually declined into a welfare-oriented society that, in fact, ignored the eventual status of its people.

While the policies were temporarily popular when advocated by charismatic generals of even elected leaders, a developing economy with uncontrolled wages eventually undermines fragile democracies with the threat of either military revolt from the right or guerilla movements from the left. As history has demonstrated, the triumph of either tendency in Latin America has resulted in catastrophe.[54]

Asia presented a different example. Singapore faced similar problems as Latin America in the 1950s and 1960s, but the democratically elected PAP found a compromise solution by forming a government-labor-business wage-control board to reach binding agreements on wages, prices, and welfare issues. Taiwan followed a similar example. In Japan, during a "spring offensive" when all unions presented their demands, compromises were worked out with companies, and at the same time sporadic wild-cat strikes were avoided. In addition, many workers belonged to "company unions" that considered the interests of the entire firm. These models were far from the American or European examples and were often regarded by Western trade union leaders as "rigged." Yet, after an initial period of suffering, the workers prospered, the countries avoided inflation, and their export goods sold well on world markets—increasing the level of prosperity for all.[55]

In a different cultural context, Mexico tried a similar approach in the late 1980s. In addition to reducing government spending and selling off unprofitable public enterprises, President Carlos Salinas de Gotari entered into a price stabilizing "social contract" similar to Singapore's, combined with debt-relief measures from the outside world that he hoped would lead to economic growth and eventually to rising wages.[56]

While political obstacles were enormous in many developing countries, some had already adapted the East Asian model with a high degree of success. This is the surest evidence that the policies followed in Asia were not bound to a particular culture, mired in time, attributable to unique historical circumstances, or checkmated by the debt crisis. In spite of vast differences in culture, politics, and resources, some other regions of the world consciously or by coincidence emulated the East Asian example. These developing societies have also begun to prosper, a hopeful indication that East Asian policies can be adapted in completely different environments.

Successes in Africa, India, Latin America, and Southeast Asia

In Africa, while incurring major debts, the economy of the Ivory Coast, a mildly authoritarian society, grew at an annual rate of 6 percent in the 1970s and 1980s. Its president, Felix Houphoüét-Boigny, had chosen a gradualist, capitalist, export-oriented path in the 1960s. In contrast, Kwame Nkrumah in neighboring Ghana opted for a socialist policy and made a wager that the Ivory Coast would collapse in ten years. Another neighbor of the Ivory Coast, Sékou Touré of Guinea, established a cruel dictatorship and set his course on creating "Marxism in African clothes."[57]

The three West African countries, ebullient with their initial liberation, had several features in common. Covered mostly by jungle, each depended on a single export (cocoa in Ghana, bananas in Guinea, and coffee in the Ivory Coast). Their unexploited areas held riches in timber, potential crops, bauxite, diamonds, and hydro-electric power. Guinea and Ghana enjoyed better ports, a larger foreign exchange reserve, and a more experienced civil service.

Both Ghana and Guinea chose authoritarian paths, tried to establish self-sufficient industries, and rejected dependence on the outside world. Guinea cut all ties with France while the Ivory Coast strengthened them and the number of French settlers increased fivefold from 1960 to 1989. In 1967, neo-Marxists such as Samir Amin predicted the imminent demise of the Ivory Coast.[58]

The prophecies proved disastrously incorrect. Although originally richer than the Ivory Coast, both Ghana and Guinea had collapsed by the 1980s. To survive, many people had to eat roasted jungle rats.

In sharp contrast, per capita income in the Ivory Coast had leapt from $70 annually in 1960 to $2,150 in 1989. The economy had been widely diversified into such new products as coffee and cotton. Small industries increased their growth by 10 percent a year. Although corruption permeated the land, the economy prospered.

Four major factors, reminiscent of the East Asian example, explained the Ivory Coast's advance. The country had diversified its products in an export-oriented direction, particularly to France. The government had opened its door to foreign influences (primarily French and Lebanese); both capital and skills flowed in. The nation emphasized education by investing 20 percent of its national budget in schooling. The government encouraged capitalism at small, medium, and multinational levels. Although burdened by tribal divisions, religious differences, corruption, and some two million refugees from poorer parts of Africa, the Ivory Coast demonstrated that economic miracles can occur in the dark continent.

All was not perfect in the Ivory Coast. The president, for example, wasted hundreds of millions on a palace surrounded by menacing crocodiles, and he built a cathedral that rivaled St. Peter's in his home village.[59] Partially because of these extravagances, the country amassed a large foreign debt, but like Korea, it paid it off through exports.

Other nations, such as Senegal, Burundi, and Botswana pursued a similar path, and their growth between 1986 and 1989 averaged almost 4 percent annually.[60] In Africa, "the list of successful policies contains nothing that would surprise an economist in South Korea or Thailand," the editors of *The Economist* commented in 1989. "Raise the prices paid to farmers; make sure interest rates are above the rate of inflation; keep the exchange rate competitive; keep the budget deficit low; give state firms tight financial targets, but managerial economy; do all these things and you will at least set the framework for an economy to grow."[61]

In India, as in Africa, two different economic strategies were followed with strikingly contrasting results. The Punjab, although wracked by religious discontent and virtual civil war, became India's shining example of economic advance. Punjabis grew two-thirds more wheat per acre than the agro-businessmen in America. They "exported" large amounts of rice to India's central reserves and accounted in 1986 for about 45 percent of the national reservoir. Farm income doubled between 1965 and 1985, literacy soared, and most of the untouchables (given access to jobs in new small industries) escaped their traditional slavery. The elements in this success story, similar to Taiwan's, were familiar: middle-income landowners took the lead in internal export trade with India; the government contributed the seeds, credit facilities, and irrigation necessary for a green revolution, and Sikh entrepreneurs built small-scale, labor-intensive industries. The central government pretty much ignored the Punjab and applied few socialist policies there. The Sikhs themselves deserved credit for the progress.

In contrast, the state of Bihar—potentially the richest region of India with two-fifths of the national mineral resources—followed a different path, more fully influenced by New Delhi's ostensible socialist goals. The Indian government nationized the state's more important industries, allowed the educational system to deteriorate under political pressure (students struck for the right to cheat, and won), neglected agricultural reform, and sought the elusive goal of self-sufficiency.[62]

The results were disastrous. Thirty-eight of Bihar's forty publicly owned enterprises failed to make a profit in the 1980s. Landlords treated farmers as serfs and the rural thugs hired by the landlords became prevalent. "Bihar has become a symbol of waywardness and dashed hopes," Trevor Fishlock, an expert on India, observed. "Corruption, gangsterism, intimidation and the rusting standards in public life had combined to give it a night-marish quality."[63]

In Latin America, those nations that had the most direct investment from Pacific countries and the greatest cultural contact with them were even more likely to benefit from the East Asian region. As I noted, Chile has prospered (economically) by trade in automobiles, fruit, timber, wine grapes, cooper, and gold. Costa Rica has benefited from Taiwanese influence and Singapore's investments. Brazil has a thriving Japanese community that has contributed primarily to the timber industry but is now involved in industrial production.

In predominantly Moslem or Buddhist Southeast Asia, as I have noted, the links to Confucian or Shintoist Japan have greatly increased in spite of memories of wartime horrors. "Japan is becoming the true economic engine that is driving growth in new and dynamic ways," Michael Berger commented.[64]

In Thailand, Japanese companies invested $1.2 billion by 1988. The Toshiba Co. manufactured ranges, color TV sets, and compact disc players. Seiko Epson, Japan's largest watchmaker, turned Thailand into its major producer. Toy manufacturer Bandri Co. produced for export to Japan, the United States, and Europe. Workers at Yamaha Sports, who have never seen snow, produced skis for export. Originally attracted by cheap labor, Japanese companies paid higher wages than their Thai competitors with the unwitting result that Thai companies upped their wages in order to keep workers. This unplanned event represented one more example of growth with equity in Asia.

In Malaysia, Victor Co. of Japan established the first full manufacturing plant in Southeast Asia to produce finished videocassette recorders and all of the sub-assembly parts. Malaysian workers at the Matsushita air-conditioning plant in Kuala Lumpur practiced Japanese exercises each morning and produced world-class products.

Asian Investments in the Developing Countries

In Indonesia, Japanese investment jumped from $375 million in 1983 to $9.2 billion in 1988.[65] In 1988, the Japanese government loaned $2.3 billion to Indonesia, double its loan of 1987.[66]

Japan also spread its influence in other parts of the Third World through both aid and trade. In April 1989 Japan unilaterally cut the tariffs it levied on imports from tropical countries by $3.3 billion. This move particularly helped Africa and Latin America. The Keidandren, Japan's manufacturing association, set aside a special fund to finance joint ventures in poor countries.[67]

Japan not only emerged as the biggest aid-giver in the world, but it weighed its greater influence in the Asian Development Bank and the World Bank. New and helpful suggestions, such as underwriting the conversion of much of the developing world's debts, were put forward officially by the Japanese government. Both Japan and Korea established peace corps to teach skills for fishing, farming, forestry, vehicle repair, and construction technology in developing countries. Much of Japan's aid went to Southeast Asia, but even by 1986 Japan had become the chief benefactor of twenty-five countries scattered throughout the world.

One of the major goals of Japanese, Taiwanese, and Korean aid was to encourage joint ventures and to persuade poor countries to emulate their outward-oriented policies. Cynics in the less-developed countries criticized the Asian countries for tying their aid to the buying of Asian goods (specifically designed tractors, for example, in newly developed farming areas). The cynics also wondered where they would sell their export goods. As Japan became more consumer oriented, the editors of *The Economist* argued in 1989 that "the answer could and should be Japan itself."[68]

Thus, the opening of the Pacific region offered new advantages for the Third World—huge markets in Asia, a fresh supply of foreign aid and technical advice, assistance in retiring old debts, and a proven model of development. Some of the wiser statesmen in nations from Thailand to Senegal are taking advantage of these new historical options.[69] In sum, East Asia can serve as a beacon for the Third World if determined leaders and a technically competent population have the will to follow the Pacific pattern.[70]

Notes

1. See Gustav Papanek, "The New Asian Culture: An Economic Portrait," in *In Search of An East Asian Development Model*, by Peter Berger and Hsin-Huang Hsiao (New Brunswick and Oxford: Transaction Books, 1986).
2. Chi-ming Hou, "Relevance of the Taiwan Model of Development," Chung-Hua Institution for Economic Research, 14 Nov. 1988, 29.
3. Ibid.
4. William H. Overholt, "Thailand: A Moving Equilibrium," *Pacific Review*, 1, no. 1 (1988): 7.
5. See William McCord, "Explaining the East Asian 'Miracle'," *National Interest* (Summer 1989).
6. James C. Abegglen, "The Fast Pace of Asian Change," *Tokyo Business Today*, 1 Jan. 1989, 6.
7. Yun-Peng Chu, "Towards a Theoretical Explanation of Taiwan's Development with Decreasing Inequality," Taipei, Academia Sinica, Mimeographed paper, 1988.
8. See Mancur Olson, *The Rise and Decline of Nations* (New Haven: Yale University Press, 1982).
9. Robin Broad and John Cavanagh, "No More NIC's," *Foreign Policy* (Fall 1988).
10. Jagdish Bhagwat, *Protectionism* (Cambridge; MIT Press, 1988).
11. See Felix G. Rohatyn, "Three Visions of the Global Economy," Japan Society, New York, 8 June 1989.
12. See, for example, Sylvia Ann Hewlett, *The Cruel Dilemmas of Development* (New York: Basic Books, 1980).
13. See, for example, Trevor Fishlock, *Gandhi's Children* (New York: Universe Books, 1983).
14. Ibid.
15. Karl Sax, *The World's Exploding Population* (Boston, Beacon Press, 1960).
16. Laurence Harrison, *Under-Development Is a State of Mind* (Lanham, MD: University Press of America, 1985).
17. Julian Simon, *The Ultimate Resource* (Princeton: Princeton University Press, 1981), 345.

18. See Abegglen, "Fast Pace."
19. Jeffrey E. Garten, "The New Protectionism," *New York Times*, 24 Oct. 1988.
20. Ibid.
21. Maryanne N. Keller, "Two Way Street," *World Monitor* (October 1988).
22. Peter Passell, "Shifting Toward Debt Reduction," *New York Times*, 22 March 1988.
23. Ibid.
24. Ibid.
25. World Bank, 1988.
26. Peter Kilborn, "Debt Reduction: Ways To Do It," *New York Times*, 6 April 1989, D1.
27. Ibid. D6.
28. World Bank, 5 April 1989.
29. See Selig Harrison, *India: The Most Dangerous Decades* (Princeton: Princeton University Press, 1960); and Trevor Fishlock, *op. cit.*
30. David Lamb, *The Africans*, New York, Random House, 1982.
31. See Paul Johnson, *Modern Times*, New York, Harper and Row, 1983.
32. See Fishlock, *Gandhi's Children.*
33. See Lamb, *Africans.*
34. Viswanathan Selvaratnam, "Vocational Education and Training," Chung-Hua Institution, Taipei, 17 Nov. 1988.
35. John Kenneth Galbraith, *The Voices of the Poor* (Cambridge: Harvard University Press, 1983), 13.
36. See William McCord with Airline McCord, *Paths to Progress* (New York: W. W. Norton, 1986), part 1.
37. Ann Tutwiler, Barbara Elliot, George Rossmiller, "Economic Development and Land Reform," National Center for Food and Agricultural Policy, 1989.
38. Chew Soon Bong, "Successful Economic Development Policies," Chung-Hua Institution, Taipei, 18 Nov. 1988.
39. Jan Morris, *Hong Kong* (New York: Random House, 1988).
40. William H. Overholt, "Thailand."
41. Chalmers Johnson, "South Korean Democratization: The Role of Economic Development," *The Pacific Review* 2, no. 1, 5.
42. See William McCord, *The Springtime of Freedom* (New York: Oxford University Press, 1965); and McCord, *Paths to Progress.*
43. Johnson, 4.
44. Hewlitt, *Cruel Dilemmas.*
45. Fishlock, *Gandhi's Children.*
46. McCord, *Paths to Progress.*
47. Richard Critchfield, "Science and the Villages," *Foreign Affairs* 61, no. 1 (Fall 1982).
48. McCord, *Paths to Progress.*
49. Ibid., 65.
50. Ibid., 66.
51. Sir Arthur Lewis, *Restless Nations* (New York: Dodd Mead and Co., 1964), 81.
52. James D. Cockcroft, *Neighbors in Turmoil* (New York: Harper and Row, 1989).
53. Robert Crassweller, *Peron and the Enigmas of Argentina* (New York: W. W. Norton, 1987).
54. Cockcroft, *Neighbors.*
55. Roy Hofheinz and Kent Calder, *The East Asia Edge* (New York: Basic Books, 1982).

56. See Patrick Oster, *The Mexicans* (New York: William Morrow, 1989). Also see Bill Bradley, "Urgent Relief for Mexico," *New York Times*, 17 Jan. 1989.
57. *New York Times*, 17 Jan. 1989.
58. Samir Amin, *Le Douvelopment du Capitalism en Cote d'Ivoire* (Paris: Editions de Minuit, 1967).
59. V. S. Naipaul, *Finding the Center* (New York: Alfred Knopf, 1984).
60. World Bank, March, 1989.
61. "Africa's Hope," *The Economist*, 4 March 1989, 13.
62. See James Traub, *India: The Challenge of Change* (New York: Simon and Schuster, 1989).
63. Fishlock *Gandhi's Children*.
64. Michael Berger, "The Japanese Locomotive is on the Move in Asia," *Billion* (inaugural issue 1988): 44.
65. Ibid.
66. Japanese Ministry of Finance, 1988.
67. Berger, "Japanese Locomotive," 46.
68. "Japan and the Third World," *The Economist*, 17 June 1989.
69. Ibid., 28.
70. See William McCord, "An East Asian Model of Development," *The Pacific Review* (May 1989).

Part III

THE FUTURE OF THE PACIFIC

The Pacific Ocean, its shores, its islands will become the great theatre of events in the world's hereafter.

—William Seward,
Lincoln's secretary of state, 1861

9

Perils to Pacific Progress

Japan is the next America. We will follow the
pattern of the United States and the United
Kingdom. Go to the top and will go down again.
All within the next twenty years.
—Hiroshi Takeuchi, 1988

An economist and nationalist, Hiroshi Takeuchi feared that the export
of Japanese capital, particularly to America, spelled the end of Japanese
hegemony. In fact, even by 1986, Japan's banks had purchased $520 billion
in stocks and bonds abroad, more than American, British, and Canadian
investors combined.[1] Takeuchi predicted that such investments merely
strengthened the economies of nations who competed with Japan. He
believed that only stiff measures—"a kind of Hitler regime"—would stop
the flow of capital to overseas destinations.[2]

Takeuchi's gloom and prescriptions found little resonance at home or
abroad in spite of a stock market recession in 1990. Nonetheless, objective
observers recorded three distinct perils to the Pacific renaissance:

1) Japan might indeed enter a period of economic stagnation or political
   retrogression. Some observers, particularly in Asia, even predicted a
   resurgence in Japan's militarism.
2) Economic and political developments in China suggested the possibility
   of an authoritarian retrenchment, a trend that vitally affected the
   strategic interests of America, the Soviet Union, Japan, and particularly
   the fragile status of Hong Kong and Taiwan.
3) The ever-present possibility of world recession, fueled by protectionism, threatened all of Asia, especially those areas such as Hong Kong
   and Singapore, Malaysia and Thailand that had become vitally dependent on export trade.

Each of these scenarios and their possible resolution required attention since, if any of them evolved, they could forestall the coming of a "Pacific Century" that has been predicted since Napoleon's time.

Retrogression in Japan?

Staffan Linder, the distinguished economist and Swedish politician, argued in 1986 that Pacific dynamism "is transforming world politics and economics."[3] Nonetheless, even then, he detected significant limitations on Japan's domestic economy.

"Technology can no longer be imported or improved," Linder noted, "but must be created."[4] In 1988, economist Ichiro Yoshiyama argued that "Japan's dilemma is that its industrial machine often lacks the ability to develop new break-through technologies that they can truly call their own."[5]

That pattern changed rapidly in the late 1980s. Japan began to spend a higher proportion of her national income on civilian research and development than did America. Japanese patents on new products shot up. Richard Cohon, an expert on the nation, pointed out that Japan had privatized many of its old monopolies and used $4 billion a year from the proceeds to finance new technology centers that "dwarf our own [American] public-private research and development efforts."[6] As a consequence, the Japanese took a dominating lead in superconductors, biotechnology, high-definition T.V., and microelectronics. In spite of earlier cautions, there seemed little doubt that Japan's powerful research effort would dominate twenty-first-century technology.

Another danger to Japan, Linder noted in 1986, was the "rapid greying" of the population, a development that would decrease the ratio of productive workers to dependents.[7] This trend, also apparent in Europe and America, meant that the social security and medical bills of the advanced industrial nations would increase.

Japan had relatively little apprehension on this front, however, since her national bill for the aged was remarkably, perhaps miserly, low. The country took a distinct lead in the development of robots, outmoding the usual industrial worker. Her increasing investments in developing lands with very young populations provided Japan with a sure source of labor-intensive products.

"Higher standards of living may erode the work ethic," Linder wrote in

1986.[8] That may well be true, and many older Japanese complained about the hedonism and laziness of the young.

Nevertheless, in order to avoid a political backlash, the ruling LDP government in 1989 officially encouraged people to take longer vacations, work less, and play more. In addition, the government allocated $8 trillion until 1999 to provide amenities such as sewerage and parks.[9] The reasons were clear: huge trade surpluses had not brought a good life to many in crowded Japan. The average Japanese paid three times as much as did Americans for food in 1988 and, due to government subsidies, ten times the world price for rice. Only 37 percent of Japanese homes had modern sewerage facilities. Tokyo offered one-tenth of the park space afforded by London.

Housing represented the most critical shortage. To buy a house, a Japanese worker had to pay six times his annual salary in order to purchase a home half the size of an American one. Thus, only six percent of people in Tokyo owned their own home.[10]

The blame for relative domestic poverty resulted partly from natural factors. More than 120 million Japanese were crowded on islands about the size of Montana, and two-thirds of the archipelago could not be inhabited. Hence, the price of land soared, while the value of the yen was half its value domestically as abroad.

Government policies aggravated the situation. Agricultural protectionism allowed peasants, the backbone of the LDP, to farm precious land with hardly any taxes. A sales tax enacted in 1989 raised the prices for basic necessities into a high realm. A government bias in favor of small retailers allowed the proliferation of four retail stores for every wholesaler. Rigid zoning laws kept the average building height in Tokyo below ten stories.

Although Japan had a remarkably equitable distribution of income, many Japanese saw the growing disparities between the rich (those who own land) and the average person as increasing. Seventy percent of Japanese did not believe that they were enjoying an affluent life-style in 1989, and 75 percent regarded differences between the rich and the poor as unfair.[11]

Such perceptions could well erode the Japanese virtues of self-denial, frugality, diligence, and dedication to company and country. Yet, immense expenditures on public amenities, a late-1980s dedication to production for the domestic market, and a virtually unanimous opinion among the Japanese that they were middle class could help to maintain Japan's social harmony.

On the political level, some commentators believed that the Japanese bureaucracy had neither the will nor the power to respond to new realities or to invigorate the nation. Karel von Wolferen, a Western journalist who lived in Japan, argued in 1989 that Japan was "a paralyzed superpower," unable to solve domestic problems or assume a responsible international role. Japan, he contended, was ruled by bureaucrats, the police, power-brokers in the government, and business leaders who bought political influence from the ruling party and a docile press.[12] It was a "stateless nation," a mere "system" of interest groups that was incapable of long-range decision making and unguided by transcendental values.

Vol Wolferen emphasized the submissiveness and conformity of the Japanese people. "The Japanese," he observed, "are constantly made to feel like subjects not citizens. They live in a cajoling and exhortative environment. . . . The loudspeakers on cruising police cars and on the bigger police boxes recalls a worrisome mother; something is always *abunai*, dangerous."[13]

Critics of Japan perhaps overemphasized the submissiveness and inflexibility of Japanese society. After all, the nation had been characterized by student riots, farmers' protests, and a far from quiescent press that caused the downfall of a prime minister and the jailing of a business leader. Over the decades, Japan has readily adapted to sweeping changes in the world economy. An official government policy of internationalism and Japan's assumption of a new role in international trade and aid hardly seemed compatible with a portrait of an isolated and incompetent country.

Nonetheless, many Japanese still retained the conviction that they were culturally and even radically unique. As von Wolferen warned, there were increasing xenophobic sentiments in Japan and a strengthening of "the old suspicion that, in essence, the world does not want to make room for it."[14]

Some Japanese teachers, public figures, and textbooks described Japan as a superior society victimized by the Pacific war. And, in the 1980s, popular revisionist films appeared that portrayed General Tojo as a hero, naval officers in the Pacific war as peaceful family men, and Japanese soldiers in the Philippines as "friendly, gentle, and full of good will . . . whereas United States soldiers are brutes who play football with human skulls."[15]

Tokyo police were remarkably tolerant of rightist orators who toured the city shouting nationalist slogans from loudspeakers, but the police were very harsh on leftist propagandists who tried the same tactic. Members of right-wing groups increasingly began to worship the war dead at Yasukini Shrine and other state-Shinto shrines.

A reinvigorated nationalism in Japan frightened other Asians who had long memories of Japanese military adventures. Nevertheless, for their own economic reasons, some American politicians urged a rearming of Japan, and perhaps, a withdrawal of American forces from the islands.

In turn, Japanese military commanders found the Soviet military buildup in the Pacific during the 1980s, with its threat to maritime corridors, a distinct threat. They particularly feared a Soviet reinforcement of its aircraft on the Kurile islands.[16] In addition, a possible military withdrawal of the United States from the Korean peninsula created apprehension.[17]

In response to these real or imagined dangers, Japanese military expenditures gradually exceeded an informal limit of 1 percent of the GNP in 1990. The air force acquired air-refueling tankers—which could only be used for long-range missions—and the navy planned for the launching of "defensive" aircraft carriers in the later 1990s. The navy also got four Aegis-class guided-missile cruisers. Since Tokyo extended its sea-lane defense to a (vaguely defined) 1000-nautical-mile perimeter, her fleet of blue-water ships expanded to sixty, exceeding China's fifty-three and India's thirty-one.[18]

As Japan's fleet of destroyers began to outnumber those that America had in the Pacific, other Asian nations took action. China built 110 conventional submarines and 4 nuclear submarines (the world's third-largest fleet). India, worried about her own sea routes, tripled her defense budget between 1981 and 1989.[19] An undeclared but real conflict over the control of ocean lanes began in the 1980s.

Rehinhard Drifte, a geopolitical commentator, reported in 1987 that Japan's military role "has already expanded far beyond that prescribed by its constitution. It is far larger than that tolerated by Japanese public opinion from the 1950s through the 1970s, much greater than that commonly perceived by Europe, and more powerful and perhaps more threatening than that preferred by the Soviet Union."[20]

Ironically, the potential military role of an economic colossus, such as Japan, remained largely out of her hands. American pressure for rearmament, incidents in China, a possible reunification of Korea, another Persian Gulf crisis, or a sudden hardening of Soviet policy might force Japan into a more militant posture.[21]

Powerful forces worked against such a development. Japanese public opinion and its constitution forbad nuclear arms. Japan's geopolitical situation pushed the nation to reach an agreement with the Soviet Union and China. Japan's increasing investments elsewhere in Asia suggested that economic rather than military considerations would influence policy. Japan's imports of manufactured goods from the NICs totaled $12.46 billion in 1987, a 60 percent increase from the previous year.[22] Having already forged solid economic links with other Asian nations, it would be rash of Japan to reenact her military ventures that began in the 1920s and culminated in the 1940s debacle.

Admittedly, ominous possibilities exist in Japan's future—a resurgence of militarism, economic recession, bureaucratic paralysis, an exhaustion of peoples' will to work—but I believe that this resilient, flexible, and increasingly creative country can overcome the problems it confronts. As the leader of East Asia, it has gained a grand role to play in the Pacific century.

Backward Moves in China?

A long shadow hung over the future of reform in China. May and June 1989 marked the demonstration of one million people in Tiananmen Square for democracy, press freedom, and an end to corruption. After much debate, both within the party bureaucracy and the army, soldiers fired on the crowd, dispersing it brutally.

It had all happened before. Dissent in Tiananmen Square was crushed in 1919, again in 1957, and in 1976. This time, however, the event involved unprecedented numbers of people and affected students, workers, and the army. Strong elements in the army—notably the chief of the general staff, the Beijing army commander, and the two surviving army marshals—opposed martial law.

Nonetheless, Deng and Prime Minister Li Peng restored "law and order" at rifle-point. Party Secretary Zhao Ziyang, a reformer, went into eclipse in an elite hospital. Some foreign investors scrambled to exit from the country. Many intellectuals were put in prison. College graduates, dating back to 1985, were ordered to work for two years in villages or factories to rekindle their enthusiasm for communism. These developments gave rise to the gloomy perception that China had returned to its centuries-old tradition of poverty, stagnation, and autocracy.

China's economic problems in 1987–1989 undoubtedly played a role in the uprising and its subsequent repression. In spite of immense progress, as I have noted, China encountered severe shortages, inflation, and corruption in the late 1980s. Salt, pork, sugar, and eggs had to be rationed in Beijing. These imbalances were caused in part by the reforms themselves. Industrial growth and the printing of more money by the People's Bank of China fueled inflation.[23] People panicked at the rise in prices (at least 24 percent between 1987 and 1988) and hoarded large amounts of consumer goods. The supply chain of raw materials began to falter.[24] As a result, the Chinese politburo put off indefinitely any further freeing of prices and attempted to reimpose central control.[25]

Under these conditions, corruption spread, particularly among party officials who could arrange deals to facilitate the flow of resources and products. Between 1983 and 1988, the party expelled 150,000 members for corruption, but this represented only a small fraction within a party of 48 million members. Lacking the spur of a totally free economy, corruption merely spread among party members in advantageous positions.

Even before the repression, some Chinese and foreign observers noted that the party's authority had declined. A once prominent journalist, Qi Xiangang, reported in a local newspaper in 1988 that "Revolutionary slogans can no longer inspire people's spirit as before . . . people's responses are cold."[26] The *China Economic News* observed that "the transition from the old economic order is now generally blamed to be responsible for most of the irregularities of Chinese society."[27] A Chinese economist wrote, "the challenge is whether the party is capable of leading the economy. There is already doubt among the people, and it is rising. The real issue is the legitimacy of party rule."[28]

At least temporarily, the tragic happenings of 1989 had several effects. The authority of the party declined even more precipitously for millions of Chinese.[29] One Beijing worker who actually witnessed the demonstration told me: "I no longer know what to believe, what I hear or what I saw." (Party propagandists had begun a campaign over T.V. and in the press to play down the seriousness of the rebellion.) "Frankly," the worker said, "I think my eyes are more reliable than my ears."

The legitimacy of the party also suffered badly from the repression. As the *Economist* reported, "Today's China is no longer Mr. Deng's sort of place.[30] The demonstrations in Tiananmen Square and other places represented the ideas of a better-educated, better-traveled group of people than their elders. Ironically for him, Deng had created a new class of cosmopolitans who measured their standard of living by the rest of the world. They not only resented Li Peng's austerity policies, but they wanted, in some ill-defined form, the freedoms enjoyed on the outside. The split between reformers and conservatives within the Communist party brought forth no new, charismatic leader. "The Communist party, deeply shaken and split by recent events, lacks the stamina, morale and determination necessary for the next difficult stage of riskier and unpopular economic reform," Louis do Rosario commented in 1989.[31]

The economy slid back into bureaucratic stagnation, particularly as foreign capital dried up.[32]

The chance that Beijing might halt China's uneasy transition from a centrally planned economy into a relatively free market economy particularly concerned people in those regions that had made the greatest progress. Guangdong province had a degree of autonomy from Beijing, and the economic results were outstanding. Industrial production in 1988 alone shot up by more than 35 percent; the province had attracted about 60 percent of all foreign investment in China; and it accounted for 20 percent of China's exports.

Much of this advance occurred under the aegis of Zhao Ziyang who had served as provincial administrator before his downfall as party secretary. Zhao had encouraged small, private entrepreneurs, foreign investment, and the rapid development of coastal zones. With Zhao's loss of power, official journals began criticizing small entrepreneurs and the policies followed by Zhao.[33] Beijing officials admonished Guangdong for getting "too rich" and reinstated political study sessions for local officials that had been abandoned in 1979.[34] Meanwhile, Hong Kong investors quietly began to pull their money out of the province.[35] A fear of purges and a recentralization of power threatened the once thriving province with paralysis.

In addition to the possibility of economic recession, the revolt in Tiananmen Square brought into question the loyalty of some army units and, inevitably, catapulted the army back into politics. In order to quell the uprising, Deng called in 150,000 troops garnered from thirteen armies. (By 1990, regardless of an end to martial law, troops from five armies remained stationed in Beijing.) Evidently, he did not trust the Beijing garrison to restore order and wanted a disparate collection of soldiers— many of whom could not speak the local dialect—to take responsibility.

Defense Minister Qin Jiwei, Chief of the General Staff Chi Haotian, and Beijing garrison commissioner Yan Tongmao questioned Deng's orders and fell into disgrace. The 38th Army massively refused to put down the revolt. The regime arrested its commander, Xu Qinxian, for insubordination. With two of the three members of the political commission that ruled the army out of the way (Deng was ailing and Zhao had been dismissed), the basic question remained: who would control the army?

The infidelity of many senior commanders to the party's orders and the obvious fraternization of common soldiers with students gave rise to fears of a military conspiracy against the orthodox regime. In the end, elements in the army obeyed the party's ruling leadership but at the price of possible discontent within the ranks.

The last try at a military coup—Lin Biao's attempted assassination of Mao in 1970—had ended in abysmal defeat. Nevertheless, it was not inconceivable that army commanders might decide that they could govern China far better than faltering politicians who had lost the aura of authority.

A Return to Moderation in China?

In its search for both social order and an escape route from poverty, China might still return to a policy of economic decentralization and gradual political liberalization. Clearly, there are other scenarios: a disintegration into military fiefdoms, a retreat into totalitarian domination, or simply, anarchy. Any of these possibilities, often enacted in Chinese history, could become a reality.

China has undergone so many profound changes since 1949 that a return to moderation under nominal Communist rule seems the most likely outcome of the nation's turmoil. But no future ruler can ignore certain imperatives.

A roll back of reforms that have been in place since 1978 would require harsh recentralization by Beijing. Yet, the party has already relinquished too much power to attempt a revamping of its central planning apparatus.

Even before 1989, the newly freed peasants often successfully refused to pay their grain quotas. Local officials in places like Guangdong found many devious ways (such as calling loans from Hong Kong "gifts") to avoid Beijing's central control. Enterprise managers, enjoying a degree of freedom in their economic undertakings, were likely to resist stubbornly attempts to whittle down their powers.

Any government in Beijing, however stark, has to follow one of two unpalatable policies in order to cut the rate of inflation. Either it has to reimpose price and wage controls—an enormous task for an enfeebled and discredited bureaucracy—or it must eliminate the multi-pricing system as a step toward ending corruption. In any case, as one observer noted in

1989, "The central government, its legitimacy and authority weakened by recent events, is incapable of imposing recentralization policies that run counter to the interests of provinces and municipalities. More than ever, Peking will have to solicit the help of local authorities to keep the economy going."[36]

Any Chinese government also must confront the issue that a variety of interest groups, created by a rising level of income, have new expectations and want a new standard of living. As the population again expands rapidly, China's economy has to grow or the leadership faces grave social discontent and even revolution. Newly "rich" farmers, corporation managers, private entrepreneurs, students forced into agricultural labor, "bourgeois" intellectuals, and some army officers no longer tolerate the demands imposed by a Mao or even a Deng. No Chinese government can totally suppress the reform movement, unless it is willing to cripple the economy and lose its "mandate from heaven."

One result of the proliferation in interest groups is the inability of the central bank, the People's Bank of China, to control local financial arrangements. Provinces, coastal cities, special economic zones, and individuals create their own banking facilities. Naturally, such localized groups favor nearby enterprises and generously lend to them. Technically illegal financial operations have sprung up in Guandong and particularly in Wenzhous city where lenders receive 40 to 60 percent interest.[37] Such loans inflame inflation, but there seems no way that the central bank can control them without a free market.

Still another factor points to the possible triumph of moderates in China—the army's influence. As reported, many in the military opposed the 1989 bloodshed. They included not only the high officers I have mentioned but such respected figures as the former head of the navy, the former director of logistics, and the former commanders of the highest military academy. Such officers were not "democrats," but they apparently believed that the bloodshed would weaken the unity of the army and the country. Thus, Harian Jencks flatly predicted in 1989 that "although the hardliners seem to have the upper hand in China now, moderates remain a potent political force and should reemerge in important party positions. . . . The reason, quite simply, is that they are backed by the military, and the military is the strongest political force in the country."[38]

Even if the moderates return to power, it will take time to set the economic reforms on a course that regains momentum. Reformers will be held back not only by objective economic constraints and criticisms by the outside world, but also "by the terrible disillusionment, cynicism, and fears of the Chinese people."[39] Difficult as it might be, freeing markets remains the only way to release China from bribery and the insidious influence of "connections"—the corruption that prompted the students' protest.

The great barrier, as Bette Bao Lord wrote in 1989, is that "the legitimacy of the Communist party had been destroyed."[40] Indeed, it will be a long march back to the era of reform.

The Threat of World Recession

Whatever happened in China, the specter of a world depression haunted all of Asia. The trigger of such a recession would be a politically inspired return of the Western world to barriers on world trade. As Linder commented in 1986, "The most serious threat to the world economy is Western protectionism."[41] This "white peril," as Linder called it, posed dangers to Asian countries, to developing economies, and to the highly industrialized nations themselves. Obstacles to trade increased prices to consumers, fueled inflation, ignored the fact that a new competitor might be a new customer, deprived consumers of the best goods, and kept inefficient companies in business.

Nonetheless, in spite of rational considerations, politicians eroded free trade in many parts of the world. In the early 1980s, the Reagan administration bailed out America's steel industry by enacting a "voluntary restraint" agreement on twenty-nine countries. In 1988, Congress enacted the so-called Super 301 section (one thousand pages long) of the trade law which gave any president broad powers to impose tariffs. In 1989, President George Bush named Japan, Brazil, and India as the most unfair competitors in trade. That decision gave him the right to place 100 percent tariffs on selected products and, perhaps, ruin other economies.

In Europe, where internal obstacles to trade are expected to come down in 1992, the European Commission has already barred foreign banks, imposed further limitations on the import of Japanese cars, and penalized Korea for dumping videocassette recorders on the market.[42] Such actions could exclude Asia from a "Fortress Europe" of 320 million affluent people and its allies in Eastern Europe.

The emergence of Eastern Europe from autocracy and state monopolies presents both opportunities and problems to the Pacific area. Japan, Korea, and Taiwan might benefit from joint ventures and increased investment in Eastern Europe. Yet, if further integration of Poland, East Germany, Hungary, Czechoslovakia, and Yugoslavia into "Fortress Europe" occurred as anticipated, it would only be natural for a nation such as West Germany to invest in East Germany rather than, say, in Thailand or Malaysia. Cultural links, language, proximity, and the existence of a cheap but relatively well-educated workforce would prompt such decisions.

The shock on the Pacific of increased protectionism in Europe would be enormous. The Western European community as a whole imported $42 billion worth of goods from Japan, $8 billion from Taiwan, $7 billion from Korea, $6 billion from China, and $5 billion from Australia in 1988.[43] If Asia lost those exports, the shock to Pacific countries would be great but, as I have argued, not devastating.

Europeans worried about the loss of jobs from Asian competition and demanded that Asia should grant a greater reciprocity in the trade situation. As one example, Japanese banks held 10 percent of deposits in the European community while Europe invested only 0.35 percent in Japanese banks. The Europeans wanted greater investment as a reward for European markets. (They forgot that Great Britain, at the height of its prosperity, had totally free markets and banking without demanding reciprocity from other nations.)

Originally in the postwar period, the General Agreement on Tariffs and Trade (GATT) encouraged nondiscrimination in commerce. It worked very well in the 1950s and 1960s for the Atlantic countries.[44] Non-tariff barriers in the 1970s began to offset the gains made by the unprecedented liberalization of trade.[45] Nonetheless, there was a worldwide decrease in direct tariffs between 1949 and 1979,[46] and world commerce dramatically increased. The major sectors of the world economy that gained from trade liberalization were manufacturing, service industries, and high technology.[47] Originally protected by the United States, agriculture suffered a decline in exports.[48]

As the Pacific-Asian region grew, some Americans and Europeans became apprehensive about free trade. In America, politicians, labor leaders, and businessmen argued that jobs would be lost, "the dollar will shrink, the energy import bill will rise, inflation will advance, the industrial heartland will decline, investments will be more difficult, and expanding markets will be lost."[49] Pessimists of this persuasion cited four basic problems:

First, in the face of fierce competition, they said, established industrial countries would undergo a relative decline in their share of the world market. Between 1950 and 1982, for example, the U.S. share of world GDP dropped in half.[50] World productivity as a whole, however, went up dramatically.

Second, some observers were apprehensive that industrialized countries would endanger their national security as growth occurred elsewhere.[51] Supposedly, the economic strength of a country determined its military prowess. This argument seemed outmoded in a time when relatively poor countries such as China and India could develop their own nuclear weapons regardless of the state of their economies.

Third, the costs of adjusting to a more competitive world economy bothered both Western businessmen and union leaders. Clearly, as Asia developed, some Western companies suffered. As one example, the Chrysler corporation would have gone under without aid from the U.S. government and a profound restructuring. Chrysler saved itself by retraining its workers and virtually merging with Japan's Mitsubishi. By 1988, Chrysler owned 24 percent of Mitsubishi, imported its smaller models under a Chrysler name, and bought Mitsubishi V-6 engines. A joint venture, Diamond-Star Motors, was started in Illinois with Mitsubishi leading the management. Without such changes and alliances, Chrysler would have collapsed since, as Linder observed, "a low capacity for adjustment is likely to be accompanied by a reduction in capacity for innovation."[52]

Fourth, trade frictions inevitably led to a deterioration in international relations. Many Americans blamed Japan and the Asian "NICs" as scapegoats for their internal economic problems. Some Asians began to regard Americans as an effete people, divided by ethnic tensions and unable to compete in the world market. In fact, economist Robert Lawrence demonstrated that there was no deindustrialization in America between 1973 and 1980 that could be attributed to an invasion of Asian goods.[53]

In response to Western hostility, the Pacific developed various ways of coping with the possibility of a world recession precipitated by protectionism in the early 1990s.

- Japan, Singapore, and Hong Kong had the option of creating high-technology products. Their pursuit of a knowledge-based economy would result in increased world demand for their exports and less dependence on imports.
- Direct investment by advanced Asian-Pacific countries in other Asian, European, or American economies allowed the Pacific to leap over trade obstacles and avoid barriers to markets that were wholly or partially

closed.[54] Japan, Singapore, Hong Kong, Korea, and even Malaysia vigorously investigated this option.

- In addition, because of a mutually advantageous combination of resources, technology, skills, and labor, the Pacific region could form a trading bloc of its own. While the cost in international trade would be great and the heterogenous nature of the Pacific was enormous, a Pacific home market could, as a last resort, become a reality. As one example of existing trends, Australian exports to great Britain, her traditional trading partner, dropped fivefold between 1960 and 1982. Meanwhile, Australian exports to Japan doubled.[55] If this pattern continues, "the negative effects of short-sighted protectionist measures would become more apparent in the domestic political processes of the established nations."[56]

One other major factor militated against protectionism: the increased globalization of the world economy. The official or informal alliances between various companies on an international scale provided them with a degree of safety from protectionist measures. For example, Motorola and Texas Instruments who produced semiconductors in Japan for export to the United States, were the only American companies exempted in 1985 from an anti-Japanese protectionist agreement.[57] Similarly, Ford bought 25 percent of Mazda, while Mazda made Ford products in Mexico and supplied Ford components to affiliates in Australia, New Zealand, and Texas.

Such investments, whether of Asia in America and Europe or vice versa, paid excellent dividends for the recipient country since the commitments often brought with them new technology, new management skills, and more jobs. In addition, these enterprises constituted a permanent stake in the host country and avoided the instant liquidity afforded by government bonds. In the American case, businessman Anthony Solomon observed, "This country gains handsomely from foreign direct investment, especially compared to the mess we would be in if it dried up or were curtailed."[58]

The benefits of free trade became most apparent when protectionist countries could be compared to relatively free-trade countries. India, for example, protected her industries in a strenuous fashion while Korea did not. The results became apparent as early as 1980: exports of goods from Korea exceeded those of India by nearly four times.[59]

Nonpartisan reports in both Japan and the United States suggest workable ways by which the imbalance in world trade could be redressed. The Cuomo Commission, for example, recommended that monetary policy should be coordinated for world growth, short-term political considerations should not dictate trade policy, and that both governments should develop schemes for Third World debt rescheduling.[60]

Why Asia Will Grow

The obstacles confronting the continued growth of the Asian Pacific region are real and grim. Japan might decline in her economic condition and this could be accompanied by a rise in militaristic nationalism. China could fall apart or take years to recover from the reimposition of autocracy. A world recession, brought on by protectionism, could cripple all of the growing Asian economies.

Nonetheless, there are objective factors that render such events unlikely.

Japanese innovators demonstrate new skills in creative research. The government has announced its dedication to internationalism. And the great majority of the people find any idea of a return to militarism distasteful.

In China, economic realities still encourage foreign investment. An enfeebled government has little ability to impose centralized planning. And new interest groups, perhaps aligned with the military, promise an eventual return to economic and political moderation.

The growing globalization and interdependence of the world economy and the increased importance of direct investment partially guard the world against the catastrophes of the 1930s. The gradual emergence of a new trading bloc in the Asia Pacific region offers further protection to that area of the world.

These major new developments provide grounds for limited optimism about the future of the Pacific. To assist the workings of history, however, requires foresight and statesmanship throughout the world. In the "march of folly," there are no guarantees that national leaders will have the bold imagination to grasp the opportunities offered by a Pacific century. The truth is, however, that no one can obfuscate the enormous human, material, political, and intellectual resources that underly the Pacific renaissance.

Notes

1. *Institutional Investor*, January 1987.
2. Quoted in Joel Kotkin and Yoriko Kishimoto, *The Third Century* (New York: Crown Publishers, 1988), 121.

3. Staffan Linder, *The Pacific Century* (Stanford: Stanford University Press, 1986), 1.
4. Ibid., 13.
5. Ichiro Yoshiyama, quoted in Kotkin and Kishimoto, *Third Century*.
6. Richard Cohon, *New York Times*, 1 Dec. 1988, editorial page.
7. Linder, *Pacific Century*, 13.
8. Ibid.
9. *U.S. News and World Report*, 13 Feb. 1989.
10. Ibid.
11. Poll by the Japanese Economic Planning Agency, 1989.
12. Karel von Wolferen, *The Enigma of Japanese Power* (New York: Alfred Knopf, 1989).
13. Ibid., 186.
14. Ibid., 4.
15. Ibid., 427.
16. See Laszlo Lajoa S. Bartalits and Johannes Wilhelmueg H. C. M. Schnieder, "Soviet Strategy and the Pacific Basin," in *The Pacific Rim and the Western World*, ed. by Philip West and Frans A. M. Aiting von Geusau (Boulder, CO: Westview Press, 1987).
17. Reinharind Drifte, "Security in the Pacific Basin: the Role of Japan," *ibid*. Also see Alan Ronberg, *U.S.-Japan Relations* (New York: Council of Foreign Relations, 1988).
18. Tai Ming Cheung, "Sealanes' Strategy," *Far Eastern Economic Review*, 17 July 1989.
19. Tai Ming Cheung, "Build-up Backlash," *Far Eastern Economic Review*, 27 July 1989.
20. Drifte, "Security in Pacific Basin," 128.
21. M. Kare, M. Barang, and F. Barnaby, "Asia: Theater of Nuclear War," *South*, no. 37 (Nov. 1983).
22. Lisa Shuckman, "Japanese Increase Imports from Asian Countries," *New York Times*, 25 April 1988.
23. China News Agency, 1 Sept. 1988.
24. *China Daily*, 24 Sept. 1988.
25. Yao Yiln, New China News Agency, 24 Sept. 1988.
26. Qi Xiangang, *Guamgming Daily*, 1 July 1988.
27. *China Economic News*, quoted in Edward Gargan, "China's Economy Takes Small Leap Backward," *New York Times*, 26 April 1988.
28. Quoted in Robert Delfs, "Helmsman's Lost Bearings," *Far Eastern Economic Review*, 27 Oct. 1988.
29. Louis do Rosario, "Struck Half-Way," *Far Eastern Economic Review*, 8 June 1989.
30. "Not From Guns," *The Economist*, 27 May 1989, 11.
31. de Rosario, "Stuck Half-Way," 16.
32. "Not From Guns."
33. Jiang Zemin, *Seeking Truth*, May 24, 1989.
34. See Fox Butterfield," Canton Looks Back and sees Crackdown Gaining," *New York Times*, 25 May 1989.
35. Ibid.
36. Louis do Rosario, "Stuck Half-Way," 17.
37. Elizabeth Cheng, "Local Fiefdoms Find Demands Fuel Inflation," *Far Eastern Economic Review*, 27 Oct. 1989.

38. Ibid.
39. Harlan W. Jencks, "China's Moderates Will Return," *New York Times*, June 20, 1989, p. A23.
40. Bette Bao Lord, "China's Next Long March," *New York Times*, 4 June 1989, E31.
41. Linder, Pacific Century 107.
42. European Commission of the European Economy, 23 Oct. 1988.
43. "The Growing American Fear of Fortress Europe," *New York Times*, 23 Oct. 1988.
44. See UNCTAD, *World Development Report*, fig. 81, Geneva, 1987.
45. Jagdish Bhagawati, *Protectionism* (Cambridge: MIT Press, 1988).
46. Finger, "Trade Liberalization."
47. UNCTAD, *Development Report*.
48. Bhagawati, 5.
49. Linder, *Pacific Century* 90.
50. Ibid., 90.
51. See Paul Kennedy, *The Rise and Fall of the Great Powers* (New York: Random House, 1987).
52. Linder, *Pacific Century*, 93.
53. Robert Lawrence, cited in ibid., 95.
54. Economic Planning Agency, Tokyo, 1984, pp. 62–9.
55. Linder, *Pacific Century*, 115.
56. Ibid., 117.
57. Michael Miller, "Big U.S. Semi-Conductors Expected to Sue," *Wall Street Journal*, 1 Oct. 1985.
58. Anthony Solomon, "Checking the Spread of New Xenophobia," *New York Times*, 31 May 1988.
59. Bhagwati, *Protectionism*, 93.
60. Ibid., 75.

10

The Asian Renaissance

> *The rise of the East is a magnificent achievement,*
> *a triumph of the human spirit and will that is in*
> *itself good. It is now up to the West, at least*
> *as much as the East, to ensure that it does not*
> *become injurious.*
>
> —Robert Elegant

The Asian Renaissance

The Asian renaissance adds immeasurably to our store of knowledge concerning how and why countries develop. What has happened on the Pacific Rim is unprecedented and differs substantially from the other "three worlds of development."

Compared to Western industrialized nations, the first and second tiers of the Pacific Rim have advanced in a much shorter period of time. They have done so while lacking resources and colonies; they have moved forward economically without the civil violence that the older Western nations suffered; and they have distributed their new wealth to all strata of their societies. An historic alliance between government and business promoted the changes, avoiding much of the chaos involved in genuinely laissez-faire capitalist expansion.

Unlike the Soviet bloc, the Pacific advance took place in the absence of revolution (as traditionally understood) and in partnership with older capitalistic nations. The social order was not destroyed in Asia but subtly and gradually altered. Indeed, former ruling classes sometimes took the lead in promoting economic progress. In contrast to Russia's suppression of kulaks, the peasants of Japan, Taiwan, Korea, and post-Mao China have gained from the changes. Private enterprises, encouraged and assisted by government, served as the engine of change rather than nationalized industries run by government bureaucrats.

The successful Pacific regions were distinguished from the rest of the Third World by their emphasis on mixed capitalism rather than some form of state socialism, their willingness to adopt foreign ideas and technology, and their relative success in combatting corruption and personalism. While the Asian governments often intervened economically, they did so to build an infrastructure and to correct distortions in the free market. They largely avoided the lures of self-sufficient industrialization, the promises offered by import substitution strategies, and the snares of an anti-dependency path. Unlike Africa, they rewarded proficient farmers, where that was appropriate, rather than ignoring their welfare or herding them into collectives. Unlike Latin America, they launched successful programs of land reform and birth control. Unlike the Middle East, they sponsored secular education and allowed women to enter the work force.

The pragmatic model developed by the Pacific countries offers a dramatic alternative to the brutalities of laissez-faire capitalist development, the crumbling command economies of Eastern Europe, and the stagnation of Africa and Latin America.

In fact, the Pacific Rim now represents a "fourth world" of development emulated in some regions of Latin America, South Asia, Central America, and increasingly, in the former Soviet bloc. This trend is particularly evident in countries such as Thailand, Chile, Costa Rica, and the Ivory Coast that have already forged economic links with the more advanced Asian regions. With Asian as well as European aid and investment flowing into previously Communist countries, we can reasonably anticipate the emergence of new miracle economies in China's Guangdong province, certain parts of Siberia, and countries like Hungary.

As I have argued, a recreation of Asia's example in other parts of the world fortunately does not depend on unique cultural factors, receptive social structures, or particular political systems. If a region encourages entrepreneurial tendencies, follows policies that eliminate obvious structural obstacles, and provides and stable government that is reasonably free of arbitrary dictatorial methods, there is every reason to expect that it too can move forward within the constraints imposed on all nations by world economic conditions.

Culture and the Pacific Model

On a cultural level, reference to the virtues extolled by Confucius does little to explain Asian growth or to predict which other culturally divergent regions may adapt a Pacific strategy and enter a new era of economic growth.

Certainly, some elements in the highly diluted form of Confucianism that prevails in Asia may have proved useful to Pacific leaders in implementing the reconstruction of their societies: its secular rationalism, its high valuation of education attainments, and its glorification of social cohesion.

It must be recognized, however, that other central traits of Confucianism may well have hindered economic change. The Confucian idolization of the cultured gentleman of leisure and its disdain for merchants hardly fits the requirements of an economically active society. A Confucian emphasis on the importance of the family as the central building block of a good society is difficult to reconcile with the prevailing meritocracy of many Pacific nations and their stress on achievement rather than nepotism as a path for advancement. The unquestioning Confucian reverence for hierarchy seems ill-adapted to Pacific nations that must depend upon an infusion of new ideas and innovations, sometimes corruptive of the old hierarchical ways, that are essential for their very survival in a competitive world market.

In truth, a Confucian or Oriental culture—so long treated as an unsurmountable obstacle to economic progress—cannot seriously be considered as the dynamic reason for Asian growth today. Max Weber was wrong at the beginning of the century; neo-Weberians are equally wrong at the end of the century.

It is tempting for some to argue that cultural barriers preclude various areas in the Third World from copying the Asian model. The other-worldliness and fatalism of some traditional religions, the Moslem insistence on excluding women from the workplace or schooling, and the Latin Catholic concern with salvation in the next world hardly encourage a creative and critical spirit of wordly economic enterprise and social mobility.

At this point in history, however, it is wise to withhold a final judgement. After all, Catholic nations from Chile to the Ivory Coast have more or less copied the Pacific model with great success. Predominantly Moslem countries such as Malaysia have consciously followed the Japanese example and prospered. Buddhist Thailand, while still hovering on the third tier of Pacific growth, has surged forward over the last decade. And parts of India and specific villages on the Indian subcontinent have stirred from their long slumber.

Even Hinduism—with its abhorrence of "unreal" worldly change, its rigidly stratified social system, and its belief that *karma* determines that each person must perform tasks ordained by his caste position—is sufficiently ambiguous to allow India the flexibility for progress.

Economic transformations within India have in themselves promoted revisions in traditional culture. The creation of a steel industry, for example, has allowed castes of iron craftsmen to emerge as steel workers in advanced industries. By the simple expedient of changing the entire caste's name, the steel workers have adjusted to a new economic environment and simultaneously maintained vestiges of their religion. The extension of roads to distant villages and the coming of bicycles has allowed untouchables to escape from bondage and given them the means to find jobs in nearby cities. Such apparently minor changes have been more effective than laws passed in New Delhi that free the untouchables from servitude. Similarly, the founding of public schools in many districts has broadened the horizons of women and given them the means to escape male domination.

Indian migrants have assumed a critical role in Southeast Asia, parts of Africa, and portions of the Caribbean. Indians are disproportionately represented as doctors and lawyers, merchants and entrepreneurs in Kenya, Singapore, Malaysia, Guyana, Trinidad, and other areas. The concept of *karma* has not shackled their energies or inhibited their exploration of new worlds. Indeed, for some castes, an energetic pursuit of a commercial role in life fulfills their religious obligations. Who knows? In the century to come, the idea of a predestined *karma* may come to be regarded as the best explanation for Indian dynamism.

The truth is that cultural imperatives do not explain the Pacific Rim's revolution or predict which other areas of the globe may soon match or exceed the Asian miracle. At best, to proclaim the supremacy of culture does not do justice to Asian diversity; at its worst, it is redolent with ethnocentrism.

Social Structure and Asian Growth

Sociologists have long subscribed to one of two enduring positions: Marxists have asserted that the economy, particularly control over the means of production, determines other institutions in a society such as the class structure, the family, religious institutions, the political order, gender differentiation, the educational system, and even science. For the dedicated Marxist, only the arrival of a socialist economy can liberate humans from such other forms of despotism as political dictatorship, the rule of men over women and children, and the tyranny of superstition. The collapse of Marxist myths in Asia and the Soviet bloc has, of course, undermined these convictions. Nonetheless, few would deny the truth of a diluted version of Marxism: the nature and structure and dynamism of an economy vitally affects other social institutions.

A second position, subscribed to by structural-functionalists, posits a grand synthesis between all of the major elements in a social system. Changes in one institution such as religion necessarily involve alterations in other spheres, such as the economy. Similarly, alterations in the economy, such as the swift advance of Asia towards industrialization, require changes in the educational realm to buttress and further economic growth. An exclusion from social status may motivate particular groups— eighteenth-century Quakers in England, Sikhs in India, Chinese in Southeast Asia—to seek out entrepreneurial roles since they could not aspire to higher ranks in the traditional hierarchy of their societies. In general, the structuralists assign an equal or greater role to social rather than to economic factors as the generators of change.

In the Asian context, some observers have attributed Pacific advances to diverse social institutions that predated the era of fantastic economic growth. Some say that Japan's solidarity as a nation and its racial exclusiveness made possible an ethic dedicated to the country's economic superiority, just as it once was conducive to the nation's military expansion. Others contend that the Orient's low evaluation of women allowed the use of female labor in minimally paid and unprotected occupations. Scholars have also maintained that the paternalistic authoritarianism characteristic of some Asian countries made possible economic growth. And observers have argued that Pacific workers, dependent at best on weak trade unions, accepted lower wages in exchange for the opportunity to work and for job security during the initial stages of the Pacific advance. Whatever the merits of these assertions, the most striking features of successful Asian nations was the rapidity with which their social systems changed to meet new economic requirements and challenges, and the ability of their economies to close the gap between rich and poor.

In this light, a position that acknowledges the supreme importance of the political realm best explains the Pacific's epoch of economic growth. The social structure of these nations did not trigger economic change but merely accommodated it. Alterations in social patterns (often deliberately planned by the political elite) were both a stimulant and a response to economic progress introduced by political decisions.

Firm government policies, for example, initiated the process of land reform. The traditional land tenure system of Japan, Korea, and Taiwan as well as the collectives imposed on China by Mao blocked agricultural progress. Once political forces had removed these obstacles and the big land-holding class (or Communist cadres) had lost their overwhelming significance, the peasants responded with a rise in productivity, savings, investment, and rural industry. The resulting improvements paved the way to further development.

In addition, a majority of people in Japan, Taiwan, and Korea severed their ties with rural life and moved into cities. This vast migration took place in one generation and subjected people to all of the influences of urbanization: a move away from the extended family, pervasive exposure to the mass media, new foci for work, and fresh perspectives on authority, time, causation, science, and progress. As the traditional rural structures crumbled, the new urbanities immersed themselves in the privileges, rewards, and tensions of an urban existence.

Educational systems, too, were revamped to meet the requirements of a modern economy. Compulsory schooling provided mass literacy while technical institutes and universities offered more advanced knowledge. The educational system emerged as the single most decisive way of sifting out young people of differing abilities and eventually determining their careers. As merit became a universal standard in Pacific societies, the influence of the family and other social ties was rapidly eroded.

With education extended to virtually all segments of society, the traditional dichotomy between male and female roles also changed. Women began to enter the work force not just as menial laborers but as business administrators, scientists, technocrats, and even legislators. Indeed, in a country such as Singapore, young women began to outnumber young men in such "male" occupations as the law, business, and accounting.

The supposedly "Asian" emphasis upon savings and investment for the future made its appearance only when policy decisions engendered economic stability, high rates of bank interest, and good returns on export-oriented industry. In many Asian societies, savings were low or peasants hoarded what little surplus they had in anticipation of bad times ahead.

With the creation of a reliable banking system, government incentives for savings, fiscal arrangements designed to curb inflation, and special institutions such as Singapore's Central Provident Fund came new and significant inducements to save and invest in productive endeavors. The famed Asian propensity to save emerged *after* the various governments eliminated obstacles to economic growth and stability. These fiscal changes and the people's growing faith in the future broke down the structural dependence of the peasant on the village moneylender.

These examples could be multiplied: for sound economic reasons, the Pacific governments endorsed equality between the sexes, freeing women for participation in their economies. In Korea and Taiwan, political elites realized that the first stages in economic growth required peasant participation and initiated "land to the tiller" programs that would ensure enthusiastic participation. In Singapore, a progressive government policy of creating public housing designed to mix various ethnic groups went far in reducing linguistic, religious, and racial tension and conflict. In Malaysia and Thailand, governments officially welcomed the introduction of foreign ideas and enterprises as stimulants of economic change while, in contrast, Burma closed her doors and retrogressed.

Government initiatives in the Pacific area often ran counter to the wishes of the old social elite, its traditions, and its values. Yet the political leaders of the Pacific nations generally exhibited the determination necessary to free their peoples from centuries of ignorance, poverty, and ill-health. Thus, conscious government policies played the most significant role in transforming old social structures into new societies responsive to the elite's demands for economic growth.

At times, external forces served a vital role in generating social change and in the promulgation of new policies. The early Japanese occupation of East and Southeast Asia was one such promoter of change. Whatever its evils, Japanese militarism stirred or sponsored nationalist sentiments in nations such as Thailand and Indonesia, built an infrastructure of roads and ports in Taiwan, created a rudimentary industrial base in Korea, and everywhere eclipsed the power of the traditional ruling classes and demonstrated the impotency of Western colonialism.

After World War II, American intervention in Japan, Korea, and Taiwan brought about its own series of changes. And the dominance of the American market between 1960 and 1990 inevitably influenced the goals and styles of Asian export production.

Decisions made abroad and the domestic policies they necessitated critically affected the Pacific in many specific areas. MacArthur's policies, for example, molded post-War Japan and significantly directed land reform. American engagements in Korea and Vietnam brought unexpected profits to Japan and provided some of the capital for the nation's industrial expansion. America's aid agencies on Taiwan introduced and financed agricultural change. The loss of the British naval base forced Singapore to seek other sources of revenue than those produced by her entrepôt activities. A subsequent influx of Dutch, French, and American firms shaped the first industrial base of the country and, indirectly, led to the use of English as a common language of instruction and commerce.

By 1990, the Pacific nations, particularly Japan, became major forces interacting among themselves. An infusion of Japanese capital and technology has invigorated Malaysia, Thailand, and Indonesia. Japanese aid programs play a major role in the Philippines. Taiwan, Hong Kong, Korea, and Japan are all instrumental in the development of China. Singapore helps to shape the fate of northern Sumatra, southern Malaysia, and the Chinese coast. Hong Kong capital and refugees have redirected the orientation of Australia.

Thus, a combination of factors—external influences, the responsiveness of internal political elites, wise governmental policies, and the forces unleashed by economic change itself—have induced the dynamism that is now so apparent in the once dormant Pacific nations. Throughout the area, political elites have taken the lead in generating changes that have made their own societies more amenable to economic progress.

The Pacific Strategy

Whatever their political origin—elected officials (in Japan, Malaysia, and Singapore), military officers (in Korea, Indonesia, and Taiwan), an enlightened monarchy (in Thailand), Communist reformers (in post-Mao China), or colonial officers (in Hong Kong)—the political elites of the Pacific Rim chose a common pragmatic path to economic progress.

Politically, as I first advocated in *The Springtime of Freedom*, Pacific leaders (with the sudden and possibly temporary exception of Deng in 1989) have maintained stability while gradually decentralizing the centers of economic power. They have created or nurturered a basic consensus without the total suppression of dissent, and they have undermined the power of traditionalist groups who sought to hold back progress while encouraging a pluralistic economic structure. They have put their faith in the villagers' potential while realizing that tutelage from above may be required. And they have understood that history is not always on their side.

In 1965, when I first put forward this message in *The Springtime of Freedom*, I could rely only on the histories of exceptional nations, such as Denmark, that had long ago followed such policies. Most of the Third World—China under Mao, Indonesia in the throes of revolution, Africa responding to the glittering appeals of charismatic leaders—consumed its own children under the illusion that sacrifice now would bring freedom and abundance sometime in the future. These dreams faded, and with them the hope that unrestrained despotism would produce affluence.

Tempered by experience, new leaders emerged throughout the Third World and particularly in Asia. Men like Lee in Singapore, Prem in Thailand, Mahathir in Malaysia, and Deng in China jettisoned ideology in a very practical search for approaches that would create wealth for their peoples. In 1986, I celebrated the accomplishments of such leaders in *Paths to Progress*, for they had demonstrated viable and palatable solutions to creating a high rate of economic growth, facilitating literacy, and improving health, while maintaining reasonably open political systems under a growing rule of law.

By 1990, as military dictatorships in Taiwan and Korea gave way to new political realities, it became clear that most Asian leaders had recognized that the imposition of untrammeled dictatorship can exert a high economic price. They realized that an uncontrolled authoritarian system would decrease the flow of information from the people to the elite; it could destroy the individual's ability to change things; it could waste national resources on prestigeful largesse and transform the usual social conflicts that always attend economic change into violently fatal battles. The sad records of Mao and Pol Pot, Sukarno and Ne Win provided widely recognized evidence.

Impressed and informed by the mistakes of the past, Asian elites set out to find new paths. They recognized that the fate of developing nations depends primarily on the courage and wisdom of their leaders, and that the quest for bread and freedom could not be brought to a successful conclusion without moral, economic, and political assistance from richer nations. In order to fulfill their missions, the Asian leaders devised a set of pragmatic policies that could well be called "The Pacific Strategy":

• The political elites formed an interlocking directorate between government and business, with the government generally ruling fiscal policy and providing an infrastructure of schools and transportation, ports and utilities, clinics and community meeting halls.

- The various governments encouraged capitalistic enterprise (under whatever name) initially based on labor-intensive, export-oriented production that catered to the comparative advantage of the particular region and, in some cases, sponsored the entrance of multinational corporations to exploit that advantage.
- The Pacific elites pursued an economic strategy that avoided inflation, eased the costs of businesses that sought to enter the world market, fostered a high degree of return to investors, and provided incentives for investment in enterprises that heavily used abundant unskilled labor.
- The governments themselves maintained remarkable stability and, for the most part, avoided arbitrary personalistic decisions. Because of a heavy use of unskilled labor, the income of the poorest segments of these societies dramatically increased, ex-peasants could be readily absorbed into the new industrial economy, and the gap between rich and poor often decreased. This pattern of growth with equity undoubtedly contributed to relative political tranquility. Where reasonably free elections were held as in Japan, Singapore, Malaysia, Thailand, Korea, and Taiwan after 1989, the ruling party remained in power and preserved governmental continuity. This held true for the LDP in Japan, the PAP in Singapore, Umno in Malaysia, and the KMT in Taiwan, because the majority were genuinely satisfied with government policies, the pace of progress, and the condition of life. Although not above manipulating the political process to their own advantage, such parties depended primarily upon their record of success rather than brutal and random suppression as the prime instrument for ensuring political stability.
- At the beginning of economic growth, government sponsored land reforms spurred higher food production and light (privately owned) rural industries. These developments allowed the Pacific countries to move toward industrialization, to accumulate capital in the countryside, and to absorb excess workers no longer needed on the land.
- All of the Pacific governments expansively invested in human capital, notably through their educational systems, encouraged a high rate of savings, attempted to control population expansion, and rewarded their peoples generously in a meritocratic fashion. These social policies undergirded and made possible economic progress.
- Perhaps of most lasting importance, the political and economic leaders of Asia have pursued an eminently flexible policy of modernization. As the Pacific economies have matured, the leaders have managed to shift gears with unequaled speed, peacefully, and usually about five years before the rest of the world has recognized a new economic trend or imperative.

Japan shed "rusting" and labor-intensive industries first to the NICs and now to the third tier of Southeast Asia and the fourth tier of China.

By 1985, Japan concentrated instead on skill-intensive, high-technology industries. By setting world standards for investment in research and new products, Japan took the lead in developing micro-chips and superconductors, aquaculture and advanced automobiles, ceramic industries and laser-beam surgery. Simultaneously, the nation wisely embarked on the production of consumer goods for internal consumption and planned the expenditure of trillions of dollars for building long-neglected parks, recreational areas, and travel sites.

The NICs have exhibited similar resourcefulness. In the 1960s, for example, while most developing countries wasted resources on abortive attempts to build heavy industry and an "import substitution" economy, Singapore concentrated on the light, labor-intensive production of shoes, plywood, textiles, and hand-assembled machine parts. Then, just before China and India became serious competitors, Singapore abandoned its own light industries in favor of multinational assembly operations.

In the 1970s Singapore offered tax incentives, a stable labor situation, and a solid infrastructure to attract foreign corporations possessing the capital, technology, managers, and markets necessary for export industrialization. The swamps of Jurong were transformed into fourteen thousand acres of roads, buildings, railroads, power stations, and a port to handle the requirements of the new industries, and Singapore emerged as the world's third-largest petrochemical center and a major electronics producer.

In the 1980s, with Hong Kong and Taiwan undercutting the computer market, Singapore again consciously changed direction to emphasize telecommunications, aircraft maintenance, medical research, biogenetics, robotics, and the high-speed digital transmission of financial transactions. Singapore's educational system produced the people to staff these new enterprises, and by the late 1980s fully two-thirds of all workers were engaged in service or high-tech industries. Thus, through governmental planning and economic foresight, Singapore was able to move from its status as an entrepôt into labor-intensive industries, then into assembly and light-manufacturing production and, by 1990, into high technology— all within the short time of thirty years.

As steady wage increases have lessened their capacity to compete in markets that reward labor-intensive industries, Taiwan, Hong Kong, and Korea have all moved upscale in productive undertakings and launched into complementary service industries.[1] They have, in addition, shown a marked interest in China, Malaysia, Thailand, and Indonesia as markets, sources of raw materials, and new sites for labor-intensive industrialization. Their freshly created wealth allowed Tokyo and Taipei, Hong Kong and Singapore to take on vital roles as Asian financial centers, investing not only in Third World countries but also in Canada and California, England and Ireland. Newly founded industries in Southeast Asia and China found a ready market for their consumer goods in the more advanced Asian economies. As Eastern European countries open their doors and underdeveloped areas respond to the Pacific strategy, the benefits of Asian expansion will spill over into these areas. The old distinctions between different worlds of development will become increasingly irrelevant as the twenty-first century unfolds.

The Emergence of One World

The overall rise of Asia with unprecedented speed raises the question of whether the great ascent marks the coming together of "one world"—free from poverty, free from autocracy.

At the extremes, two opposing visions of the future dominate intellectual discussion in Asia, America, Europe, and indeed, the Soviet bloc.

Integrationists argue that increasing economic, political, and cultural similarities throughout the world mean the "end of history" as we have known it. An American State Department official, Francis Fukuyama, has contended in *The National Interest* that the decline of fascism and communism as well as changes in the Soviet Union and Asia, signaled the final victory of liberal democracy and some form of capitalism.[3]

Although he noted that Asia might create its own distinctive system, Fukuyama believes that "the triumph of the West, of the *Western idea*, is evident first of all in the total exhaustion of viable systematic alternatives to Western liberalism."[4] He asserts that this phenomenon has prompted changes in the intellectual climates of China and the Soviet Union. In addition, it extends to "the ineluctable spread of consumerist Western culture in such diverse contexts as the peasant markets and color television sets so omnipresent throughout China . . . the Beethoven piped into Japanese department stores, and the rock music enjoyed alike in Prague, Rangoon, and Teheran." Fukuyama contends that "anyone familiar with the outlook and behavior of the new technocratic elite now governing China knows that Marxism and ideological principle have become virtually irrelevant as guides to policy."[5]

From the point of view of Soviet officials, as Daniel Patrick Moynihan has reported, their deepest concern is with the economic promise and threat of Asia, not ideology. They are wary about "the widening gulf between the Soviet Union and the advanced capitalist nations. . . . They were talking of Korea, Taiwan, Singapore, Coolie labor, Asian hordes. Of a sudden flooding of world markets with micro-circuitry whilst Soviet Russia was left peddling fish eggs and furs, the trading goods of a hunter-gatherer society."[6]

Other writers partially accepted Fukuyama's thesis, derived from Hegel, but disagree that mankind has truly reached an "end to history" and international conflict. Clearly, Gertrude Himmelbarb has noted, the idea of liberal democracy has not become universalized.[7] Fukuyama agreed that it would take a long time for China and the Soviet Union to become full-fledged liberal democracies. Moynihan has commented on the continuing importance of ethnic conflicts throughout the world.[8] And Stephen Sestanovich considers the issue of nationalism as unresolved.[9] Discussing the Soviet Union and the United States, Daniel Bell has said, "I don't think that there is a convergence between the two societies."[10] He cites "extraordinary civilizational differences," particularly the lack of a "civil society" in the Soviet Union: voluntary associations, an independent church, trade unions, etc. He regards such a civil society as a necessary "political setting for a market economy."[11] The same argument applies to China.

At an opposite pole from Fukuyama are the *rejectionists* who believe that "Japanese and other East Asian societies are creating a completely new form of polity and economy."[12] S.N.G. Davies, for example, notes that the rejectionist position—shared by Lee in Singapore, Mahatir in Malaysia, and Nakasone in Japan—involves the assumption that the value of individual autonomy is absent in Asia and that a "group ethic" dominates the region. Davies argued that such societies place a greater emphasis on family life, social order, and the supremacy of authority than the West's supposedly anarchic individualism. Davies reported that capitalism in East Asia appears under an ideological guise where "consensus is seen as the supreme value, not conflict; cooperation with the model of social interaction, not competition; the acceptance of central and authoritative direction by government the basis for social and economic progress, not a pluralistic and conflictual pork-barrel politics."[13] Davies remained reasonably skeptical but argued that communalism in Asia seemed to dominate individualistic strains. Japanese businessmen with whom I talked largely agreed, but one, a forty-year-old stock-broker, entertained the once unthinkable idea that he would desert his company if another one offered a higher salary.

In the context of Indonesia and Sri Lanka, as well as ancient China and India, Nathan Keyfitz argues even more strongly that "unity, wholeness, was and is the supreme virtue."[14] In Indonesia, he said, harmony and cooperation supposedly guide politics. The same was true of the economy. Although that often-invoked ideal theoretically guided Indonesia, the fact is that revolutions have erupted from time to time in Sumatra, the Celebes, Timor, and West Irian. This appeal to unanimity allowed both Sukarno and Suharto to suppress dissent. Nonetheless, Keyfitz contends that the average Indonesian assumes "that the social order is fragile, and once it is weakened anything could happen. The opposite of the existing order is not some alternative order but chaos. Individuals would run amok; whole populations could take to senseless violence."[15]

Indeed, in Indonesia, a brief flirtation with parliamentary democracy resulted in seventeen governments in five years. Later autocratic regimes bloodily suppressed various rebellions in Indonesia, taking at least 500,000 lives. Quite correctly, Keyfitz asserts, such rebellions, as well as pervasive corruption by the economic elite, "by no means lessens the need for consensus."[16] He concludes that a presumed Asian preference for unanimity and social cohesion provides the only viable alternative to chaos or the use of naked force.[17] Yet, how is this consensus to be achieved? By government slogans? By economic growth? Or by the usual method of "naked force"? Total disorder and brutal repression, not consensus, seemed the rule in post-independence Indonesia.

In spite of an assumed Asian penchant for consensus, the actual creation of national ideologies for Asian nations has proven to be a difficult undertaking. Mao tried a Cultural Revolution and it ended an abysmal failure. Suharto's Indonesia created its "Pancasilia," a pithy collection of five vague ideals to which every Indonesian—Islamic or Christian, Javanese or Sumatran—is supposed to adhere. The creed did not stop corruption in the ruling class or halt insurrections in Timor and Irian. Malaysia propagated its "Runkun Negara," a dictum of Malay virtues that the Chinese and Indians ignored, and Malays have virtually forgotten.[18]

Singapore presents the classic case of a government that attempted to inculcate its diverse citizens with a common core of values. In 1982, Lee's regime announced that Confucianism would be taught as moral instruction in secondary schools. Indoctrination in the core values of Confucianism would presumably provide a corrective to such "Western" attributes as materialism, hedonism, and individualism. Lee feared that the cosmopolitan nature of Singapore would breed "excessive" individualism. He stressed the idea that the survival of society was of far greater importance than individual interests. For him, the family represented the basic unit of society.

President Wee Kim Wee defined Confucian core values in 1989 as "placing society above self, upholding the family as the basic building block of society, resolving major issues through consensus instead of contention, and stressing racial and religious tolerance and harmony."[19]

Few quarreled with such general ideals, but Singaporean skeptics feared that the supremacy of supposedly Confucian values (as well as the Mandarin language) in the schools was merely a cloak for Chinese chauvinism and political autocracy. The critics asserted that such policies imposed a fake ethic on the 24 percent of the population who were not Chinese (and even on those Chinese who were Christians or Daoists).

Further, the critics said, Confucianism had always served the interests of autocratic rule and encouraged unthinking obedience. Indeed, as *The Straits Times* editorialized, "Singapore is pointed out as an example of a desirable style of leadership, or maximum government, where the populace instinctively appeals to the government for solutions to their problems."[20] They feared that Confucianism would merely serve to reinforce authoritarian rule and that "it may turn out to be a convenient basis for labelling individuals or groups who do not share the ideology as 'anti-national.' "[21]

Indeed Singaporeans—like the early Japanese and other Asian populations—wanted "to have it both ways, to be modern and traditional at once, to modernize, but not Westernize."[22] Would this prove possible? Or would a new "one world" inevitably emerge? The answer differs in three major realms: the economy, the polity, and the culture.

Convergence in the Economic Sector

At the end of the twentieth century, the increased globalization of national economies meant a convergence of interests, forms of production, and even styles of management between East and West.

Although a pronounced trend, this process was hardly inevitable (as some determinists believed). Both political events and a possible world recession curtailed the prospects for modernization.

In China, political repression forced foreign businesses to reassess their future. In 1989, Hopewell Holdings of Hong Kong halted work on two coal-fueled stations; Mitsubishi Motors drastically slowed its China-based truck production; Gaz de France suspended its construction of a Chinese pipeline network.[23]

Yet, because China's share in the Asian Economy was so great (25 percent in 1989 of intra-Asia trade) and because foreign companies had invested some $11.5 billion in China between 1979 and 1990, an indefinite cut-off in foreign contacts was unlikely.

In Korea, however, precisely because of the "consumerism" fostered by its dynamic development, the country was in danger of losing its comparative edge in world trade. Between 1988 and 1990, strikes led to wage increases that averaged more than 20 percent a year,[24] and exports fell drastically. As pent-up consumer demand made up for lost exports, social scientists worried whether Korea could pay its bills. In 1989, for example, the domestic demand for Korean cars, two million a year, exceeded the foreign demand.[25]

Although growing consumerism at home or political instability could temporarily derail the Asian economies, the longrun trend is clear: the Pacific region has decisively left behind its former colleagues in the underdeveloped world.[26]

Taking the industrialized countries as a whole, the degree of trade interdependence increased through good times and bad at an approximate rate of 2.8 percent a year.[27] Direct foreign investments by multinational corporations in developing countries as well as industrialized ones steadily increased.[28] Cross-investments and joint production ventures also become increasingly common and resulted in "incestuous cross-country relationships."[29] "Offshore production" by foreign affiliates for export became a dominant trend for corporations in the United States,[30] Sweden,[31] and Switzerland.[32]

The interdependence of the world economy was a two-way street. In 1988, for example, General Motors owned 42 percent of Isuzu of Japan, had a fifty-fifty arrangement with Toyota to produce cars in California, controlled 5.3 percent of Suzuki stock, and built a joint venture plant with Suzuki. In turn, Isuzu and Fuji created an assembly plant in Indiana with General Motors supplying major components for the Isuzu vehicle.[33]

In Europe, a similar Asian-Western synthesis of productive facilities grew astonishingly. In 1984, Japan invested $1 billion in Europe; by 1989, that figure jumped to $9 billion annually.[34] Great Britain benefited in 1989 alone by Toyota's creation of a $1.2 billion auto plant in the Midlands and

Fukitsu's building of a $680 million semiconductor factory in Northeast England. Simultaneously, Nissan announced an expansion of its plant in Newcastle from 60,000 cars a year to 400,000.[35]

As I already noted, interdependence within the Asian region also grew. In 1989, fueled by political uncertainty in China, Hong Kong capitalists quadrupled their investments in Thailand while Taiwanese entrepreneurs doubled their investments there.[36] Meanwhile, Singapore created a low-cost but high-technology manufacturing center in southern Malaysia.[37]

Even an advocate of dependency theory such as James Mittleman argued that "underdeveloped countries must learn to exploit international market forces and to hitch them to the domestic economy."[38] He added, "just as production is increasingly international, struggles in various parts of the global economy must be intertwined. As the ideological struggles intensify, moralizing about the evils of exploitation should not replace sober analysis of the crisis."[39]

Highly protectionist countries such as France and Italy began reconsidering their policies. Receiving only 1 percent of Japanese foreign investment in 1989, Italy dropped its quotas on forty-two Asian-made products in the hope of improving economic relations.[40]

In fact, economic interdependence often brought mutual advantages to all concerned. As Staffan Linder observed, "The scope for fruitful exchange increases, there are wider markets and better sources of goods and services; capital and investment opportunities (both domestic and foreign) are more plentiful; there are new technologies to use, new methods to emulate, more competition, and the stimulus of faster feedback."[41]

The interaction between Asian and Western economies had a long history. For centuries, the transfer of technology went from East to West.[42] Indeed, Linder noted, "The westernization of Asia was preceeded by the still more significant contributions made by Asia to Europe. Present-day interdependencies are merely a continuation of this process."[43]

The further globalization of economics had a far-reaching impact. As Clark Kerr demonstrated, industrialization entailed a growing convergence among various societies in their use of technology, their ways of mobilizing resources, and their patterns of work.[44]

Although recognizing that "every land moves towards its future in terms of its own past, its own institutions and traditions,"[45] Kerr foresaw an increasing similarity in the use of science, the nature of economic rewards, the dominance of bureaucracy in industrial societies, the preeminence of managers, and a high degree of planning. This drive toward "convergence,'' Kerr and others maintained, was a predictable result of the fact that industrialization required common skills, attitudes, and behavior.

An example of the necessary attributes involved in the process of industrialization occurred in Egypt where I once worked. The Fiat Co. built a steel plant and an automobile factory to produce the Misr car. They recruited workers from the peasantry around Helwan. The peasants often used the word "bokhra"—meaning everything from "tomorrow," to "immediately" to "next month." In other words, they did not possess the concept of precise timing required in an automobile factory.

After training, an Egyptian peasant was promoted to supervise the coke ovens. One day, I witnessed the Egyptian asking his Italian superior for permission to go to the bathroom. The Italian said, "When will you return?" The Egyptian answered "bokhra." Believing that the peasant meant "immediately," the Italian assented.

An hour later, the Italian saw smoke emerging from the Coke plant. The worker had not come back and the coke oven had burned out. It cost 2 million Egyptian pounds to repair. The damage resulted from a simple misunderstanding, but the lesson was clear: people had to alter even their concept of time if they wanted to operate a factory in an efficient manner.

Industrialization depended, of course, on unique historical factors, culture, and the governing elite. Political ideologies might well remain unchanged as the actual industrial organization of different societies proceeded toward uniformity. Capitalist societies tended to stress productivity and consumption while, until the late 1980s, socialist societies emphasized equality and social welfare. In 1983, Kerr maintained, "What the West seems to have, efficiency and freedom, dissidents in the East want. What the East seems to have, equality and stability, dissidents in the West demand."[46]

Nonetheless, since that time, both socialist and Asian societies have moved increasingly toward market-oriented policies, allocated an important role to independent managers, and in the process, exhibited greater ethnic and political tensions. China's progress has suffered from political repression while the future of reforms in the Soviet Union remains in doubt.

In many ways, capitalist societies have also moved closer to the socialist model by restricting pure laissez-faire competition, providing greater social welfare, and engaging in long-term planning.

For good or evil, the century has been marked by a trend towards mixed economies and economic uniformity produced by industrialization. Some scholars, notably Colin Turnbull, lament the death of old cultures.[47] And, as Peter Berger noted, the coming of modernity "seriously weakened those definitions of reality that previously made [the] human condition easier to bear."[48]

Even Fukuyama, the prophet of "an end to history," predicted that the future would be "a very sad time." He commented that "In the post historical period there will be neither art nor philosophy, just the perpetual caretaking of the museum of human history."[49]

By some standards, the costs of economic modernization may be great. Lee in Singapore, Mahatir in Malaysia, and nationalists in Japan tried to repair the cultural damage and restore a real or imagined tradition. Nonetheless, the coming of modern science, technology, medicine, and education in Asia increased the length of man's life, decreased infant mortality and adult illiteracy, opened new perspectives, and provided options for both social and geographical mobility.

Pacific growth provided a powerful "demonstration effect" in other regions, suggesting invigorating new approaches. The success of market, mixed economies in Asia entailed the growth of new sources of capital, new technologies, and new strategies that could be of aid to many nations.

Whether the globalization of the world economy and the growing commonality in the industrialization process will result in basic political alterations in Asia remained in question.

Democracy in the Future?

Economic development, Chalmers Johnson has pointed out, creates a more "pluralistic" society where a wide spectrum of interest groups compete for power. The progress of the economy depends on satisfying the desires of these varied groups. Pluralism may lead to liberalization—a greater realm for a free press, a free judiciary, and free expression. In turn, according to Johnson, liberalization *may* turn into democracy (access of the citizen to the corridors of power), but it may just as easily create the strains that reproduce authoritarianism.[50]

In Asia, some trends in the late 1980s suggested that the deep yearning for social order and cohesion would lead to a continuation of the perceived Asian willingness to submit to authoritarian rule. China exhibited few signs of retreating from its form of totalitarian rule without a major struggle. Lee in Singapore reasserted his control over dissenters. Mahatir in Malaysia tried to crush his opponents. Indonesia endured military rule. According to Davies,[51] Keyfitz,[52] and to some degree, Lucian Pye,[53] this was the normal course for traditionally authoritarian Asian societies. Keyfitz contended that underlying traditions taught that "within the deepest layers of peoples' minds, pluralism would indeed lead to chaos."[54]

Did tradition dictate the perpetuation of authoritarian power? Some countervailing forces in Asia indicate that this is not the necessary fate of the Pacific Rim.

Economic modernization in Asia, with its concentration on human capital and education, created new groups of engineers, scientists, business leaders, lawyers, and technocrats who are necessary to the economy. They could, of course, be bought off or simply crushed by a sufficiently powerful regime. *If*, however, further economic development was to proceed, these new interest groups had to be accommodated within the old structure.

In fact, population pressures, shortages of land, and the renewed expectations of their peoples pushed the Asian nations, including China, down the road of economic modernization.

In China, for example, the government wanted to continue the process of economic modernization even in the political turmoil of the late 1980s. However much they may have desired it, party conservatives could not ignore the technocrats, local enterprise managers, "rich" peasants, and university students who had a direct interest in further economic reform and political liberalization.

Further, certain legal and political changes—decentralization of industry, bankruptcy laws, direct elections of city and university officials—had already been put in motion. They could be reversed, but only at great economic cost. Thus, even in retrogressive times, it seems likely that the liberalizing effects of economic and technological advancement will bring about a greater measure of reform and decentralization.

Deng in China, Lee in Singapore, and Park in Korea had, quite inadvertently, built a pluralistic social structure with depositories of power independent of the group that controlled the government. As their economies became more complex and dependent on educated people, tendencies towards a politically more open order were created. This development made it improbable that aspiring leaders would reverse the pace of their robust economies by attempting to reimpose tyranny.

In Taiwan—once the exiled home of the ruthless dictator Chiang Kai-shek—the forces of modernization produced a relatively liberal social order. I found in 1988 that 239 fledging newspapers published freely, thirty-four competitive political parties had emerged, the government allowed peaceful demonstrations of opposition, and people spoke their minds openly. In Korea, opposition parties controlled parliament in what was once a military dictatorship. In Singapore, George Yeo Yong Boon, an influential general and finance minister, said "Singapore cannot become a great nation in this information age without a lively democracy."[55] In Japan, the Socialist Party had an imminent opportunity to take over the government. In Thailand, highly competitive groups—bureaucrats, the press, allies of the monarchy, businessmen, the military, and the intelligentsia—juggled for power in a free environment.

William Overholt's observations about Thailand applied to much of Asia and, indeed, to other developing areas:

> Competition among institutions creates alternative power bases for individuals and groups. The competitive pursuit of different goals by different institutions, and widespread recognition that such competition is legitimate, creates space in which individuals and groups pursue their own choices. By limiting the extent to which any institution can circumscribe choices, it creates freedom.[56]

This movement of most of Asia away from autocracy offered substantial hope that the forces unleashed by economic development would lead to political liberalization.

Sporadically, as in China and the Philippines, the demand for greater liberalization boiled over into violence. Usually, however, the evolution took place peacefully. As the Trilateral Commission, an influential group of American, Japanese, and European statesmen observed, "Without such political evolution, economic progress cannot continue for another two decades as it has over most of the last 30 years. *This is the central challenge for the region over the next decades*. Political structures and institutions must now catch up to the economic achievements of the region, before the cushion afforded by economic growth erodes.[57]

Cultural Change?

In the long run, the coming of factories and schools, televisions and motorcycles, clinics and newspapers undermined traditional cultures in Asia.

In spite of frantic efforts to revive Confucianism in Singapore, a Malay ethic in Malaysia, or Shintoism in Japan, Asian societies have been invaded by a world culture that particularly attracted young people.

In Japan, for example, Robert Christopher, an astute observer of Japanese character, noted in 1989 that there were remarkable changes in attitudes and behavior from merely a decade ago. Fathers have begun to assume the wife's role in child care. Individualism, "doing your own thing," has gained in popularity particularly among *shinjinrui*, a "new breed" of young and affluent people. Half of all married women hold full-time jobs and the divorce rate has soared. Young people have begun to change their jobs at will, and only 26 percent of white collar workers believed that they should sacrifice their outside life for the good of the company.[58] The Ministry of Education imports 3,000 teachers of English annually to "internationalize" Japanese culture.[59]

In contrast to a frenetic devotion to work that once pervaded Japan, corporations in 1988 spent $34 billion on entertainment, "a sum roughly equivalent to the entire gross national product of Ireland."[60] Undoubtedly, Christopher observed, "the most pregnant of these changes is an erosion of the group ethic that has traditionally dominated Japanese life and behavior."[61]

Throughout Asia, new social relationships, new occupations, and new political influences increasingly replaced old loyalties. Modernization in Asia required wrenching changes in man's perception of causality, his concept of progress, his view of nature, his sense of time, and his relation to the old social order.

Cultural interaction between East and West worked both ways across the Pacific. Joel Kotkin and Yoriko Kishimoto predicted an American resurgence in the Pacific era because Asian migrants would invigorate America with entrepreneurial skills and open a fresh network of relationships with Japan, Taiwan, China, Singapore, and Korea.[62] Asian immigrants, they argued, were "children of America's open system" and "represent the most crucial asset, the key ingredient for prevailing over an ascendent Asia."[63] Kotkin and Kishimoto contended that "the large infusion of Vietnamese and Chinese has been essential for the staffing of high-technology manufacturing plants in the Silicon Valley companies."[64] They foresaw that California—"the most multiethnic, Pacific-oriented region of the world—presents the face of America abroad."[65] Indeed, another observer, Kenichi Ohmae predicted "the Californization of the Free World."[66]

Nonetheless, elements of the old culture survive in Asia or are actively strengthened. Perhaps disturbed by the rapid pace of economic modernization or the cultural void in their lives, people often seek to identify themselves with their ethnic group, their traditional religion, or a new political faith.

Ethnic categories remain strong in Japan where Ainus and Koreans are despised by many. For most Japanese, foreigners remain outside the pale. An ingrained ethnocentrism even led one prime minister to proclaim that Japan had been superior for 2,000 years because "no foreign races" had been allowed into the country. In turn, other Asian societies, particularly China, evince concern that a form of Japanese "neo-imperialism" might emerge in the future. Throughout Southeast Asia, hostility towards Chinese minorities threatens burgeoning economies. Economic modernization has failed to eradicate many of the ethnic divisions.[67]

Religious tensions also infect parts of Asia and make the coming of "one world" a tumultuous process. Both Malaysia and Indonesia suffer from a resurgence of Islamic fundamentalism that threatens the unity of these countries. In Singapore, Lee's attacks fell disproportionately on Christians who, nonetheless, gained adherents. Korean Christians also increased their strength and were often in the forefront of challenges to the establishment.

Politically, some people turned to socialism as a faith that provided a sense of community and meaning, as well as a "science" that predicted future happiness. As Peter Berger pointed out, the first stages of modernization often produced anomie and a feeling of homelessness. "Modernity has accomplished many far-reaching transformations," he argued, "but it has not fundamentally changed the finitude, fragility and mortality of the human condition."[68]

For hundreds of millions, the ideology of socialism in Asia temporarily filled people with enthusiasm and elan. By offering a hope for the future, Sukarno's Indonesian socialism, Mao's "great leap forward," experiments in Burmese socialism, and the slogans of Ho Chi Minh in Indo-China gave meaning to life for many. When vibrant new societies failed to blossom and their economies stagnated, however, leaders in East and Southeast Asia turned to more pragmatic policies: a move toward free-market economies, a recognition that new technologies might offer more than old ideologies, and a greater openness to the ideas that flowed back and forth across the Pacific.

Thus, as the century ends, old cultures live on side by side with modern technology and new political styles. This melange was nowhere more evident than in the once-remote hill towns of Thailand, where monks garbed in saffron silks learn English from well-thumbed books, Japanese motorcycles and American rock 'n roll tunes blare in the town squares, and the girls in Dior dresses (imported from Taiwan) mix with boys in leather jackets and blue jeans. The Thai sun, bright red and huge, sets equably on ruined pagodas atop a mountain peak and the jet port that lies below in the Golden Triangle. East has met West and, for good or evil, no one will ever be able to separate them.

Notes

1. Of the NICs, Korea was the slowest to move into high technology. Its dependence on high-wage, capital-intensive industries may well cost it a competitive edge in the years ahead.
2. These troubled economies will probably benefit the most from Western European investment, aid, and advice, particularly from Germany. The opening of the Soviet Union and Eastern Europe could divert some West European capital away from the Pacific Rim since the former Communist countries offer the advantages of proximity and a well-trained work force.
3. Francis Fukuyama, "The End of History," *The National Interest*, no. 16 (Summer 1989).
4. Ibid., 3.
5. Ibid., 11.
6. Daniel Patrick Moynihan, *The National Interest*, no. 16 (Summer 1989) no. 16: 30.
7. Gertrude Himmelfarb, *The National Interest* (Summer 1989): 25.
8. Moynihan, *National Interest*.
9. Stephen Sestanovich, *The National Interest* (Summer 1989) no. 16: 33.
10. Daniel Bell, "Reflections of a Bourgeois Menshevik," *Society* (Sept./October 1989): 13.
11. Ibid.
12. S.N.G. Davies, "The Capitalism/Socialism Debate in East Asia," *Society* (March/April 1989): 39. See also Lucian Pye, *Asian Power and Politics* (Cambridge: Harvard University Press, 1985).
13. Ibid., 33.
14. Nathan Keyfitz, "The Asian Road to Democracy," *Society* (Nov./Dec. 1988): 71.
15. Ibid., 73.
16. Ibid., 71.
17. Ibid., 76.
18. N. Balakrhisnan, "Pledge of Allegiance," *Far Eastern Economic Review*, 9 Feb. 1989.
19. Wee Kim Wee, Singapore Parliament, 9 Jan. 1989.
20. "Confucianism and Democracy," editorial in *Straits Times*, Singapore, 1 Aug. 1988.
21. Balakrhisnan, "Pledge," 34.
22. Lynn Pan, "Playing the Identity Card," *Far Eastern Economic Review*, 9 Feb. 1989, 30.
23. Nina McPherson and Scott Savitt, "China's Self-Inflicted Economic Wounds," *Billion* (Aug. 1989).

24. "The Korean Struggle to Capture Lost Successes," *Billion* (Aug. 1989).
25. Ibid.
26. See S. Linder, *The Pacific Century* (Stanford: Stanford University Press, 1985).
27. Michael Michaely, "Exports and Growth: An Empirical (1977): Investigation," *Journal of Development Economics* 4 (1977): 49–53.
28. Jagdish Bragwati, *Protectionism* (Cambridge: MIT Press, 1988) 74.
29. Ibid., 75.
30. Robet E. Lipsey and Irving Kravitz, "The Competitiveness and Comparative Advantage of U.S. Multinationals, 1957–1983," NBER Working Paper 2051, 1986.
31. Magnus Blomstron, *Swedish Multinationals Abroad* (New York: NBER, 1986).
32. Silvio Borner, *Internationalization of Industry* (Berlin: Springer-Verlang, 1986).
33. "Mixing Cultures on the Automobile Assembly Line," *New York Times*, 5 June 1988.
34. Japanese Ministry of Finance, April 1989.
35. Steven Greenhouse, "Europe's Agonizing Over Japan," *New York Times*, 30 April 1989, 3.
36. *The Economist*, 26 Aug. 1989.
37. Ibid.
38. James Mittleman, *Out From Underdevelopment* (New York: St. Martin's Press, 1988), 169. Mittleman contended that other developing countries had little to learn or gain from Japan and the NICs. Among other reasons, he cited the absence of land reform in other areas, a lack of contact with the Japanese market, a drought in international aid, and an unwillingness to open markets. I examine these arguments in chapter eight.
39. Ibid., 169.
40. *The Economist*, n. 36.
41. Linder, *Pacific Century* 70.
42. Ibid., 73.
43. Ibid., 71.
44. Clark Kerr, *The Future of Industrial Societies* (Cambridge: Harvard University Press, 1983).
45. Ibid., 23.
46. Ibid., 96.
47. Colin Turnbull, *The Lonely African* (New York: Simon and Schuster, 1962).
48. Peter Berger, Brigitte Berger, and Hansfeld Kellner, *The Homeless Mind* (New York: Random House, 1973).
49. Fukuyama, "End of History," 18.
50. Chalmers Johnson, "South Korean Democratization," The *Pacific Review* 2, no. 1 (1989).
51. Davies, "Debat in East Asia."
52. Keyfitz, "Road to Democracy."
53. Lucian Pye, *Asian Power and Politics* (Cambridge: Harvard University Press, 1985).
54. Keyfitz, "Road to Democracy," 76.
55. George Yeo Yong Boon, quoted in *Far Eastern Economic Review* (Sept. 1989): 122.
56. William Overholt, "Thailand: a Moving Equilibrium," *Pacific Review* 1, no. 1 (1988).
57. Richard Holbrooke, Roderick MacFarquhar, and Kazuo Nukazawa, *East Asia in Transition* (New York: Trilateral Commission, 1988), 51.

58. Japanese Productivity Center, 1989.
59. Japanese Ministry of Education, 1989.
60. Robert Christopher, "The Japanese Mind Revisited," *Billion* (Aug. 1989).
61. Ibid., 81.
62. Joel Kotkin and Yoriko Kishimoto, *The Third Century* (New York: Crown Publishers), 1988.
63. Ibid., 63.
64. Ibid., 177.
65. Ibid., 228.
66. Kenichi Ohmae, *Triad Power* (New York: Free Press, 1985), xxvi.
67. See Moynihan, *National Interest*.
68. See Berger et al., "Homeless Mind."

Annotated Bibliography

The literature on the East Asian "miracle" and its implications for other developing regions has become so vast that it would require a separate volume to do justice to it. I have included here only those books and articles that I have found most significant. Marxist, "dependency theory," and "world systems" literature has been largely omitted since the facts of Pacific growth so obviously contradict these writings.

Abegglen, James. "The Fast Pace of Asian Change." *Tokyo Business Today* (Jan. 1989). A good account of Asian growth by a noted expert.

Adshead, S.A.M. *China in World History*. London: Macmillan, 1988. A fine history of China's relations with the outside world.

Adshead, S.A.M. "Mao to Modernity: China Joins the World Order?" *Pacific Review* 2, no. 3 (1989). An instructive analysis of factional battles within China.

Aikman, David *Pacific Rim*. Boston: Little Brown, 1986. A vivid description of various countries within the Pacific Basin.

Ajami, Fouad. "The Fate of Nonaligned Nations." *Foreign Affairs* (Summer 1982).

Alagappa, Muthia, ed. *In Search of Peace*. Kuala Lumpur, Malaysia: ISIS, 1988. A thoughtful anthology on conflict reduction in the Pacific.

Amnesty International. *China: Violations of Human Rights*. London: AI Publications, 1985. Documents curtailments on political and cultural expression.

Andaya, Barbara Watson, and Leonard Y. Andaya. *A History of Malaysia*. London: Macmillan, 1982. The standard history on the subject.

Andrews, John. "Singapore: Lee's Creation and Legacy." *Far Eastern Economic Review*, 22 Nov. 1988. An excellent description of the city-state.

Asia Year Book, Hong Kong. An annual anthology listing basic statistics.

Awanohara, Susumu. "Japan and East Asia: Towards a New Division of Labor." *Pacific Review* 2, no. 3 (1989). Points to the rise of regional cooperation in Asia.

Belassa, Bela, et al. *Development Strategies in Semi-Industrial Economics*. Baltimore: Johns Hopkins Press, 1982. An incisive collection of articles on the topic.

Baran, Paul. *The Political Economy of Growth*. (New York: Monthly Review Press, 1956. A dated but still classic statement of Marxist faith. Useful for its discussion of India.

Barnett, A. Doak, and Ralph N. Clough, eds. *Modernizing China*. Boulder: Westview Press, 1985. An excellent anthology on the problems and opportunities confronting China.

Bauer, Peter. *Rhetoric and Reality*: Cambridge: Harvard University Press, 1984. A vigorous defense of capitalism in developing nations.

Berger, Peter. *The Capitalist Revolution*. New York: Basic Books 1986. An outstanding analysis of capitalism, using East Asia as a prominent example.

Berger, Peter, and Hsin-Huang Michael Hsiao, eds. *In Search of an East Asian Development Model*. New Brunswick and Oxford: Transaction Books, 1986. A fine anthology of articles explaining Asian growth, with particularly excellent contributions by Peter Berger and Gustav Papanek.

Bergsten, Fred. "What to Do about the U.S.-Japan Economic Conflict." *Foreign Affairs* (Summer 1982).

Bergsten, Fred, and William Cline. *Trade Policy in the 1980s*. Washington, D.C.: Institute for International Economics, 1982. A discussion of world trade problems and protectionism.

Bhagwati, Jagdish. *Protectionism*. Cambridge: MIT press, 1988. A distinguished analysis of the perverse effects of protectionism.

Bonavia, David. *The Chinese*. New York: Lippincott, 1980. A well-written summary of Chinese character and events.

Bong, Chew soon. "Successful Economic Policies." Taipei, Chung-Hua Institution, 1988. A fine history of strategies that worked in Asia.

Borown, Ian. *The Elite and the Economy in Siam*. Singapore: Oxford University Press, 1988. A fine history of the early modernization of Thailand.

Bradley, William, et al. "Thailand: Domino by Default?" Athens, OH: Ohio University Center for International Studies, 1978. An interesting analysis of Thailand's weaknesses.

Breslin, Shavn. "China in Crisis." *Pacific Review* 2, no. 3, 1989. Discusses the influence of various factions within China after the 1989 events.

Broad, Robin and John Cavanaugh. "No More NICs." *Foreign Policy* (Fall 1988). An argument that world conditions will not allow the transformation of any more developing countries into industrialized ones.

Brugger, Bill. *China: Liberation and Transformation*. Princeton: Princeton University Press, 1981. A discussion of China after revolution.

Buss, Andreas E., *Max Weber in Asian Studies*. Leiden: E.J. Bull, 1986. A discussion of Weber's contributions.

Butterfield, Fox. *China*. London: Hadden and Stoughton, 1982. A well-written description of China under Mao.

Chandra-Sehkar, Scripati. *Red China*. New York: Praeger, 1961. An early, unbiased report on Mao's China.

Cheung, Stephen N.S. "Will China Go Capitalist?" London: Institute of Economic Affairs, 1982. Early reforms in China under Deng.

Chi, Yan-Peng. "Towards a Theoretical Explanation of Taiwan's Development with Decreasing Inequality." Taipei: Chung-Hua Institution, 1988. A convincing analysis of Taiwan's growth.

Ching, Frank. "The Emergence of Greater China." *Billion* (Jan. 1989). An interesting speculation about the possibility of a reunion among China, Hong Kong, and Taiwan.

Christopher, Robert. *The Japanese Mind*. New York: Simon and Schuster, 1983. Emphasizes the group loyalty of the Japanese.

Cima, Ronald J. "Vietnam in 1988: The Brink of Renewal." *Asian Survey* 29 (1989).

Cline, William R. "Can the East-Asian Model of Development Be Generalized?" *World Development* (Feb. 1982). A thoughtful analysis of a difficult question.

Coombs, Philip. *The World Crisis in Education*. New York: Oxford University Press, 1985. A general explanation of the educational problems facing the Third World.

Davies, S.N.G. "The Capitalism/Socialism Debate in East Asia." *Society* (March/April 1989).

Denison, E., and W.K. Chung. *How Japan's Economy Grew so Fast*. Washington, D.C.: Brookings Institution, 1976. An early explanation of Japan's rise to affluence.

Donowaki, Mitsuro. "The Pacific Basin Community: The Evolution of a Concept." *Speaking of Japan* (March 1981).

Dore, Ronald, ed. *Aspects of Social Change in Modern Japan*. Princeton: Princeton University Press, 1973. A balanced view of the Japanese "miracle."

Dore, Ronald. *Taking Japan Seriously*. Stanford: Stanford University Press, 1987. A challenging description of some of the lessons that Europe and America could learn from Japan.

Drysdale, John. *Singapore's Struggle for Success*. Singapore: Times Books, 1984. An admiring portrait of Singapore.

The Economist Intelligence Unit. *Towards the Pacific Century*. EIU Special Report no. 137, London, 1983. A early account of the Pacific basin's expansion.

Edwards, Michael. *Asia in the Balance*: Baltimore: Penguin Books, 1962. An early but still relevant account of Asia's influence.

Elegant, Robert. *Pacific Destiny*. New York: Crown, 1990. An exciting narrative of Asia.

Emmott, Bill. "The Limits of Japanese Power," *Pacific Review* 2, no. 3 (1989). Argues that Japan's capital surplus has peaked.

Esman, Milton. *Administration and Development in Malaysia*. Ithaca: Cornell University Press, 1972. An excellent description of overcoming problems in Malaysia.

Fei, John C.H. *Growth with Equity: The Taiwan Case*. London: Oxford University Press, 1979. A fine statement describing Taiwan's ascent.

Feuctwang, Stephen, ed. *The Chinese Economy*. Boulder: Westview Press, 1988. A definitive anthology on China's economy and the obstacles to development.

Fishlock, Trevor. *Gandhi's Children*. New York: Universe Books, 1983. A description of India that suggests the difficulties of that nation in following the NICs example.

Franz, Uli. *Deng Xiaoping*. Boston: Harcourt Brace, 1988. An interesting account of Deng's life, revealing some of his early authoritarianism.

Frazier, John. *The Chinese*. New York: Summit Books, 1980. A portrait of Chinese society.

Fukuyama, Francis. "The End of History." *The National Interest* no. 16 (Summer 1989). An audacious proposal that "Westernization" has triumphed throughout the world.

Galenson, Walter, ed. *Economic Growth and Structural Change in Taiwan*. Ithaca: Cornell University Press, 1979. Explains some of the reasons why Taiwan prospered.

Garside, Roger. *China after Mao*. New York: McGraw Hill, 1981. An excellent description of early reforms in China.

Geertz, Clifford. *The Religion of Java*. New York: Basic Books, 1960. A classic description of a religious mood that still affects politics in Indonesia.

Greene, Felix. *Awakened China*. Garden City, NY: Doubleday, 1961. A dated but fascinating account of Mao's China.

Harding, Harry. *China's Second Revolution*. Washington, D.C.: Brookings Institution, 1987. An excellent record of the problems and achievements of post-Mao China.

Harrison, Lawrence. *Under-Development Is a State of Mind*. Lanham, MD: University Press of America, 1985. An argument that cultural factors are the main obstacles to development.

Heilbroner, Robert. *An Inquiry Into the Human Prospect*. New York: Harper and Row, 1974. A dramatically pessimistic discussion of the problems of world development.

Heilbroner, Robert. *Marxism: For and Against*. New York: W.W. Norton, 1980. A sophisticated consideration of a once dominant theory of development.

Heng, Liang, and Judith Shapiro. *Intellectual Freedom in China After Mao*. New York: Fund for Free Expression, 1986. An informative description on limits to freedom of speech in China.

Hewlett, Sylvia Ann. *The Cruel Dilemmas of Development*. New York:

Basic Books, 1980. Set in the context of Brazil, a strong argument that the nation cannot copy the Far Eastern example.

Hinton, William. *Fanshen*. New York: Random House, 1966. An eloquent description of a Chinese village under Mao.

Hirschmeier, Johannes, and Tsuneko Yui. *The Development of Japanese Business*. Cambridge: Harvard University Press, 1975. A description of an original model of development.

Hofheinz, Roy, and Kent Calder. *The East Asian Edge*. New York: Basic Books, 1982. A reasonable assessment of the reasons for Asian achievements.

Holbrooke, Richard, Roderick MacFarquhar, and Kazuo Nukazawa. *East Asia in Transition*. New York: Trilateral Commission, 1988. An influential examination of Asia's future.

Horowitz, Donald. *Ethnic Groups in Conflict*. Berkeley: University of California Press, 1985.

Hou, Chi-Ming. "Relevance of the Taiwan Model of Development." Chung-Hua Institution, 1988. An argument that some of Taiwan's policies could be successfully adapted in other regions.

Inoguchi, Takashi, and Daniel Okimoto. *The Political Economy of Japan*: Stanford: Stanford University Press, 1988. A thoughtful examination of Japan's development.

Jackson, Karl. *Traditional Authority, Islam and Religion*. Berkeley: University of California Press, 1980. An authoritative account of political ideas within Islam, a topic of particular importance in Southeast Asia.

Japanese Economic Planning Agency. "White Paper on National Life." Tokyo, 1988. An important document urging Japan to change its economic priorities.

Japanese Ministry of Health and Welfare, "White Paper," Tokyo, 1988. An influential examination of the gap between wealth and welfare in Japan.

Johnson, Chalmers. *MITI and the Japanese Mind*. Stanford: Stanford University Press, 1982. A fascinating analysis of Japan's prime economic coordinator.

Johnson, Chalmers. "South Korean Democratization: The Role of Economic Development." *Pacific Review* 2, no. 1, 1988. An excellent analysis of the possible emergence of democracy in Asia.

Johnson, Paul. *Modern Times*: New York: Harper and Row, 1983. A major account of modern history, including the rise of Asia.

Kaneko, Kumao. "Organizing Pacific Cooperation and Japan's Role." *International Affairs* (Nov. 1988). Outlines the possibilities of regional cooperation.

Kennedy, Paul. *The Rise and Fall of Great Powers*. New York: Random House, 1987. A massive and erudite examination of the relation between economic, military, and political power.

Kerr, Clark. *The Future of Industrial Societies*. Cambridge: Harvard University Press, 1983. An interesting examination of "convergence theory."

Keyfitz, Nathan. "The Asian Road to Democracy." *Society* (Nov./Dec. 1988). An argument that Asia will create its own political forms.

Koo, Bon-Ho. "An Overview of Korea's Economic Development." Taipei, Chung-Hua Institution, 1988. A reasonable explanation of Korea's rise.

Kotkin, Joel, and Yoriko Kishimoto. *The Third Century*. New York: Crown Publishers, 1988. A lively account of the impact of Asian immigration upon America.

Kuo, Shirley. "Development of the Taiwan Economy." Chung-Hua Institution, Taipei, 1988.

Kuo, Shirley. *The Taiwan Success Story*. Boulder, CO: Westview Press, 1981. An explanation of Taiwan's growth.

Lamb, David. *The Africans*. New York: Random House, 1982. A discussion of the many failures and few successes in African development. Relevant to any discussion of whether the Asian model can be generalized to other societies.

Lampton, David, and Katherine Keyer. *China's Global Presence*. Washington, D.C.: American Enterprise Institute, 1988. An excellent anthology on China's economic future.

Lane, Cristal. *The Rites of Rulers*. Cambridge: Cambridge University Press, 1981. A wide-ranging discussion of civic religions that has relevance to the decline of Marxism in Asia.

Li, Choh-Ming. *The Economic Development of Communist China*. Berkeley: University of California Press, 1963. An early but still pertinent analysis of China's economy.

Linder, Staffan. *The Pacific Century* (Stanford: Stanford University Press, 1986). An important examination of the economic opportunities offered by the Pacific basin and its "demonstration effect" on other developing societies.

Little, I.M.D. "The Experiences and Causes of Rapid Intensive Development." Bangkok, International Labor Organization, Working Paper, 1979.

Little, I.M.D. *Economic Development*. New York: Basic Books, 1982. A very sensible analysis of the process, including the rapid rise of Asia.

Lyons, Nick. *The Sony Vision*. New York: Crown Publishers, 1976. A description of one of Japan's great corporations.

MacDonald, Donald Stone. *The Koreans*. Boulder, CO: Westview Press, 1988. A portrait of the politics and economies of the two Koreas.

McDonald, Hamish. *Suharto's Indonesia*. Victoria, Australia: Fontana Books, 1981. An excellent report on political conditions in Indonesia.

MacFarquhar, Roderick. *The Origins of the Cultural Revolution*. New York: Oxford University Press, 1982. A definitive exploration of Mao's grand experiment.

Malenbaum, Wilfred, and Wolfgang Stopler. "Political Ideology and Economic Progress: the Basic Question." *World Politics* (April 1960). A classic comparison of China and India.

Mamata, Satoshi. *Japan in the Passing Lane*, London: George Allen and Unwin, 1983. A searing diary by a Japanese journalist of his actual experiences in an auto factory.

Mao, Yu-Kang. "Land and Agricultural Policies in the Process of Economic Development of the Republic of China on Taiwan," Chung-Hua Institution, Taipei, 1988. An interpretation of the premier role of land reform in Taiwan's development.

Mende, Tibor. *China and Her Shadow*. Bombay: Asia Publishing House, 1961. A first-hand account of life under Mao.

Mittleman, James. *Out From underdevelopment*. New York: St. Martin's Press, 1988. An argument that few developing countries can emulate Asia's success.

Morishima, Michio. *Why Has Japan Succeeded?* Cambridge: Harvard University Press, 1982. An early analysis of Japanese ascendancy.

Morris, Jan. *Hong Kong*. New York: Random House, 1988. An eloquent description of this unique city.

Mosher, Stephen W. *Broken Earth*. New York: Free Press, 1984. A controversial recording of village life in China.

Myrdal, Gunnar. *The Asian Drama*. New York: Pantheon, 1968. A classic examination by a Nobel economist of Asia's problems.

Nakane, Chie. *Japanese Society*. Berkeley, University of California Press, 1985. A classic description of the Japanese.

Nathan, Andrew J. *Chinese Democracy*. Berkeley: University of California Press, 1985. A good account of the Chinese political ethos.

Ohmae, Kenichi. *Triad Power*. New York: Free Press, 1985. An examination of the reciprocal influences of the West on Japan and Japan on the West.

Okabe, Tatsumi. "China's Asian Policy: Chance or Challenge?" *Japan Review of International Affairs*. Tokyo (Spring/Summer 1987). Analyzes changes in China's policy.

Okita, Saburo. "Pacific Development and Its Implications for the World." Pacific Economic Cooperation Conference, Seoul, 1985. Argues that a benign division of labor is taking place in the Pacific.

Okita, Saburo. "The Outlook for Pacific Cooperation and the Role of Japan," *Japan Review of International Affairs* 1, no. 1 (1987). An authoritative presentation.

Oster, Patrick. *The Mexicans*. New York: William Morrow, 1989. An examination of Mexico's problems and opportunities. Relevant in an era of Japanese expansion into Latin America.

Overholt, William H. "Thailand: A Moving Equilibrium." *Pacific Review* 1, no. 1 (1988). A brilliant discussion of Thailand's evolving democracy and the various interest groups within the country.

Paloczi-Horvath, George. *Mao Tse-Tung*. Garden City, NY: Doubleday, 1963. One of the best biographies of Mao's younger years.

Papanek, Gustav. "The New Asian Capitalism: An Economic Portrait." In Berger and Hsiao. A convincing analysis of how economic and social policies affected the growth of Asia.

Peck, Perry, ed. *Roses and Thorns*. Berkeley: University of California Press, 1983. A good anthology on Dengist reforms.

Perkins, Dwight. *China: Asia's Next Economic Giant*. Seattle: University of Washington Press, 1986. A reasonable estimate of China's economic possibilities.

Prestowitz, Jr., Clyde V. *Trading Places*. New York: Basic Books, 1985. An attack on Japanese trading practices from an American viewpoint.

Pye, Lucian *Asian Power and Politics*. Cambridge, MA: Harvard University Press, 1985. A brilliant description of different political styles in the East.

Pye, Lucian *Politics, Personality and Nation Building*. New Haven: Yale University Press, 1962. A subtle and sophisticated analysis of differences in political approaches in Southeast Asia.

Rabushka, Alvin. *Hong Kong*. Chicago: University of Chicago Press, 1979. A strong defense of Hong Kong's free enterprise policies.

Rabushka, Alvin. *The New China*. Boulder, CO: Westview Press, 1987. A vigorous argument for free market policies.

Rahman, Tunku Abdul. *Contemporary Issues in Malaysian Politics*. Petalung Selangor, Malaysia: Pelunduk Publications, 1984. A brilliant analysis by the country's outstanding leader.

do Rosario, Louise. "Growth Faces Many Hurdles." *Far Eastern Economic Review*, 2 March 1989. An excellent description of obstacles to China's economic development.

Scalapino, Robert A. "Asia's Future," *Foreign Affairs* (Winter 1988). A thoughtful examination by an authority on the Pacific.

Scalapino, Robert A., et al., eds. *Asian Political Institutionalization*. Berkeley Institute of East Asian Studies, University of California Press, 1986.

Schell, Orville. *Discos and Democracy*. New York: Pantheon Books, 1989. A journalist's brilliant account of the tension between autocracy and democracy in China.

Schell, Orville. *To Get Rich is Glorious*. New York: Pantheon Books, 1983. A fine description of life in post-Mao China.

Scott, Paul D. "The New Power of Japan." *Pacific Review* 2, no. 3, 1989. Argues that Japan must become increasingly globalized.

Segal, Gerald. "Sino-Soviet Relations: The New Agenda." *The World Today* (June 1988). Analyzes the possible impact of changes in foreign policy.

Shi, Maung Maung. *Burmese Political Values*. New York: Praeger, 1983. A subtle analysis of power in Burma.

Simon, Julian. *The Ultimate Resource*. Princeton: Princeton University Press, 1981. A persuasive argument that man's ingenuity can overcome many of the barriers to development.

Singh, Bilveer. "Gorbachev and a Pacific Community." *Pacific Review* 1, no. 3, 1988. A thoughtful evaluation of the Soviet role in the Far East.

Smith, Michael. *Asia's New Industrial World*. London: Metheun, 1985. A brisk discussion of Asian nations, their problems and achievements.

Southeast Asian Affairs, Singapore, Institute of Southeast Asian Studies. An annual anthology describing political and economic conditions in the region.

Sowell, Thomas. *Marxism.* New York: William Morrow, 1985. An excellent discussion of Marxism and its faults.

Taylor, Jared. *Shadows of the Rising Sun.* New York: Quill, 1983. Some warnings concerning the ascent of Japan.

Tolchin, Martin and Susan. *Buying Into America.* Armonk, NY: Times Books, 1988. The impact of Japanese investment in America.

Trasker, Peter. *The Japanese.* New York: E.P. Dutton, 1987. An authoritative account of Japanese society.

Tutwiller, Ann, et al. "Economic Development and Land Reform: Japan, Thailand, and South Korea," Washington, D.C.: National Center for Food and Agricultural Policy, 1988. Describes some of the distinctive contributions of land reforms to Asian development.

Vogel, Ezra. *Japan As Number One.* Cambridge: Harvard University Press, 1979. A brilliant description of Japan's success and its possible lessons for America.

——— *One Step Ahead in China.* Cambridge: Harvard University Press, 1989.

Von Vorys, Karl. *Democracy Without Consensus.* Princeton: Princeton University Press, 1975. An analysis of the maintenance of democracy despite intense ethnic conflict.

Wang, Kwei Cheong. "The Singapore Experience of Economic Growth." Taipei, Huang-Chou Institution, 1988. An explanation of Singapore's rapid growth.

Watanabe, Toshio. "Asia: Its Growth and Pains." Nihon Hoso Shuppan Kyokai, Tokyo, 1988. A sweeping account of Asian growth.

Ward, Barbara. *New Perspectives on Economic Development.* Oxford, Oxford Conference on Tensions in Development, 1961. A distinguished economist's original contribution to the study of development. Still relevant.

Weber, Max. *The Religion of China.* Gelncoe, IL: Free Press, 1951. A classic, if mistaken examination of the tension between Confucianism and capitalism.

Weiner, Myron, and Samuel Huntington, eds. *Understanding Political Development.* Boston: Little, Brown, 1987. An outstanding anthology.

Wen Wei Chang, David. *Deng Xianoping.* London: Macmillan, 1988. A summary of Deng's career before the tragic events of 1989.

West, Philip, and A.H. Alting von Geseuau, eds. *The Pacific Rim and the Western World.* Boulder, CO: Westview Press, 1987. A penetrating anthology on American strategy in the Pacific basin.

Westphal, Larry, and Kwang Suk Kim. "Industrial Policy and Development in Korea." World Bank Staff Working Paper, Washington, D.C., 1977. An argument for directed development.

Wolfe, M.J. *The Japanese Conspiracy.* London: New English Library, 1984. A condemnation of Japanese economic practices.

von Wolferen, Karl. *The Enigma of Japanese Power*. New York: Alfred Knopf, 1989. An argument that Japan does not have a responsible central government or a capitalistic economy.

World Bank. *China: Long Term Issues and Options*, Washington, 1985. A balanced estimate of China's economic potential.

Wu, Yuan-li. "Chinese Entrepreneurs in Southeast Asia." *American Economic Review* (May 1983). An excellent analysis of the economic influence of overseas Chinese.

Yong-Dong, Kim. "Socio-Cultural Aspects of Political Democritization in East Asia." Washington, D.C.: American Enterprise Institute, 1988. A good discussion of the impact of culture.

You, Poh Seng, and Lim Chong Yeh, eds. *Singapore: 25 Years of Development*. Singapore: Times Press, 1985. A good introduction to the means by which Singapore achieved an advanced economic status.

Yun, Ken. "Crossing the Yellow Sea," *The China Business Review*. (Jan. 1989). Describes growing intra-Pacific ties.

Zhongmei, Yang. *Hu Yaobang*. Armonk, NY: M.E. Sharpe, 1988. An account of a tragic political reformer.

Index